SISTER OF THE ROAD

Born in the shadows of a railroad yard, of a wandering mother who took her lovers where she found them and a father who was scarcely conscious of her arrival in the world, Bertha Thompson took to "the road" as soon as the restless impulses of adolescence stirred in her. As a result of her early environment, abnormal persons interested her more than normal, wanderers more than those who settled down in homes, criminals more than law-abiding citizens. She wanted to see how they lived, live as they did, know what they were like.

As a result of her restlessness and curiosity, she became, in fifteen years of wandering, a hobo, traveling from one end of the country to the other in box-cars, "decking" passenger trains, and hitch-hiking; member of a gang of shoplifters, with whom she traveled, as the mistress of one of the men, for months; a prostitute, working in a Chicago brothel; the mother of a child of an unknown father; and a research worker for a New York social service bureau.

SISTER OF THE ROAD is Bertha's own story of those fifteen years and the record of her conclusions about them. Gifted with a naturally keen intelligence, fearless of consequences to herself, willing and eager to do and be everything which other members of her group did and were, her story is a mine of little-known information and a succession of moving human stories about that vast and growing army of homeless, jobless, wandering women who live by begging, stealing, cheating, prostituting themselves, and occasionally working at legitimate jobs.

Added to the running narrative is an appendix containing the tabulated results of Box-Car Bertha's observations and study of her own problem, which alone constitute a sociological text-book on one of the most fascinating problems of modern society. Seldom has any document combined knowledge with frankness and readability in so startling and informative a revelation.

BOOKS BY DR. BEN L. REITMAN

THE SECOND OLDEST PROFESSION

SISTER OF THE ROAD

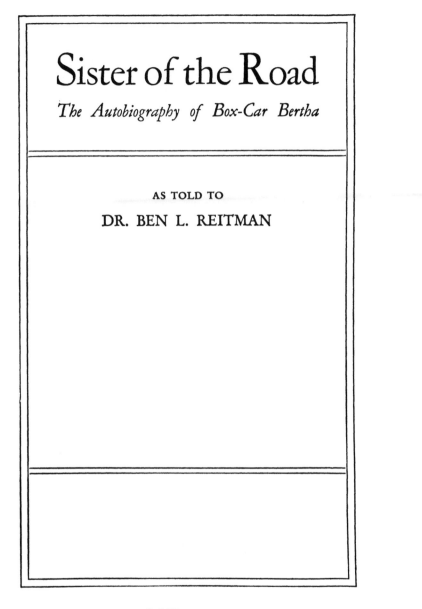

Sister of the Road

The Autobiography of Box-Car Bertha

AS TOLD TO

DR. BEN L. REITMAN

M Evans

Lanham • New York • Boulder • Toronto • Plymouth, UK

M. Evans
An imprint of The Rowman & Littlefield Publishing Group, Inc.
4501 Forbes Boulevard, Suite 200, Lanham, Maryland 20706
http://www.rlpgtrade.com

10 Thornbury Road, Plymouth PL6 7PP, United Kingdom

Distributed by National Book Network

Library of Congress Cataloging-in-Publication Data Available

ISBN 13: 978-1-59077-466-3 (pbk: alk. paper)

♾™ The paper used in this publication meets the minimum requirements of American National Standard for Information Sciences—Permanence of Paper for Printed Library Materials, ANSI/NISO Z39.48-1992.

Printed in the United States of America

SISTER OF THE ROAD

ONE

I AM thirty years old as I write this, and have been a hobo for fifteen years, a sister of the road, one of that strange and motley sorority which has increased its membership so greatly during the depression. I have always known strange people, vagrants, hoboes, both males and females. I don't remember when I didn't know about wanderers, prostitutes, revolutionists. My first playhouse was a box car. Conductors in freight yards used to let me ride in their cabooses. Before I was twelve I had ridden in a box car to the next division and back.

Police and pinches, jails, bughouses, and joints seem to have been always a part of my life. When I knew that a man was stealing, or a woman hustling, or some poor girl going nutty, or that a guy was on the lam, or learned that a pimp was living with four women—it all seemed natural to me, an attitude given me by my mother, to whom nothing was ever terrible, vulgar, or nasty. Our family never had any hard luck, because nothing seemed hard luck to it, nor was it ever disgraced for there was nothing which it would acknowledge as disgrace. When my mother changed her "husband," I simply took it for granted. When I was pinched the first time for riding in a box car, it didn't seem unusual to me. Many of the men and women I knew had been arrested for the same thing. In my world somebody was always getting arrested. My mother was arrested when I was a baby because she wouldn't marry my father. As I grew up, if we missed a meal or two now and then, or a half-dozen meals, it wasn't anything to get excited about. All my life I have lived with hungry and lonely people.

My mother wasn't what the world would call a good woman. She never said she was. And many people, including the police, said she was a bad woman. But she never agreed with them, and she had a way of lifting up her head when she talked back to them that made me know she was right. I loved her deeply from the first day I can remember until she died. I love to think of her. Her example and influence and sacrifice (she always denied that she ever made sacrifices for her children) proved that she loved us and that she was a woman of rare courage and of fine principles all her own. I remember her first when she was cooking in a railroad camp for a section gang not far from Deadwood, South Dakota. The man whom I called "father" was the foreman of the gang laying the tracks of the Northwestern. I was the oldest of mother's four children. Each of us had a different father.

"Hobo, hobo, where did you come from?" is the earliest chant I learned. There were always wandering men, and even then a few women traveling on the railroad and on the highway. I read an article the other day saying that now women hoboes and tramps have so increased that one out of every twenty persons on the road is a woman. I don't know what the percentage was when I grew up, but I remember some of these women very vividly, probably because there were so few of them then.

I heard Harry Hopkins, relief administrator, speak this year. He says that now we have 6,800 transient women in the country. This count is taken from the government shelters and transient bureaus. There must be twice that many actually unattached and hitch-hiking and riding freights and walking about the country. That would make 13,600 women, "sisters of the road," as the men call us. No wonder people are writing books about us!

My childhood was completely free and always mixed up with the men and the women on the road. There weren't many dolls or toys in my life but plenty of excitement. We were set down on side tracks in the midst of vast hills and ravines. We used the river for swimming and washing. I learned my first spelling from the names on the box cars. What early geography I knew I learned by asking the men about the towns and cities, the names of which were chalked on the cars. I learned numbers by counting the cars on long freights.

I don't ever remember anyone telling me a real fairy story in my whole childhood, but the tales of the gandy dancers, and of the bundle stiffs, of their jobs in the wheatfields of Minnesota and the rides on the blinds to and from them, and the breath-taking yarns of mushing in Alaska, or getting pinched in San Francisco, or of drunken brawls in New Orleans' dives were thrillers I remember to this day.

Some of the men in the gang had their families with them. Half the kids boasted that their cradles had been handcars. We took for playthings all the grand miscellany to be found in a railroad yard. We built houses of railroad ties so big that it took four of us to lift one of them in place. We invented games that made us walk the tracks. We crossed pins on the main tracks and let the big engines crash over them and leave tiny pairs of scissors for us. We played with the men's shovels and picks and learned to use them. And we lined up to wave with ceremony to the passenger trains that thundered by.

We girls dressed just like the boys, mostly in hand-me-down overalls. No one paid much attention to us. They saw to it that we had something to eat and a place to sleep at night. And they saw to it that we did our simple chores. But the men never thought of changing their conversation in front of us. The men worked hard and the women worked harder. Mother was always busy cooking and serving meals and cleaning, and she taught me and the other girls how to cook and clean and to wash men's clothes.

"Bertha," she would say, "as long as you can keep men clean and well fed and love them a little, they'll be perfectly satisfied. They're all babies. They need to be looked after. Teach them to depend upon you. But never let them make a slave of you."

Mother was a handsome blonde, straight-shouldered, deep-breasted, with penetrating steel-grey eyes, and with a sort of glow about her that attracted everyone, especially when she talked. She was the kind of woman who looks after everyone, and everybody called her "Mother Thompson" even when she was so young that all the tramps (as well as all the others) tried to make love to her.

Her father, Moses Thompson, was a Kansas pioneer, who spent his whole life trying to right the wrong of the oppressed. He was an abolitionist. When he was yet in his teens he worked with John Brown and he served in the Civil War. Later he was one of the earliest workers for the emancipation of women, and published, at Valley Forge, Kansas, a little paper, *The Women's Emancipator*, advocating votes for women and freedom from marriage. He was one of the committee that in the Eighties organized the famous free-love convention at Worcester, Massachusetts. He served three terms in jail, two for sending birth control information through the mail (the federal authorities called it obscene), and one for admitting that he advised his daughter, my mother, against marrying the father of her child.

When mother was twenty, grandfather was living on the farm and publishing his little paper. Walker C. Smith, an active free-thought and eugenist propagandist, a man of forty, stopped in while making a tour of the west. He had corresponded with grandfather. He stayed at the farm and became mother's lover the first week. Grandfather knew it. He urged her not to marry. During the last months of her pregnancy, the neighbors began to talk, and five days after I was born, the village parson, the sheriff, and three good citizens came and asked bluntly whether mother was married or intended to marry.

"No, my daughter is not married," grandfather told them, "and, what is more, she is not going to be married. She and Smith love one another and they have a child because they wanted one. They are both intelligent and healthy, and that's all a child needs in its parents."

Someone swore out a warrant for the whole family, and two weeks later they were tried at the county seat. Mother and father were sentenced to six months in jail. Grandfather was fined a hundred dollars and costs, which he promptly refused to pay. So he was sent to jail too. All of them enjoyed their stay there. Grandfather wrote a series of articles which were published in the New York and London liberal papers. Father caught up on his back reading. Mother did the jail cooking and sewing, nursed me, and studied Esperanto and socialism.

"When we all got out of jail, the liberals and the radicals in Kansas City gave us a great mass meeting," mother said. "There had been a lot of publicity. You made your first public appearance there, in my arms, held high for all those people to see."

My father did not go back to the farm with mother and grandfather.

In the spring of 1906 grandfather died, and mother, for no particular reason (and against her better judgment, she said) married a young tow-headed farmer, Toby Miller, and moved to a large farm near Bismarck. During the next two years my sister, Ena, and brother Frank were born. But only Ena was Toby's child. Frank was the son of a traveling physician named A. H. Wright. Mother met him at a carnival. Her husband, Toby, made the best of it. He knew of the relationship, and later that Frank was not his child, but he treated the little fellow, as he did me, like his own.

When I was five, again without any good reason that mother could ever remember or of which I have any recollection, she hitched up a team, took us three children and a valise of clothes and drove into Bismarck. Before nightfall she had found a job as cook in a nearby construction camp, and within a month was living with the foreman of the gang, who always referred to us as "my wife and children." Eleven months later my sister, Margaret, was born.

Mike Blake, our new father, was a husky silent man, heavy-handed with the men, but having for my mother a respect and devotion, and for all of us a rough tenderness. He gave us children as much care as if we had been his own. He worked hard and drank hard. Drunk or sober, he was good to mother. And if he was ever jealous—and he had much cause—he was most successful in hiding it.

This period with Mike left an impression on me. There was security in the rough way he bossed the men and mother and us. Mother seemed to take a fierce delight in the heaviest kind of work for him. By watching her there I learned the urge I now know so well, for serving men who work and drink and talk. Across our box car threshold came many men, those of the gang who missed women folk and who had talk to offer, and various dirty, footsore, gay and bedraggled hoboes, all of them bringing in to us the world of careless living detached from the rest of the world.

There were few women hoboes those days. The only two I remember seemed to have about them something of my own mother's way of raising up her head proudly with an idea and of telling a funny story or in talking without embarrassment about hustling and living with men and leaving them.

I saw one (in dusty black sweater and striped overalls) flip a freight that had stopped at our switch to take on an empty, and ride the rods right out of our camp, waving to mother in our doorway and to the gang who held up their shovels in astonishment. I had seen her bundle her things together on mother's table a few minutes before. She had a book along. She had been in Detroit. She spoke of a child in Memphis. She was going to talk at an I. W. W. meeting on the coast. She and mother laughed together because the men wouldn't be able to get at her on the rods. I knew that she had spent a couple of nights over in the men's shacks. Mother knew it. We didn't think anything about it. But the look on her face as she talked about going on west, and the sureness with which she swung under the freight car, set my childish mind in a fever. The world was easy, like that. Even to women. It had never occurred to me before.

One other woman I remember, older and more battered looking, who traveled with a whole gang of men, and rolled out of an empty with them one day when a freight slowed up around our curve. One of the men had had a meal of mother's on a trip the other way a few months before. These men treated the woman with them as if she were a man. She wore skirts, though. She carried her own water and washed out her underwear and some of their shirts, borrowing soap from mother. She smoked, rolling her own. I was interested in this. Mother never had.

This woman was going off somewhere to some man, or away from some man, I don't remember which. It seemed natural to me that she should be going to a man or away from a man. And not important. Far more important to her, and to the men hoboes she was with, was food, and a place to wash, and the hills they had come through, or an idea someone had given them in another camp.

Much as I liked our life along the railroad, I don't remember being upset at all or wondering about it when, at the time I was eight, mother left Mike and the box cars and took us to Aberdeen and opened a boarding house. The boarders were mostly railroad men, show and carnival people, and the kind of folks who don't like to stay at hotels. We always got labor people and strikers and radicals. Practically all the hoboes who passed through Aberdeen stopped at our house for a meal and a wash-up. Often they slept in the big barn. When a hobo would knock at mother's back door and begin, "Lady, will you—" she always snapped back, "You're a professional bum. Only the professionals on the road call me 'lady'."

But she always fed them and talked to them.

These and the railroad hands and the I. W. W. men filled up our boarding house. Every night there would be a discussion about sex and strikes and socialism. All the agitators stayed there. I learned afterward that "Mother Thompson" became known that year from coast to coast among the radicals and the hoboes.

We had a woman hobo now and then, but they were still few enough in those days to cause a little stir, even among the men hoboes. They were almost always alone.

Once in a while they traveled in pairs, but very seldom with men. Some of them were hitch-hiking. There weren't very many automobiles then, and they always told of wild and exciting rides with strangers across the long stretches of prairies. They explained that alone they could get rides from men in cars easier than if they were with men, and that food and shelter and a little money now and then came easier that way.

Most of the women on the road in those days were agitators, it seems to me. They wore their hair bobbed, long. They talked excitedly and got the men hoboes all roused up to go on to San Francisco or wherever they were going for some meeting. Now and then one of them seemed to be just hoboing without purpose, as hundreds of women are doing now, having no place in view except some city they had heard about or liked on a previous trip. Mother accepted them all.

Since then I have thought a lot about why women leave home and go on the road. I've decided that the most frequent reason they leave is economic and that they usually come from broken or from poverty-stricken homes. They want to escape from reality, to get away from misery and unpleasant surroundings. Others are driven out by inability to find expression at home, or maybe because of parental discipline. Some hobo their way about to far away relatives, or go to seek romance. The dullness of a small town or a farm, made worse by long spells of the same kind of weather, may start them off. Or some want better clothes. But others are just seized with wanderlust. The rich can become globe-trotters, but those who have no

money become hoboes. Some of the women I knew way
back there in Aberdeen fell into this class, I guess. And I
did, too, when I first took the road, wanting freedom and
adventure such as they had, with maybe a few of the
other things thrown in. But I never wanted to leave home
because home wasn't exciting.

Ena and I went to public school a little over two years
in Aberdeen. I don't remember much about it. We also
went to Sunday School and to every revival and to any
kind of meeting that came to town. We played with a lot
of kids who ran around as we did. Mother took us to hear
everybody, quoting grandfather, "The more you hear,
the more you learn, the better you will be to judge for
yourself."

Aberdeen had "a line," a row of houses of prostitution
just outside the city limits. There were fifteen girls working in there. They were not allowed to visit generally in
the town. They were not even permitted to shop. They
had to go direct from the depot to the joints. The police
watched them closely. But they let them come to our
house. They would come in for a meal. Sometimes their
lovers and their pimps would stay as paying boarders.
Sometimes the girls would take me to their joints for a
visit. I was fascinated. Quickly I learned how they conducted their business. I suppose you will be horrified when
I say that it did not disgust me. It seemed like any other
business to me.

Mother did not seem to have any objection to having
me visit these girls. She did not seem to mind their talk
in front of me. She accepted it as she did the stories other

women and men brought in of labor meetings in Birmingham and of hoboing across the country for Idaho apple picking. It may seem unkind and undaughterly and disloyal of me to relate these things about my mother, but if I am to tell an honest story of my life and the influences that moulded it, I must begin it, as I have, by telling about my mother.

TWO

I WAS eleven years old when the United States entered the World War. Some of the railroad men got passes for our whole family, and mother left her boarding house and took us to Little Rock, Arkansas, to a co-operative colony in the hills. A woman hobo, who had stayed with mother the winter before when she was sick, had told us about it, and several of the labor leaders had been there, and urged mother to try it. We found there thirty-five families, socialists, anarchists and free-thinkers, all opposed to war, weary of the struggle for existence, blaming capitalism for their difficulties, all wanting economic security and mental peace without too much of an effort. They were living in houses and cottages they built themselves clustered in a beautiful valley. A group of socialists had purchased the property and invited others to join them there. There was one central lodge where the affairs of the colony were discussed. Those who came with money or earned any while there put it into the common fund. All worked the land. By the time we arrived there was a well organized co-operative farm experiment under way.

There were seventy-one of us children. We went to a school conducted in an old barn by two remarkable teachers, Bill White and his wife, Edna. They had taught school in the east, but had been forced to leave when the school board discovered that they had never been legally married. They had come to the colony in the hopes of establishing a modern Francisco Ferrer school.

We did not get much regular school work, probably, but we did have some reading, writing, arithmetic, spelling. Mostly we learned about inconsistencies of religion, and about governments, labor, and economics. We were taught that the capitalistic system was wrong and that people are poor because they are exploited and do not get the full product of their labor. We were shown that the government protected the private property of the rich, and that without government and violence the rich could not continue. We were taught also in the colony the dignity of labor and were made to feel the need for preparing ourselves to live in a free co-operative society. The only textbooks I remember we had were William Morris' *News from Nowhere,* Oscar Wilde's *The Soul of Man Under Socialism,* Emile Zola's *Labor,* and Walt Whitman. We had to recite one of Whitman's poems every day.

Besides our teachers, two persons in the colony played important parts in my development. One was Edwin C. Owen, then only 19 years old, a sweet young poet, blond, with a small moustache, with a voice so rich, even with his English accent, that every word he spoke sounded like music. He read Byron and Shelley and Strindberg and Ibsen to us, and poems of revolt, among them C. E. W. Wood's *The Masters—Makers of Bloody Revolution,* so that even after all these years I remember such lines as, "The end is always packed in the beginning! The apple is in the bud, and the worm is in the blossom." He read us Eltzbacher's *Anarchism,* and attempted to explain Tolstoy and Prudhoun and Godwin and Tucker. He would say, "The holding of property is robbery, and marriage is an outlawed institution. 'My house,' 'my dog,' 'my wife'— men make their gods. But gods do not make men."

Owen was studying shorthand in the colony, and typewriting, and he had me study with him. I have never been without a typewriter since, when I could help it. Even in jails I have been permitted to use one, and I have constantly practiced shorthand. This has helped me to earn my living many times, but more than that it has made it possible for me to take down quickly and keep notes of many important things people have said. If you don't judge my grammar or my spelling too severely, I am a fair stenographer.

Another man at the colony who meant a great deal to me was Herman Baginsky, a pudgy little fellow with intense eyes and bulged forehead. This comrade came from Germany but had worked at his trade as a tailor for over thirty years in New York. He had saved a few thousand dollars. He was weary of the city and had come to the colony in order to live simply. He was a believer in free love and was trying to write a book on love.

"When women learn the technique of love and become economically independent, and understand birth control, they will be free," he used to say. "Marriage is slavery for a woman. Children are born by accident."

While we were at the colony we lived in a little cottage by ourselves. Mother made our expenses by doing the cook-

ing and washing in the big house where most of the unattached men lived. I have learned since that she took care of
some of the sex needs of those men, too, but as I remember
it, she was always eneregtically scrubbing and cooking for
them, always gay and friendly, ready to tell or to listen to
a good story. I remember her reading a great deal, studying books against war, and in groups at night talking pas-
sionately against it. When she was serious, there was not a
soul in the colony who would not listen. I remember her
face all lit up with feeling when she once told a group of
the women that she and they had no right to have more
sons to give to the land for cannon fodder.

My brother and the rest of us children worked four
hours a day in the colony. One of the rules was that
everybody had to do some kind of useful work. If a
child was old enough to play, he was old enough to do
something useful, even if it was only fetching the water
from the well or carrying a broom.

When we had been at the colony about eleven months,
James Wilson, a dark-haired powerful man of thirty, who
looked like the New Yorker he was, and who spoke with
an Eastern accent, came to stay a week. He was an active
anti-militarist.

"I have a heart lesion, and would have been excused
from military service in any case," he told us. "But I am
not satisfied because I do not have to go to war. And it
does not make me happy that I can die quietly in bed. All
war is stupid. It is cruel and expensive and outrageous.
That which we gain by violence, somebody with more
violence will take away from us."

When he left the colony, he took mother with him. Baginsky and the other colonists said they would look after us while mother went crusading through the country. I remember that I didn't have a doubt in my mind about the need of her going or the rightness of her cause.

In the time that followed, we children were greatly concerned in the affairs of the colony. The school flourished. The common cause—of finding a way to live without exploitation—became part of us. Many leaders of various movements came to speak to us. There was talk of expanding the farm by pushing it farther into the hills. There were quarrels over housing and regulations. We all felt that the colony was very important. We were being watched. I remember feeling disgraced when the war fever got hold of a couple of our younger boys and they left to enlist.

Now and then a woman from the outside came to the colony. Some of them hoboed their way in; they were always on some kind of a crusade, and, after a quick conference with our leaders and an envious glance at our wooded valley, they were off again. Those women were older than the women on the road now. They were out with a purpose. I remember three particularly; radical women who caused quite a stir because of their manner of traveling. They stopped on their way from a conference to maneuver a strike in California. Agnes was from Vassar. Ray was from a group of garment workers. Mamie had a father who was an active socialist in Pittsburgh. All three women wore trousers.

They didn't have time to ride freights or to hitch-hike,

and from New York to Little Rock they had decked a Pullman on the fastest passenger train, climbing up on top while it waited in the station, and, after it started, sprawling on their stomachs and bracing themselves with their hands over the sides, with only the little ventilator shutters between their legs keeping them from flying off into space. Their brown, rather harsh and purposeful faces, and their ringing voices as they spoke to our group in the evenings before they took a Ford back to Little Rock to deck another train at midnight, seemed very dramatic then. They risked their lives hoboing.

Another woman hobo came walking into camp with a man comrade. She wore men's clothing, too, but she dressed up in a red blouse for her talk to the group in the evening. When she was told who we children were, she put her arms around us and said that she had heard mother in a wonderful speech in Boston, and that we must be brave until her work was over. She waited at the colony two days until two other comrades came for her in a car and they went off to a free-speech fight in San Antonio.

Mother was gone for almost a year. When she returned to the colony she brought with her a grand young man, an Irish poet, John Carney, who was connected with the Irish Labor movement. He was tall, thin, serious, and only twenty-four years old. Mother had picked him up in Greenwich Village, in New York. Although he was eleven years younger than mother, she had taken him for her man and in two days we were off for Seattle, Washington, with Carney and mother. We started out by day coach, though we didn't have money enough to make the whole trip. We stopped off for a week in Bismarck, running into mother's husband, Toby, and having a fine visit with him. He urged mother to leave us children with him, but she refused.

"Whenever you or the children want to come and live with me, the home is still yours," he said. He was very good natured about it, and learning that we were broke, insisted on buying us tickets to Seattle. Carney urged us to go that way, saying he would be on the same train. He managed this by riding the rods and decking the coaches as far as Butte, Montana. There, as we left, mother was watching, and saw that he could not make it, so she pulled the cord and stopped the train and we got off. Carney chided her for being so loyal, but she smiled in deprecation.

"Well, we started off together and we are going to travel that way," she said.

That night, while we were yet in the yards, a railroad detective picked us up and took us to a police station. Mother, who did all the talking, explained that her husband had a job in Seattle, if he could only get there. The officer looked at Carney skeptically.

"You mean your son, don't you?" he grinned.

They kept us in jail all night but in the morning took us to the city hall and gave us tickets to Seattle. Mother said nothing about having first class tickets in her pocket all the time.

In Seattle we first went to the I. W. W. hall, and one of the fellow workers showed us to a cozy little apartment on a hill not far from the waterfront. From our window we could see the tops of the boats going out, and around the corner was all the exciting activity of the harbor.

Good living seemed ahead. But in less than a week Carney was gone. There was a bitter free-speech fight going on at San Diego.

"Where there is a struggle, that's where I want to be," he told us. "You have nothing to worry about. You are strong. You can work. And if you need any help, the I. W. W. will look after you."

We kissed him good-bye lovingly. When next we heard of him he had been killed in a labor riot.

Mother soon had a job cooking in a short order restaurant. She registered as a special student at the University of Washington and put us four children in school. We had all been irregular, and lacked proper credits, but upon examination we were placed. I started work in Seattle High School.

We managed pretty well during the next two years. Mother was a good provider. Her work at the restaurant was hard and of long hours, but she came from it as if it had not touched her and entered upon our own life with gayety and enthusiasm. In addition to everything else she made our clothes for us, designing them to suit our hair and coloring as well as our figures, and did it so well that I had the feminine satisfaction of seeing the other girls in high school envying me for my clothes. But most of the girls of my own age seemed rather silly to me then. School did not matter a great deal, anyway. It seemed ridiculous to study Latin grammar when the whole exciting world was waiting outside.

About half the time we were located in Seattle, we spent in Home Colony, an anarchist settlement near Tacoma, living about with different families in the group. This was a free-love colony, started by a group of anarchists who bought the land and organized vegetable, fish, and chicken-raising projects. Each family had its own house.

Everyone there made us welcome. We swam and fished, dug clams, worked in the vegetable gardens, helped pack eggs, and all of it seemed play to us. There were a number of fine sturdy clean youngsters about my own age. We studied hard, and in the summer evenings we sat around a fire near the water and someone read to us. In this group I first became acquainted with Shaw, Darwin, Emerson, Huxley and Lenin.

While I was at Home Colony I met David Kaplan, a fugitive. He had been indicted with Matthew Schmidt and the McNamara brothers for blowing up the Los Angeles Times building. The McNamara brothers had been caught and sent to San Quentin, but Kaplan and Matthew were being sought by the whole country. We took long walks in the woods together and I asked him if he were not afraid in the colony since the Burns agency had offered five thousand dollars reward for his capture. But he shook his head.

"If a man is an anarchist or an honest union man or labor leader, I don't mind letting him know who I am," he said. "I have traveled all around this country and in England and in South Africa. Thousands of my comrades know who and where I am and not one would think of betraying me."

A little later someone did betray him, however, Donald Voss, the son of one of the women in the colony. I remember sitting one day in the doorway of this woman, Gertie Voss, his mother, an ardent freethinker, when she said, in speaking of the rights of women, "A mother has a right to throw her baby in a stove and burn it up if she wants to." When I heard later of her son's betrayal of Kaplan, I regretted that she had not exercised her right.

While mother was attending classes at the university she met E. A. Orr, an instructor in political economy. He came regularly to the Saturday night group of literary people, radicals, anarchists and a few professors she had gathered around her. Mother was very much attracted to Orr, and he soon became her lover. She made no effort to hide her feelings. She had never learned how to lie or to deceive anyone, and whenever she had a new lover she was very enthusiastic about him and took us children into her confidence.

When I was sixteen the men began to notice me, and I them. When I had gone swimming naked, or taken sunbaths in a mixed group, occasionally one of the older boys had attempted to touch my body, or make remarks about it. But no one seriously tried to bother me, and I can honestly say that I had never really wanted to come close to any man. I had heard so many discussions, and read so much about sex, and had become accustomed to nakedness so naturally that I had no curiosity about it. I had often said that I would never marry, and that whenever a lover really wanted me, or I wanted him, I would take him.

"Mother, what should I do when some man tells me he wants me?" I asked her once.

Her large grey eyes smiled at me as she answered, "Babe,

if a man wants you and you want him, just take him. There isn't much to it. I have had all kinds of lovers, and it never did me any harm. Don't be afraid of life and love and nature. Anything you want to do is all right with me. Men can't do you any harm. Nobody can hurt you but yourself. Every experience you have makes you all the more fit for life. Men are wonderful. When you get tired of them, or they of you, leave them without bitterness or regret. No matter what happens to you, I'll stand by you."

Professor Orr, the young instructor, came often to our house. He stayed late, often stayed all night. He brought us good books and talked to us all as he thought we were intelligent persons. Often he took the whole family riding. But one evening he asked me to go for a ride alone with him. We drove a long way through the hills. Then we stopped and he began to make love to me. I found that I wanted him to go on, and he became my first lover. It never occurred to me that I was showing any disloyalty to mother in letting him. Later, though, he intimated that possibility.

"What do you think your mother will say when she knows?" he asked.

"Let's ask her," I answered, without hesitation.

So we went home and told her about it. For a moment a strange, drawn look crossed her face. Then she smiled quietly and turned to Orr.

"Do you think, then, that you are strong enough for the two of us?" was all she asked him.

E. A. O. never made romantic love to me. "I want

you," he would say, or "I need you," or "your body is grand." Our affair lasted for nearly a year. Mother never mentioned it again, but continued her own relationship with him.

Even with E. A. O., Seattle became monotonous to me. It was late spring. I was nearly seventeen, weighed about a hundred and sixty pounds, was built, E. A. O. said, "like a truck horse," and I was restless. I walked along the water-front and the freight yards. I read the ads of the excursions to the east and the south and the north. I remembered women I had seen getting off freight cars, women hitch-hiking. Over at I. W. W. hall I met a number of women hoboes who had been tramping about the country, and listened eagerly to their stories. Ena was restless, too, and bit by bit we decided that we wanted to take a look at the world and see for ourselves what it was like. Ena was fourteen, blonde, and dainty, with small wrists and ankles, childlike still, yet showing clearly the attractive woman she was about to become. After a few days of planning, I spoke up for both of us.

"Ena and I want to go out on the road," I told mother. "Ena wants to go to school in the east. She has some talent to write and draw. I think the east has more opportunities. . . ."

Mother put her arms around both of us, saying, "I knew you were getting ready to leave me," she said gently. "I want to tell you something before you go. I've always been a rough-neck. I never had any morals, nor did I ever teach you any. But I've been a happy mother. I'm proud of both of you. Remember that I never made any sacrifice for you, nor did I give up any pleasure or good times for you. I never did anything different because I had children. And so don't either of you ever do anything for me that isn't easy and natural for you to do. I haven't any advice to give you. You both know plenty now. Just remember one thing, however—a woman's character, her value to the world, and her love for man is not in her hips, but in her heart and head."

E. A. O. bought us tickets on the boat from Seattle to San Francisco. A gay little crowd came down to see us off and sang I. W. W. songs and a parody on "We'll never say good-bye in heaven." Ena and I had light woolen dresses, new coats. Mother had packed our grip, and had given us an extra dress apiece, extra shoes, underwear, stockings, and a few toilet necessities.

"That's all you'll need," she said, "and baggage is a nuisance."

We moved into San Francisco bay next morning while the sun was coming up deep red on the water's edge. I was up and dressed and on deck. My heart throbbed as deeply as the ship's engines. I was wildly happy with life and in anticipation of the future.

Some of the girls we had known in the colony met our boat at San Francisco and took us to their home. In less than a week, both of us were working, Ena as a children's maid in a home near the Presidio, and I as a check girl in a restaurant.

True to mother's teachings, we began to go to lectures. One of these was by the famous New York anarchist, Enrico Mallettini, a short, stubby, fiery orator. He did things to the crowd; things that made them rise out of themselves and believe what he said and cheer and shout. When, after the meeting, I was introduced and he looked at me directly, something so violent happened to me that I could say nothing. I wanted nothing in the world but to be close to him, to listen to him, and to make him a part of myself.

When Mallettini left for Los Angeles two days later, Ena and I sat opposite him on the train. That was in June. In Los Angeles we stayed with friends of his. My life for the next weeks became a dream. Mallettini had four lectures in Los Angeles. I attended them all. He was a divine figure to me, whatever he was to the others. Every word he uttered seemed to me a miraculous revelation. When he announced that he was going to New Orleans and then to St. Louis and Chicago, I followed him to the train and asked him to kiss me. He did. I felt I had never known before what it was to kiss and be kissed. I told him then that I would see him both in New Orleans and in St. Louis.

Next day I asked Ena if she wanted to stay in Los Angeles and get a job or go with me to New Orleans, and she answered me by humming the old tune, "I'll go where you want me to go, Dear Lord."

Although we had talked a lot about hoboing, and had known folks who did it all our lives, I thought I had better know a little something about this particular trip, so we went over to Hobo College to ask about the best route. Hobo College was then over on the Mexican Plaza, a large room with maps and pamphlets and pictures of

Carl Marx and Lenin, Jack London and J. Eads How. Every type of wandering person came in and out of its doors, men and women. This day when we went over, there were only men there. They were free and generous with their advice.

"The S. P. is the best road to take," one said, "but she's a bitch, sister. The shacks are hostile, and the railroad dicks will glom you sure, unless you're lucky."

Another did his best to discourage us.

"There are damned few empties on those freights," he told us, "and you'll have to ride the bumpers or deck it. A big woman like you can never ride the rods, and the reefers are all full of ice. You might make it, if you're tough, but you're not.

"You girls'll do much better to hitch-hike. It will take longer, but it's cleaner and safer. Why don't you do something even better than that. Go to the Charities and tell them you're broke and that your mother lives in New Orleans. They'll ship you."

But I had thought of my trip in terms of hoboing and hobo I would. A short fat man of about forty, who had been on the road for twenty-five years, came up to us then and offered to help us.

"Boes, I was goin' back east next week," he said, "but if you kids want to go to-day and need the services of an expert, I'm your guide and I'll show you the ropes. Before we get to New Orleans I'll make first-class hoboes out of you. Now this is going to be a cinch. All you girls got to do is to say I'm your father, and keep your traps closed and your legs crossed. And don't ditch me for any sheiks."

In the east-bound fast freight that left the Southern
Pacific yards that night there was an empty freight car—
empty, that is, of everything except fourteen hoboes besides "Fat," Ena, and myself.

THREE

THERE was no trouble getting on. Fat had located a brakeman who said he was sympathetic to the I. W. W., and toward midnight we took a street car out to where the Southern Pacific yards began. Fat had ruled out all luggage. Ena and I had crammed our pockets with a few necessities, pencil and paper, a nail file, and soap. We wore our plaid skirts, sweaters and tams, and we pinned the little money we had into our underclothing. When we got off the street car we hung around the section gang's tool house for a few minutes while Fat talked with some other men waiting, and then he told us to keep still and follow him. We did, slipping along the line of smelly dark cattle cars and closed reefers until, without warning, he began climbing into the open door of a box car. Without a word we followed, and almost before we got our balance there was a jerk, and he pulled us down alongside of him toward the front end of the car. And with a few more jerks and stops and backings we were off.

Ena and I were too excited to move. We could see in the dark that there were other figures squatting in the ends or braced against the sides. An occasional cigarette lit up a man's face. We knew there were some other women because we heard their voices. But everyone lay low because we were still passing lights. The streets and the lines of houses began to go by faster and faster, and soon everyone was shifting around to get comfortable, and we were out in the country, with the lines of orange groves and clumps of palms flashing by. After awhile there was a little moon.

About three in the morning we stopped, and the brakeman and conductor climbed into the car with a lantern. There was a stir among the hoboes.

"Tickets!" said the conductor.

"And dig deep!" added the brakeman. "It's going to cost you two bucks apiece to make the next division." He walked towards the end of the car and took a lanky young fellow under the arms.

"How much you got?" he demanded.

"Not a nickel. If I had I'd be riding the cushions."

"Well, ride this!" and he gave him a boot in the seat of his pants that sent him sprawling out of the car. "Now if the rest of you guys think this is a charity bazaar, you'll go the same way. Two bucks. If you haven't got it, take the next train."

Four men in the car had two dollars. One gave up his watch. There were five other women besides Ena and myself. One of them took a five dollar bill from her shoe and said in a soft voice, "Mr. Conductor, we three are college girls, going back to Madison, Wisconsin, and we only have a few dollars to make it on. Will you please let us ride three for five?"

The conductor looked her over and grinned.

"All right, professor, sure!"

The other two women didn't stir. Then Fat spoke up.

"Look here, mate," he said in a wheedling voice, "I'm a union man. Used to switch on the Lehigh valley. Been working out in Los Angeles and lost my job. I've just buried my wife and I'm takin' my two daughters here back to my sister in New Orleans. Give us a break, won't you? We haven't got two bits between us."

"Sure, I'll give you a break, you big-mouthed bastard!" the brakeman answered, and his fist came up and made a lunge at Fat's jaw. But our protector dodged and started for the door, and the brakeman, satisfied, used his foot as he had on the other man, sending Fat sprawling onto the right of way. Then, to make sure that neither of the two men who had been ejected would come back, both brakemen followed them. One of them looked at us as he jumped.

"You girls stay here," he yelled back. "I'll tend to you later."

All the girls were terrified except the older two who hadn't spoken up to the brakeman. We crouched there in the half dark of the car, trembling and saying nothing. Ena was crying a little. Some of the men had liquor and offered it. The college girls refused it, but the older women took it and I made Ena swallow a little and took a big drink myself and promptly felt better. But the men were sore.

"These short-change brakies!" one of them said. "They can do that to us because we're not organized. Thank God I'm only going to Tucson on this road. Got a job in New Mexico, and look at this roll!" He held up a big wad of bills. "If the brakie'd see that he'd charge us ten apiece. If you girls need any money we'll slip you some."

All that night we sat there wondering when the brakemen would come back and what would happen when they did, while the train jolted on through the dark, shaking and prodding us in our uncomfortable seats. But, strangely enough, we saw no more of them.

When, toward morning, we pulled into the next division, the man with the roll fed everybody in the car and insisted on buying overalls and a jacket and cap for each girl. The other girls were dressed about as we were, except the older ones. One of them was in torn men's trousers and shirt. The other had on a brown wool woman's suit which was badly mussed. Both of them had their hair cut short like men's and at first glance they didn't look much like women. After we ate, the college girls went off alone into the town, but Ena and I stayed around with the men and with these women. There were piles of new ties near the tracks that made a good hiding place. The two women were waiting for a freight that would take them to a little town north of there, but had a couple of hours.

The one in women's clothes was called Maggie. She was tall and rather gaunt looking, with dark rings under her eyes. Her hair showed grey although she said she was only twenty-five. The other girl in trousers didn't tell us her name. She was smaller and plumper, and laughed a lot when she talked about herself, and said she envied us two starting out. Maggie wasn't sure it was a good thing to do, and wanted to know what our mother thought about it. Then she got interested telling about herself.

We talked a long time together, and both of them told us all about their lives. I remember being terribly excited about what they told us. They were our first women hoboes—since we were out ourselves.

Maggie said she had been hoboing all her life. She was born in London and raised in an orphan asylum. She was brought to America by relatives when she was sixteen. In New York she met some women hoboes and started on the road with two of them. She had been on the road ever since, begging and stealing and doing a little work now and then. For awhile she had been an extra at Hollywood, but not for long. She was completely frank about her sexual promiscuity and the fact that she had contracted veneral disease. She accepted the fact that it was easier for a woman to get along on the road if she was not too particular and she frankly considered her body as her working capital.

The girl in the trousers agreed that it was no trouble at all to get along on the road. She said that lots of times when she got into a strange town she hung around the depot and got acquainted with someone.

"If that don't work, I go over to one of the taverns and sit down at a table and pretty soon someone will ask me to have a drink. Yes, I drink a good deal. I can drink anything. If no one pays any attention to me I ask the bartender if I can dance. That usually makes friends for me."

These two women had happened to ride the same freight car into San Diego the winter before, and had stuck together ever since. Now they were hitting for a town where the one in the trousers had an aunt.

You might think that what they had told us would have disgusted me and warned me against the road, but it didn't. It simply excited me and made me want to go on.

They made another empty freight car when their local came in and pretty soon the college girls returned from town with some chocolate bars, and the men and they and Ena and I sneaked along down the tracks about five o'clock in the afternoon and climbed back into the same box car we had come in. The new brakeman and the conductor didn't bother us. '

The girls were really college girls, from a mid-western university. One, whom I shall call Jean, came from Indianapolis. Her father was a merchant. The one called Ida was from New York. Margaret was from Michigan. Her father was a minister. They were all in their third year of college. They had decided that they needed to try something different for a lark and had persuaded their parents that they were making a study of different types of people for their college professor. They had hoboed their way to California and this far back without a single unpleasant experience, they said. They had decided that the life of a woman hobo was as safe as the life of a college student.

Their clothes were about like ours. A little better material, maybe, but much more rumpled and soiled. They said they threw away their underwear and bought new rather than carry any with them or wash it at night.

They had money with them, and although they got a big kick out of bumming their way, they had actually paid for almost all of their own meals.

Although that was a long time ago, their story about the meals fits most of the women on the road who are out from colleges to experiment or to see just for a lark how it feels to bum rides. They can usually manage the rides, but they seldom get food free unless they repay the men who set it up for them with what every man wants from a woman.

Our men friends didn't ask anything of any of us that time, however. Times were good for them. They had made good money on the coast. They insisted they wanted to go to their new job broke. In those days many of the hoboes on the road were like that; they enjoyed beating their way about the country from job to job, making good money and spending it fast. It was just a principle of theirs to get their transportation free. When these men left us at Tucson they insisted that each one of us take five dollars. We did.

We hung around Tucson for a day, staying at a "Y" hotel that night in order to get baths. Early next evening the college girls and Ena and I got another empty box car. Ena and I were pretty new at this, but the other girls had done it before and didn't hesitate even when the train crew saw us get on. I noticed that the crew took pains that no men hoboes got into the car with us. We rode along until dark and then stopped for water. Then five of the crew walked down alongside our car and hailed us.

"Girls, get out and stretch your legs. Let's take a little

walk over here in the sage brush, smoke a cigarette—
have a drink." They spoke lightly, but to a purpose. Each
man took a girl by the arm and attempted to pull us off
in different directions. But I pulled back and faced the
one tugging at me.

"Look here, big boy," I said, "do you know what you're
doing? You're fixing to make a lot of trouble for yourselves. If you pull any rough stuff you'll hear from our
families and friends. You've all got wives and kids at
home that you don't want to hurt. Let's have a drink
and forget it."

Then the oldest man in the bunch, with Jean, spoke.

"The kid's right," he said. "Here, take this bottle. Climb
back into the car. We'll be friends."

And so the first time that a brakeman tried to take
payment from me passed off without anything happen-
ing. But the college girls were frightened and, since they
had money enough to pay their way, they left the train
at Bowie, Arizona, and bought tickets for themselves to
El Paso, where we agreed to meet them later.

We found them at the Sheldon Hotel, where we had
the luxury of a bath and comfortable beds which they
furnished us. Jean's father was fairly well off and had
apparently always given her what she wanted. She took a
liking to me and offered to help me through college. For
a moment I was tempted to go along with her—for a
little while at least, if only because it would be a new
experience, but then I remembered that Mallettini would
be in St. Louis in a few days, and that I wanted to be
where he was. My one regret about the box car trip I

had just taken was that it had been so slow. It was too late now for me to hear him speak in New Orleans. So I told Jean that if she'd help Ena and me get to St. Louis quickly we'd both be grateful.

She agreed to that and took us to St. Louis in a drawing room—the first I'd ever ridden in—then gave us some money and went on.

Ena and I rented in St. Louis a cheap room on Washington Street and the next night went to hear Mallettini. He was speaking in a big crowded hall, and had already begun when we entered, but recognized us and insisted we come up on the platform and sit by him. He was speaking in Italian. I could not understand the words, but I had a chance to watch the flow of emotion that passed over the crowd with the rise and fall of his wonderful voice.

Suddenly there was violent commotion at the back of the hall. A dozen police charged the platform. The audience lifted chairs and rushed the police. Clubs banged and men went down with bashed in heads. One of the police was just about to strike Mallettini with the butt of a gun. With all my strength I rushed him and tore it out of his hand. Someone from behind struck me a blow, and the next thing I knew, Ena, Mallettini, four other men, and I were in a patrol wagon.

They did not book us girls but took us to the women's department, where we were searched. I begged the matron to let me send a note to Mallettini, and she refused until I offered her $3.00. Then she delivered the note for me. We all spent the night in jail. There was only one other woman there, and she wasn't booked, either, but just allowed to sleep there till morning. She was an old Negro woman who had walked all the way up from Mt. Meigs, Alabama. She was in search of her son, Joe. She had put Joe through Talladega College. Her hair was in kinks. She had her few belongings in a shoulder bundle. These were spotless. Her old feet were scarred from the cotton fields. People had given her rides and food. She had not heard from Joe for eight months, but she was sure he was in St. Louis. She felt sure the police would find him for her. She was sure he needed her.

I talked with her a long time, and when I teased her a little about being a tramp on the road like myself, she objected with dignity, maintaining soberly that she had only had to travel that way to find her boy.

I have always remembered this old woman, for she was the first woman I talked to in St. Louis, where I have known more women hoboes in a short time than in any other city. And she is the only one I have ever known who felt it necessary to defend herself for being on the road.

One of the case-workers in an Alabama shelter which I visited later showed me a federal report about transients. This said that eighty-six percent of the total number of transients on the road now (those who register at transient camps and shelters) are white and native born, and that only eight percent are colored. Apparently the Negro race as a whole has the same attitude this old woman had!

When we left her in the jail the next morning, we were ably defended in court by two lawyers who represented the I. W. W. Free Speech Defense League, and were all discharged but Ena, who was turned over to the juvenile authorities. When I asked the lawyers to try to get her released they told me not to worry as the court had notified mother and they would probably send Ena home.

Mother's telegram answering the police was a peach.

"My daughter is old enough to take care of her sister," she wired. "The only things I am afraid of are the brutal police, the stupid charity workers, and the meddling reformers. Turn my daughter loose and I will be satisfied."

But it was more than two months before they did, and, in the meantime, in the Juvenile Detention Home, she had contracted scarlet fever. I was torn between my desire to see Mallettini, who had to go on to Chicago, and my duty to Ena. I wrote to him, and he replied, "Stay with Ena," and so I did.

FOUR

I SET about to find a position. Finally I spoke to the attorney who had defended me, and he offered me a place as housekeeper in his home.

He was a remarkable man. His name was Lowell Schroeder. He weighed over two hundred pounds, and was six feet tall, with dreamy brown eyes and rather long black hair that was beginning to grey. He was a successful attorney and had been in the Missouri legislature. In the last few years he had begun to devote most of his time to labor cases and to the championing of unpopular causes. His particular interest at the time I met him was unemployment, especially among unattached women.

When I came to work at his big house his wife had been dead several years and he was living with his mother and his son of fifteen. He paid little attention to me the first two weeks I was there, I thought. His mother did the cooking and I did the rest of the work. After I had been there three weeks his mother went east to visit another son, perhaps at Schroeder's instigation—I don't know. At any rate the day she left he told me gently, but quite casually and in a matter-of-fact manner, that he wanted me, and I spent the first of many nights with him. There was never any suggestion from either of us that it would be a permanent relationship. We wanted each other for the time being and took each other. Neither of us made any romantic pretensions about it or talked, or thought, about a future together.

After awhile Lowell's mother came back. She was seventy, blue-eyed, kindly, severe and a tyrannical boss of the whole household. She thought in terms of the kitchen and loved to cook and was resentful when I tried to help. Occasionally she became bitter and impossible, but I understood that I was an invader with a temporary lease and tried hard to be patient and kind. We finally became great friends.

Lowell Junior was a fine, tall, silent boy devoted to and afraid of his father. Junior and I often went for rides, walks and swims; he had an ambition to be a lawyer like his dad. He was always gentle and considerate to his grandmother and she worshipped him.

The first few weeks after Schroeder and I became lovers, I slept in my room until the family were supposed to be asleep before I went to his room. But after awhile we started to go to bed together and nothing was said about it.

While I was with him I became acquainted with a number of men whose names loomed large in the annals of unemployment and hoboing. The two most distinguished were General Jacob S. Coxey, of Massillon, Ohio, who led the famous Coxey Army March of 1894, and Dr. James Eads How, known as the Millionaire Hobo, who had organized hobo colleges all over America.

It was from Schroeder that I got my first technical

knowledge of the hobo problem. He told me that there were between a million and a half and two million hoboes roaming about the country, most of them men and boys. The most conservative estimates said that about half of one percent of them were women and girls, that is, about one woman to every couple of hundred men.

He also classified vagrants for me; as hoboes, the unattached men and women traveling around looking for work, tramps, the unattached penniless ones tramping around for excitement and adventure, like myself, and bums, who make up the third and smallest but the most troublesome type of vagrant, the type addicted to drugs and to drink and who have lost all sense of respectability. They are the barrel house habitues, the type you see lying around in alleys and parks and booze joints. A bum, he said, is not a vagrant who drinks occasionally. Most vagrants drink some. A bum drinks all the time and doesn't care anything about jobs or society. Fortunately this class is very small, and especially small among women.

General Coxey was seventy years old when I met him there. But he was the picture of vigor and health. He had sparkling blue eyes and an erect bearing which gained respect for him wherever he went.

He told me the story of Coxey's army's famous march. In the fall of 1893, he was driving from Massillon, Ohio, through muddy roads to a stone quarry some five miles beyond. The roads were in such bad condition that the horses could hardly pull the buggy through the mud. The thought came to him that it was an outrage to allow three million men's labor to be wasting, when they should be put to work in building good roads and making other public improvements.

When he got home from that trip he sat down at his desk and wrote out a program of how to finance a good road and other public improvements. It was based on the fifth clause of the eighth section of the first article of the Constitution of the United States which provides that the Congress shall have power to coin money, regulate the value thereof, and of foreign coin, and fix the standard of weights and measures. His plan was that the government should finance through community banks organized under State laws, farmers, merchants, manufacturers, partnerships, corporations, trusts, or trustees, and provide legal-tender money without interest secured by community non-interest-bearing twenty-five-year bonds for public improvements, market roads, employment of unemployed, and building homes.

The next step was to attract the attention of the nation to this plan. He attended the World's Fair in Chicago during the fall of 1893, and there met Carl Brown, who was a cartoonist and very well posted on the money question. Together they outlined a plan for the unemployed to make a march to Washington, to start the twenty-fifth of March, 1894; to arrive at Washington to make an address on the Capitol steps May first.

As soon as they announced their plan, groups of unemployed, on the Pacific coast as well as the Atlantic coast, heard of it and commenced to organize similar marches to Washington. While they did not arrive on the first of May, they came in later, about five thousand arriving in

Washington. It took the main group thirty-five days to march from Massillon, Ohio, starting on March twenty-fifth, arriving in Washington on April thirtieth so as to be prepared to appear on the Capitol steps May first.

A request was made of Speaker Crisp, of the House of Representatives, and Vice-President Stevenson, to allow Coxey to speak from the steps of the Capitol at noon, May first. This request was not granted. Neither was it denied, and the next day they proceeded up Pennsylvania Avenue to the Capitol Building, and halted the army on a side street, while Coxey started for the steps of the Capitol.

When he reached the Capitol steps he found a detail of police barring his way. "You can't speak here," they told him. He tried to read a protest which he had written out beforehand, but they wouldn't let him and led him off the Capitol grounds and let him go.

They arrested Carl Brown and Christopher Columbus Jones, who had gone on the Capitol grounds, and three days later arrested Coxey, charging all three of the men with treading upon the turf or grass and injuring the shrubbery. The men were tried and fined five dollars each and sentenced to jail for twenty days.

A bill drawn from Coxey's plan was introduced in the House of Representatives and a hearing obtained for it January 8, 1895. Such hearing was granted by William Jennings Bryan, who was chairman of the sub-committee of the Ways and Means Committee of the House of Representatives.

This was the first attempt, at any time, of the unemployed in this country to appeal to the national law makers for redress of grievances and plan to take care of all unemployed on public works when there was no demand for labor in production.

In 1914 Coxey made another march to Washington. This time he was allowed to go on the Capitol grounds and addressed the House and Senate, on the same errand and the same bill; and up to the present time that bill has been introduced into eleven different Congresses.

Dr. J. Eads How was a wizened Christ-like figure of a man, with sallow complexion and a short beard. His eyes were faded blue and apologetic, belying, along with his mild and almost tender voice, the sarcasm or stridency of his words. His grandfather Eads had built the great Eads bridge over the Mississippi at St. Louis. His father had been president of the Wabash Railroad.

It was his money, his love for the down-and-out unemployed homeless men and women that had rented old halls for them to meet in, and had brought before them professors, labor leaders, heads of radical movements, doctors, lawyers, economists, the best there were who talked to them of social and economic situations and of their own predicament. In Chicago, in Los Angeles, in St. Louis, and in Pittsburgh and New York, wherever Dr. How could find someone who would organize the speech schedule, and buy the milk and doughnuts or coffee and buns that went with the lectures, he paid the bills. He gave the unemployed a forum, a place where they could express themselves. He had made the unemployed conscious of their need for knowledge. He had made them realize that the only power for their liberation lay in being informed.

I also met a number of women hoboes, among whom three of the most interesting were Dorothy Mack, Lena Wilson, and Leg-and-a-Half Peggy.

Dorothy Mack was a stout girl of twenty-four, with dark brown eyes and hair combed back from her face like a man's. She had been on the road as a hobo for over five years. Usually she traveled by hitch-hiking. She said that most of the time it was simple and good fun, though often she found men difficult. More than once she had been dumped out of a car in the country because she wouldn't give a man what he wanted. She had worked for all kinds of commercial firms demonstrating furniture, cosmetics, cleaners, and other things sold in department stores or drug stores. She said she could take any line of merchandise and get a little space in a store and get a crowd of women around her and sell it. But she didn't like to stay very long on any one job. When she had worked for a few months she got rested and hit the road again.

Lena Wilson was a tall, red-haired woman with kind blue eyes. She was a typical soap-box agitator and box-car propagandist. She had been a member of the Socialist Party for almost a quarter of a century and said it was a full-time job. She had spoken in nearly every state in the Union. Like most agitators, she seldom paid any train fare.

"The railroads rob the workers," she said. "Why shouldn't we rob the railroads?"

She had been on the road for thirty-five years and traveled with the roughest and toughest kind of men. She had slept in box cars and in the open—with crooks and with murderers.

Leg-and-a-Half Peggy was born in the slums of Chicago, one of eleven children. Her leg had been cut off by the propeller of a speed boat when she had fallen out of it. She told me her story at great length but it was such a constant repetition of one sex adventure after another that it seems to me to add little to the story of the sisters of the road. Peggy was a prostitute as well as a tramp, and whenever she had to make a little money she sold her poor mutilated body to a man. And apparently there were plenty of takers.

Several years later I happened to run across Peggy in a Chicago department store. She was well dressed, buoyant, and happy. She had quit "hustling" and had settled down with one man, had finally married him, and seemed to have got completely over her desire for the road.

One morning in spring, while we were having breakfast, Ena came walking in, looking well and strong. She had developed considerably since I had seen her and she was glowing and happy. She had been sent home by the Juvenile Court some months before, but had not stayed long. And meanwhile she had taken her first lover, a young poet, with whom she had hoboed her way to St. Louis. She wanted me to join them and go to New York where the young poet hoped to get a job and publication for his poems.

The idea appealed to me. For several weeks Schroeder

had been going to meetings and social gatherings without taking me along, and several times he had stayed out all night without making any explanation. So I knew that he was tired of me, or had another woman, or both, and when I told him that I was going away we were both relieved.

FIVE

A WEEK later Ena, her poet lover and I got a ride with a sister of one of the men in Mr. Schroeder's office as far as Alton, Illinois, and from Alton got an empty box car with two men hoboes on a midnight freight.

It was a bumpy ride, full of scrapings and stoppings at every little jerk-water town in Illinois. Toward morning a brakie found us, but we gave him fifty cents apiece to shut him up. We ran into only one woman on this trip, but her story was worth all the discomfort we had. She and two tall, lanky southern male hoboes, all of them drawling in their talk, got on towards morning when we stopped and switched about in a little spot. The brakie had tipped us off that we had about an hour's wait, and we had gotten out to stretch ourselves. As it was getting light we walked around the quiet streets and up past the little red brick store buildings and the court house square that then had hitching posts around it. When we got back in our box car we found the girl and the two men there before us.

Her name was Virginia Hargreaves. She was thin, raw-boned, rather attractive in her overalls and heavy boy's sweater. Her husband had left her and she had attached herself to the two older men hoboes and was trying to make Chicago where a girl friend of hers had a job in a "house." She said the two men had helped her all the way from Alabama. Part of the time they had come in box cars, part of the time on the road hitch-hiking. They had hustled food for her and in return she had given them what sex expression they wanted. She was pretty cynical about men generally. After the train got rolling she told me how she lost her husband on her first hobo trip, on her wedding night.

Virginia was seventeen and had lived all her life in a small Georgia town. Hargreaves was the son of a farmer who had been dispossessed. They scraped together five dollars, bought a marriage license, gave the preacher fifty cents to marry them, and immediately after the ceremony hopped on a freight train intending to spend their honeymoon with relatives in Alabama.

When they got on the freight it was already moving, so they climbed up the ladder and got on top of an empty. It started to rain and soon poured down. They decided to swing down from the top and jump inside, a feat quite common among hoboes and sisters of the road.

Hargreaves held on to his wife's hands while she swung over the roof of the car and let her body down. She was in overalls. As her legs began to descend a pair of arms took hold of them and helped her into the car. Her husband attempted to follow her, but the train had gained speed and was jerking so badly that he was afraid he couldn't make it. He put one leg down slowly, then yelled after her, "I can't do it. I'll fall off!" He swung back and flattened himself on the top of the car, holding the sides for support. Hanging over the edge, he looked inside the car. What he saw made him wild.

The arms that had helped his wife down belonged to a male hobo, and were now around Virginia, struggling with her. But Hargreaves wasn't man enough to make another attempt to do anything about it. He simply lay there and watched while the hobo raped his wife.

The train thundered on a hundred miles through the mountains. Finally, when they came near a small town and the train slowed down to about twenty miles an hour, the hobo jumped off. When the train stopped, Hargreaves climbed down to his wife. He was beside himself with rage.

"You had no business leaving me on top of the car," he shouted. "It was your fault. You sure as hell can beat it. I'm going back."

And he did.

Virginia and her men were willing to risk the railroad dicks in Chicago, but Ena's poet had been picked up twice in the yards there, so we got off the train when it slowed up in Berwyn and rode into the city on a street car. We had sent our baggage on by American Express and walked through the Loop to get it on Randolph Street. Ena's poet suggested we go over to the Near North Side close to the Dill Pickle Club and Bughouse Square. Here we found a little three-room housekeeping apartment with two beds, and proceeded to settle down and look around.

The first thing I did was to hunt for Mallettini. I could find no trace of him. I wrote to the paper of which he was editor, and got an evasive answer, "The last we heard of our comrade he was touring the South."

I had fifty dollars, which Schroeder had given me, and for about a month we bummed around the city doing nothing. We spent much of our time in front of the Drake, the hotel that later played an important part in my life. In the evening we drifted over to the famous Bughouse Square, in front of the Newberry Library on Walton Place, between Clark and Dearborn Streets, where there were always exciting soap-box orators who said what they pleased and always found an audience.

No less than ten men who spoke there that first summer claimed to be king of the hoboes. One, who signed himself Dan O'Brien, Rex, an Irishman with a fine distinguished head, and who was seventy years old, always said that he was going to run for president. But the night I heard him he admitted that if the crowd didn't give him a good collection he'd have to "carry the banner."

Another king of the hoboes that I heard was Al Kaufman, a stuttering, handsome Jew of twenty-five, who claimed to have traveled 300,000 miles on thirty cents and his nerve. Another was Thomas Fitzgerald, a shrivelled hobo of fifty, who had tramped through every state in America and had been in fifty jails. By far the handsomest of these kings was Gus Schaffy, a scholar, an actor, and an impresario. When anyone challenged his kingdom he quoted, "They can copy my ships, but not my brain!"

The best known king was Jeff Davis, of Cincinnati.

He was tall, loose-jointed, partially bald, humorous in face and speech, and with a flare for organizing. He had a passion for denouncing all the other kings and for getting his name in the papers and in the movies. Later I attended several of his hobo conventions, and saw him just a few months ago in Pittsburgh in charge of the big hobo jungle jamboree of the 27th conclave of International Itinerant Workers Union.

That summer there were also a number of women, each of whom claimed the title, "Queen of the Hoboes." Among these were two elderly women who were not only queens but champions of the working class. Both were widows of Chicago anarchists of Haymarket Riot fame who were hanged November 11, 1887. The better known of these two was Lucy Parsons, who invited me to her home and gave me a copy of her book, *The Life of Albert Parsons*. Her skin was quite clay-colored, like that of a Mexican, and I learned that she was born in El Paso and had a full-blooded Indian father. She was bent over with age, yet her hair was hardly grey at all. I got a big thrill out of hearing from her the speeches of the earlier Chicago anarchists, her husband and Louis Lingg, when they were on trial for their lives.

The other anarchist widow was Nina Van Zandt Spies, a large breezy woman who wore many underskirts and walked with a cane and always had her hair flying about from under a pokey hat. Formerly she had been very beautiful, they told me. When I knew her she wore bifocal glasses and peered over them intently. She harbored many stray dogs and cats in her apartment, and the story went, until the health department interfered, she had kept a horse there too. She had a voice that sounded aristocratic, and whenever she spoke in Bughouse Square she thrilled her audiences as she told the story of "how they murdered my dear innocent husband."

The most popular queen was "Red Martha," keeper of the famous Martha Biegler Boarding House. Her place reminded me of my own mother's "Mother Thompson's Boarding House." Red Martha was originally from a little town in Illinois, and had taught in the socialist league. She was short and fat when I knew her, with her red hair greying. She had been a typesetter. Practically all of the more or less intellectual hoboes and sisters of the road who have visited Chicago in the last twenty years have stayed at her place. When any of us hobo girls were broke or hungry, we always knew where we could get a meal and a bed, and no questions asked.

By far the best known of the queens was Lizzie Davis. I saw her that first summer and later in New York, and got the end of her story a long time after, back in Chicago.

Lizzie was a large girl, with shoulders as broad as a man's. She was not bad looking, but was not the type of a girl men chose first on a dance floor. She was born in Tennessee, in the late nineties, from an enviable American racial stock, but from an environment that, our professors say, is so often the primary factor in the production of the maladjusted and the malcontent, a home in which there was domestic discord and desertion. In addition she had a nervous, puritanical, inexperienced mother who had to make a tremendous struggle to provide for her children.

As a child Lizzie was timid, imaginative and misunderstood, she said. The urge of love and life and the desire for freedom and adventure was always burning in her soul. And in a small country town there was no place for expression. At seventeen she attempted to escape by the way of matrimony and found out what so many women have learned to their sorrow that those who marry to escape drabness and the monotony of existence only find themselves in a worse jam. Through devious paths she found herself on the road as a hobo.

Lizzie had known practically every kind of social outcast that is mentioned in the police record. She had also met the other groups of higher-up and distinguished students, including professors, Freudian analysts, and novelists. She often quoted, "God, what things are there I haven't done to find a little adventure, love and peace!"

She told me her story several years ago when I ran into her in Cleveland:

"I've been everywhere hoboing, traveled the freights on deck," she said, "in the box cars, rode the bumpers, rode in the engine and the cow-catchers. I've beat the passenger trains by telling the conductor I lost my ticket, by hiding in the ladies' toilet, by riding the blinds and by decking it. I made the Twentieth Century right out of the Grand Central depot.

"When it comes to hitch-hiking, there's nothing to it. Anybody with a skirt on can hitch-hike. I go down between New York and Chicago just like a business man.

It never takes me more than three days and I always end up with more money than when I started. I go down to Palm Beach and Muscle Shoals in automobiles just as if I owned a fleet of them. I'm no beauty, and I never wear very good clothes, but I bet just as many men make love to me and try to sleep with me as they do with the beauties."

Lizzie's claims to fame were many. She was not like many women on the road whose place in the sun depends upon the fame of their lovers. And she had a group of sweethearts, as fine a group of men as ever went unhung.

Lizzie was a genius in her own right. She was a grand scandalmonger, and she did not like her scandal vicariously. She liked it straight. She knew the dirt about everybody. She knew if a man was "queer" or if a woman would take money or drinks for her favors. She knew the best neighborhood for panhandlers and when hostile bulls were on the beat. The lesbians and the fairies and the "queens" could keep nothing from her.

If there was anything radical, questionable, dangerous or sordid in the neighborhood, Lizzie was always a part of it. If there were any new perverted, vicious, crooked, anti-social terrible men in the community, Lizzie wanted them as lovers. Her love for the abnormal, the seared and the sordid, was only equalled by her admiration for good literature and scientific psychological research. Her devotion to the notorious gangster was only paralleled by her devotion to her son.

For Lizzie had a son. That is, she gave birth to a son. Really she never had him. The man who was his father knew Lizzie too well to let her bring up the boy. Lizzie's son was brought up in private schools, in special schools. He went to forty schools in twenty states, and was kicked out of most of them. He was Lizzie's son and he wanted to be with his mother, but the father, who also was a queer duck and lived on the fringe of criminal racketeering, spent his money on the kid's schooling and always had a five or ten dollar bill for Lizzie.

She always reminded me of a large turbine engine, throbbing away. She had tremendous sex appeal, in spite of her hundred and seventy pounds and her ill-fitting, shabby gowns. She'd steal a new dress and in two days it would look as though it had been slept in for a month. I've heard more than one woman say, "How in the hell can those fine looking young men stand for that woman?" Her chief asset and the most outstanding thing about her was her naturalness. It was not in her to be artificial or conventional. She had an uncanny ability to understand the psychology and behavior of social outcasts. She'd be walking down the street and meet a group of perverts and in five minutes they'd be standing on the street telling her everything they knew. They confessed their sins and their hopes to her.

Often she would meet a prostitute, get acquainted with her and go home with her and stay up all night or day talking. She would often watch how the girl turned her tricks. She knew all about prostitution but she was never a prostitute herself.

She was very popular and yet very much hated by the I. W. W. and labor leaders. She was often invited to their conferences. Men could talk freely and bitterly when she was in the room. The drunks liked to have her around, because she always stayed sober and when their money was gone, she knew how to get a bottle on tick.

A group of gangsters conspiring to rob and kill would permit Lizzie to stay in the room, having full confidence that she would not betray them. She was fearless and suspicionless, and had all the faith of a Seventh Day Adventist that she could get out of a jam.

One day she burglarized a home and was caught in the act by the police and dragged to the station. The next morning she looked the Judge square in the face and said, "Yes, I broke into that home to get some letters that my lover had written to one of your high school teachers." The Judge believed her, turned her loose, and the school board turned a high school teacher loose the next day.

She was a shop-lifter and seemed so clumsy at it that everyone marvelled that she didn't get caught, but she never did. She would go into a department store and paw over a lot of lovely gowns, find one that fitted her, put it under her arm and walk away with it. She not only stole her own clothes, but when she'd meet some poor ragged outcast, man or woman, she'd say, "Come along with me and I'll get you some clothes." And she always made her offer good.

She was a crude panhandler. She looked overly well fed, was haughty and often insulting. She had a simple technique when panhandling.

"Mister, wouldn't you like to give me twenty-five

cents?" she'd gurgle a smile and approach a stranger. "I need fifty cents for my room rent."

Although she begged considerably, she never liked it. She followed her primary behavior pattern. She was the fourth generation of hard-working American women, and she worked when she wanted to. She was a stenographer and typist. Most of the time she worked in the better shops and offices where they needed someone to address envelopes. Lizzie could do two thousand envelopes a day. She could sit at a machine and type for fifteen hours straight. She would get tired working and hobo for a time and become weary of hoboing and work.

There was no peace for her, no matter what she did. No man satisfied her no matter how much she loved him.

We met a number of homosexuals that summer, both male and female. There were several tea shops and bootleg joints on the near north side of Chicago that catered to lesbians. But I didn't like most of these women. There was only one that I became well acquainted with and she told me her story.

She called herself "Yvonne the Tzigane." She said she was a gypsy, come from a family of migratory entertainers. She was born in Paris, France. Her mother was a dancer from Russia, and her father was a well known artist. She was trained as an acrobatic split dancer and came to America in 1921 with a troupe of dancers and played all over the Keith circuit now known as the Orpheum. But she became tired of the stage and in 1925 took to the road. Her first trip from coast to coast in 1925 took her eighteen days. When she was thirteen years old she was seduced by a woman and lived with her for two years. Since then she had had several lesbian relationships which lasted varying lengths of time. She had had one male lover, also, and had born a child by him, but the child had died. She seemed to feel that there was little difference between a hetero-sexual and a homosexual relationship. On the whole, she felt a hetero-sexual relationship was better for a woman, since she believed that men were more dependable than women.

She said that there were a number of lesbians on the road and that usually they traveled in small groups. Apparently they had little difficulty in getting rides or obtaining food. The majority of automobilists, she said, sensed that they were queer and made very little effort to become familiar.

She told me that among the lesbians on the road there were always a number who were bi-sexual; that is, who liked both men and women and also another group who were prostitutes, selling themselves to men for money but having women sweethearts.

Many of the lesbians in Chicago hunted in packs and traveled in automobiles. There was a group of these who had a magnificent apartment on North Dearborn Street near the Park. I met a number of them there at a soirée called "Mickey Mouse's party." Half a dozen of them were wealthy women. Four of these were legally married and two of the four had children. They were there ostensibly as sightseers, but actually they had more than a superficial interest in these lesbian girls. But they were constantly being exploited. The lesbians would get their names and addresses and borrow money by saying, "I met you at Mickey Mouse's party."

Besides the kings and queens, there were hundreds, not dozens, but hundreds of articulate hoboes who spoke on the Square. Drunk or sober, ragged, and often unable to speak clear English, they could always get a crowd to listen to what they had to say. Many speeches started with, "When I was in Leavenworth," or, "When I was in the can in Detroit," or, "When they had me locked in in New York." And, "Fellow workers: I just came in from a hobo trip!" Or, "I haven't worked for seventeen years. I'm staying down at the Shelter House." And many of them began, "For the last three weeks I've been sleeping in Grant Park."

Not only did the hoboes talk about themselves, but everybody else talked about the hoboes and about unemployment.

Several of the regular speakers were brilliant. John Burns, tall, lanky and hatchet-faced, had a powerful way of talking. He had the manner of a politician, and I learned that he often electioneered for the Republican campaigns. He understood and explained the psychology of the hobo, the gangster and the criminal. Happy Jimmy Rowan, an I. W. W. veteran, told convincing stories of early hobo hardships. David Tullman, a short, stocky Jew with horn-rimmed glasses, knew a great deal about history, economics, and psychology, and talked on these subjects with wit and humor and many long words. He had much to say about hoboes. All this was an education to me. Not only at Bughouse Square, but at many forums, hoboes and vagrancy were the chief topics of discussion.

Always after meetings on the street, or at the Square, or at the Bug Club in Washington Park, or in any of the forums, a crowd of speakers and initiates would get together in the Penny Cafeteria, or in the home of one of our friends. We would talk for hours, often all night. Few of the speakers were working and everybody slept late. We women hoboes often slept out on the grass all night, or we might sleep anywhere. Ena and I must have slept in two dozen different houses or halls that first summer, although we always had our own room. Often I would bring a number of girls home with me, and occasionally a man would come.

Girls and women of every variety seemed to keep Chicago as their hobo center. They came in bronzed from hitch-hiking, in khaki. They came in ragged in men's overalls, having ridden freights, decking mail trains, riding the reefers, or riding the blinds on passenger trains. They came in driving their own dilapidated Fords or in the rattling side-cars of men hoboes' motorcycles. A few of them even had bicycles. They were from the west, south, east and north, even from Canada. They all centered about the Near North Side, in Bughouse Square, in the cheap rooming houses and light housekeeping establishments, or begged or accepted sleeping space from men or other women there before them. Some of them had paid their own way on buses or passenger trains but arrived broke to panhandle their food or berths with men temporarily able to keep them. A few had been stow-aways on Lake boats, and I remember one who said she stowed away on an airplane from Philadelphia. Not a few of them had their ways paid by charity organizations believing their stories that they had relatives here who would keep them.

On arrival most of them were bedraggled, dirty, and hungry. Half of them were ill. There were pitiful older ones who had been riding freights all over the country with raging toothaches. In Chicago they got themselves to clinics, and although they couldn't get any dental work done free they could usually get the old snags of teeth taken out. Some were obviously diseased, and most of them were careless about their ailments unless they had overwhelming pain.

The bulk of these women, and most all women on the road, I should say, traveled in pairs, either with a man to whom by feeling or by chance they had attached themselves, or with another woman. A few had husbands and children with them. There were a number traveling with brothers. Now and then there was a group of college girls. A few women traveled about with a mob or gang of men. These were of the hard-boiled, bossy type, usually, who had careless sex relations with anyone in their own group, and who, therefore, never had to bother to hunt for food or shelter. I do not remember, during the first years, seeing many pairs of lesbians come in off the road together, but of course they are common now, women who are emotionally attached to each other, even though, on the road, or while they stop, they give their sex to men or to other women in exchange for food, transportation, and lodging.

These women were out of every conceivable type of home. But even that first summer I could see what I know now after many years, that the women who take to the road are mainly those who come from broken homes, homes where the father and mother are divorced, where there are step-mothers or step-fathers, where both parents are dead, where they have had to live with aunts and uncles and grandparents. At least half the women on the road are out of such homes.

Many others, I have found, are graduates of orphan asylums. Shut up and held away from all activity, such girls have dreamed all their childhoods about traveling and seeing the world. As soon as they are released they take the quickest way to realizing their dreams, and become hoboes. Not a few are out of jails and institutions, choosing the road for freedom, the same way, regardless of hardship. Among these are actually many paroled from institutions for the feeble-minded and insane.

During my years in and out of Chicago I talked to hundreds of these women. How they managed without money on the road always fascinated me. Many worked from time to time. Some were typists, some file clerks, and carried with them recommendations from companies they had worked for. I knew one that first summer who was a graduate nurse. The only thing she carried with her on the road was a conservative looking dress which she could put on when she wanted to register for a job. She'd stay on a case, or a couple of cases, until she got a little

money again, and then she'd pack the good dress away
and go out on the road in trousers, hitch-hiking.

The bulk of the women on the road made no pretense
of working, however, even when they stayed for weeks
or even months, as they do in Chicago or any other big
center. I have already explained how they get by, by begging, stealing or hustling, or with help from the welfare
agencies.

Today, of course, all over the country there are state
relief stations, federal transient bureaus, travelers' aid
offices, but in the earlier days the missions and the private
charities would help transients, especially women. Some
of the girls made a specialty of all the words and attitudes that went with "being saved," and used them all
successfully to get the watery soup and the coffee and
bread that were put out by rescue missions in the name
of the Lord. Some of them made up circumstantial stories
of their Jewish ancestry (being Irish) and got emergency
help from Jewish agencies. Or they manufactured Ro-
man Catholic backgrounds (being Jewish) and got help
from Catholic missions. Others had acquired the language
of various lodges and fraternal organizations and in the
name of fathers and brothers and uncles who were Ma-
sons, Moose, Woodmen, Kiwanians, they were given
food or clothes or money for transportation.

But the great group of hobo women practiced none of
these tricks. Most of them weren't clever enough. Instead
they begged from stores and restaurants; from people on
the road or on the city sidewalks. A lot of them didn't
bother to beg rooms. If the weather was good they slept

in the parks with the men, or alongside them, cleaning up in the morning in the toilets of the libraries or other public buildings. And on the near north side there were dozens of people in studios and rooming houses who would let any of them in for a bath or clean-up.

One of the roughest, toughest and smuttiest flats we used to gather in was Tobey's. Tobey ran a bootleg joint on Hill Street, near the elevated, and this side of hell there was no worse conglomeration of human beings. Tobey was a rebel and a freethinker. He was tough and vulgar, a vicious, crooked, frightful sort of man. The vile, filthy language that he spouted, and the degrading way in which he handled his women were almost unspeakable, but I doubt if any aristocratic apartment of a wealthy bachelor in town attracted such a varied assortment of brains and talent as did Tobey's lousy flat.

Many of the best known labor leaders, the ones who not only believed in, but practiced, violence, came to his place for a loud drink, and quite a number of distinguished professors and literary men could be found there often. The poets, the real ones whose books did something for the community, came often.

I shall never forget the first night that Lucille Donoghue, the wife of the star reporter, Terry Donoghue, brought me to Tobey's. The place was stuffy and crowded with half-drunken men and soused women. Two of the "heavy men" (burglars) I met that night were killed by policemen soon after.

I despised Tobey, with his heavy jaw and penetrating eyes, the moment I laid eyes on him. He leered at me, and attempted to put his dirty hand under my dress before he had talked with me five minutes. About twelve o'clock two cabs stopped in front of the place, and a group of actors and newspaper men came in. Among them was Earl Ford, who was playing in *The Front Page,* and some of the stars from *My Maryland.*

There was no piano, but there was music. There was no modesty or decency, but there was genuine intellectual activity. I was amazed at how clearly the drunken, brutal Tobey could think. After Earl Ford downed a pint of "moon," he recited part of *The Ballad of Reading Gaol.* I left the party with a bunch of actors. Ena refused to leave, and when her poet attempted to drag her out, Tobey broke a china cuspidor over his head.

In practically every large city that I have visited, except those in the South, I found hobo colleges, unemployed councils, and radical forums that were run especially for the hoboes and the unemployed. They were nothing new to me. But the most interesting of them all was the one in Chicago, located in an old bank building at Washington and Desplaines Streets. The director was a physician, and the superintendent was John Burns, the Bughouse Square speaker I have already mentioned. For months I attended the meetings regularly. There were three each day, one at ten in the morning, the others at three and eight in the evening.

The staff at Hobo College was drawn from many walks of life some of which had nothing to do with hoboing. It was here that I not only heard but met Richard Bennett, the actor. He made a delightful and humorous speech and invited the whole audience to come to his play. We all loved him in *They Knew What They Wanted,* and after the play we all ganged into his dressing room and had a grand time. Mary McCormic sang for us at the College, and afterwards gave the superintendent fifty dollars and sent him out to buy food for the crowd. Gilda Gray, the dancer, and her husband and publicity man, came over and danced and sang for us. Her husband got a taxi and brought us some wonderful cakes from the swellest baker in town and a whole milk can full of steaming coffee.

There were a good many authors at the College. Jim Tully came and made an arrogant speech. He was short, ferocious and red-headed, with a very dramatic manner. He brought with him Daniel Hennessy, a newspaper man who had written several good books on hoboes for the Haldeman Julius Little Blue Books. Professor Nels Anderson, author of *The Hobo,* and several other textbooks on sociology, also spoke to us. He had a strong, rugged, purposeful face and a rare way of telling a funny story, but the thing I remember most about him was a certain sweetness and tolerance that showed in his lips and in his voice as he talked of conditions on the road and of the things he and we had done and were then doing. Professor Edwin Sutherland, author of a splendid book on criminals, also gave us a fine talk.

Besides these men we heard some of the most noted professors and sociologists in America, Professor E. A. Ross, of Madison, Professor E. W. Burgess, of the University of Chicago, and Professor Herbert Blumer, secretary of the

American Sociological Society. Professor Blumer was a former college football star, large and dominating in body but with scholarly eyes and quietness of manner.

I am mentioning all these illustrious names to make it quite plain that the hoboes are not a bunch of dumb ignoramuses, and that they have an interest in and capacity for good lectures and for worthwhile intellectual food. Besides having the finest type of teachers, the most profound professors, and the ablest adult educators come to Hobo College, the students themselves, the hoboes, became able to think and talk more clearly. By far the most brilliant teachers and the most inspiring speakers who taught at the College belonged to us and came from the life we knew. One of these was Franklin Jordan, the man who later became "my heart." Although I saw Jordan every day, and fell in love with him the very first time I laid eyes on him, we did not become intimate until much later.

I had many jobs in Chicago that first year. One was as a typist and clerk in a big mail order house. One was addressing envelopes for a politician. And the last was as an office girl for a woman physician, Dr. Hope Stone.

Dr. Stone and I met at one of the radical forums and liked each other almost at once. She was small, decisive in manner, clean cut in features. She asked me to work for her. She had an enormous practice and maintained an elaborate suite of offices in a large downtown building. There were on the staff besides myself, a secretary, a nurse, a confidential clerk, her sister, who looked after her finances, and two assistant physicians.

Dr. Stone was an abortionist, now in business for herself, but once had been the assistant of a Dr. Cooper. Old Dr. Cooper had been an abortion specialist for thirty years, and the rumor was that he averaged ten curettages a day for the entire time. There is no proof of this, but if true, then he lessened the population by a hundred thousand souls during his lifetime. But even if it is only one-half or one-fourth true, he has more than 25,000 abortions to his credit. A number of people who are familiar with the abortion business in America told me that other men have performed even more than that number.

There was not a single day during the six weeks that I worked for Dr. Stone in which there were less than twenty-five patients. They were not all operated on, but fully two-thirds were—an average certainly of fifteen operations a day. On the same floor with Dr. Stone there were two other abortionists, and in the same building, four more.

No one ever saw Dr. Stone operate. A patient came into the office. I took her name and address and asked who sent her to see the doctor. A large part of the doctor's practice was referred to her by other physicians. She kept one little cozy office, down the corridor, far away from the operating room, where she would meet the doctors who sent her patients, give them a drink and pay them their commissions.

After I talked to the patient I would admit her to the secretary's office, where the secretary and patient would talk over the business side of the visit. It was a cash business, but not a cold and cruel cash business. Dr. Stone was kind and often operated for nothing, sometimes even giving the penniless patient some money from her own purse. After satisfactory financial arrangements were made (and an effort was made to get cash . . . cash in advance,) the patient was sent into the examining room. I saw over six hundred patients in the six weeks of my stay there. The average fee was $50. Often, though, it was $25. A good many times it was $75, and sometimes $100. It was not unusual to get $150, or $200. Nor was it rare to get $10. Or nothing at all.

Dr. Stone examined every patient herself.

"This kind of practice isn't at all hazardous if you can choose your patient," she told me. "Most of the fatalities in interrupted pregnancies come from infections, and I have never yet had an infection. Nobody goes into our operating room who is not sterile, and the patients are prepared in the most careful manner. I always make an examination and a smear of a woman. If she is infected I will not operate. And I never take a case after four and a half months unless they can go to a hospital. Women who are weak, or who have tumors or diseases, I refuse to operate on. I turn down half a dozen cases every day, no matter how much money or influence they may have."

Dr. Stone interviewed all comers. I've seen policemen bring their wives and officials their stenographers. She didn't care who knew she was an abortionist. If they had the money and were physically fit for the operation, she took them. Everybody in the building knew what she was doing, and it seems that everybody in town knew it too. I asked Miss Jensen, one of her nurses, if there wasn't any danger to it.

"Sure . . . there's danger," she answered me. "The police and the City Hall know what she is doing. But nearly all of these men want a good reliable abortionist at some time or other. Dr. Stone is careful and skillful, and she will operate for a low fee. Whenever any of the Police Court attaches, or one of the State's Attorney's men have a friend that needs an operation, they send her to the doctor and she takes care of them without charge. They say that she pays a big graft . . . but I think this service to the powers that be is all she gives for protection. I've been with her five years, and we've had only four deaths in all that time. That is much less than any doctor would have had if he had treated half as many legitimate patients. And not a fifth as many deaths as for a doctor with an equal number of full term obstetrical cases."

It's difficult to say what percent of Dr. Stone's cases were married. They nearly all lied about it. The married women said they were single and the single women said they were married. But I should say they were about half and half.

I used to think that the doctor performed all the operations herself. But I learned, to my surprise, that she did not do a single one. She would examine the patient, and if everything was satisfactory, would take her into another room and put a sheet over her head. Then one of her assistant doctors would perform the operation. Quite often they would give the patient gas, and in that case the patient could never tell how long an operation lasted.

SIX

ENA and I were drinking considerably and hanging around Tobey's. She had lost her lover because of Tobey and had forgotten all about her New York plans. But suddenly she became nauseated with Tobey's filthy talk.

"I'm sick of Chicago, Bertha," she complained. "Come on south, or any place with me, will you? Let's take our time and travel by freight."

Meanwhile I was getting restless, too. I had stayed too long at a job, so I agreed.

The night before we left I spent in Franklin Jordan's arms—one fleeting happy night.

Ena and I took an Illinois Central train, in an empty box car with four men hoboes, on the fifteenth of December, in bitter cold weather, and arrived in Nashville two days later. We rode the front end of a passenger train from there to Chattanooga. When the conductor found us half frozen on the blinds and asked us where we were going, we said "Chattanooga." He took us into the coach and let us sit down. The passengers took up a collection and paid our fares, and one older woman, plainly dressed, invited us to her home in Chattanooga. We accepted, and stayed three days. Then I noticed she was a little too interested in Ena and sat watching her across the living room in the evenings. One night she asked Ena to sleep with her and Ena made some excuse, and the next day we got out of town.

While roaming around the town the day before we had met a pair of twins, the Morgan sisters, Pauline with the buck teeth, (that was the only way I could tell her from the other) and May. They lived down beyond Jacksonville, Florida, and urged us to go along the road with them. It was on this trip that we stopped at a very important hobo camp on the outskirts of Jacksonville. The girls had stopped there before.

Camp Busted, as it is called, was about three miles from the edge of town, on the banks of a little stream and hidden from the tracks and the highway by a cluster of trees. When we arrived, about four o'clock in the afternoon, there were already thirty men, fifteen women, and eighteen children, all white. At the edge of the camp were four or five dilapidated cars and one truck. There were also motorcycles and a couple of bicycles.

"We're just about to get supper," said a large greasy-faced woman in overalls. "Have you girls any vittles or money to throw in the pot? If you ain't, you're welcome jes' the same. But there's lots of things more we need for supper. Got plenty of vegetables, but we need butter and some condensed milk and some dessert. An' if you got any money, we gotta buy some cheesecloth and cotton for some o' the ladies here. And somebody's got to go down to the doctor or the dispensary and get a bottle of cough syrup."

"An' if you kids can panhandle," spoke up a lank, worn, bald-headed man of fifty, named Tulliver, "I wish you'd bum an axle for me. That ole Chevy of mine . . . if it wasn't for Mr. Jamison with his truck, my wife and two kids would have starved to death in that swamp."

May took hold of my hand and said, "Box Car, let's go to town and get what they want."

And then Don, a boy of about fifteen, offered to drive us in. As we left, his sister, Susie, approached him.

"Don't forget the tickets for the gas," she said, and handed him a length of rubber hose.

We left Don in the town siphoning gas from a Peerless into a milk bottle.

"I never take gas from anybody unless his car cost over two thousand," he told us. "These folks with Fords and Chevies are as poor as I am."

"Do you know how to beg, Bertha?" asked May.

"Not very well, I'm afraid."

"Just watch me, then."

The first place we stopped was a big drug store.

"I want to see the manager," said May.

"Yes, ladies. And what can I do for you?"

"We girls are sick and haven't any money. Will you trust us for some Kotex?" she asked, without any embarrassment.

The manager blushed furiously and hemmed and hawed.

"Why certainly," he said, avoiding her eyes. "Is there anything else you'd like?"

"Well, it would be very kind of you to give us a soda. And we *could* use a little face powder."

As we walked out with the things, I whispered, "You forgot the cough syrup, didn't you?"

"No, I didn't. I believe in dividing my patronage."

Next we visited the "Famous Grocery and Meat Market."

"Hello," said May to the manager. "How's business?"

"All right, thank you, miss. What can we do for you?"

"We're broke. We're from out at the hobo camp, and we need a lot of things."

His eyes grew hard and his mouth set in a firm line.

"Then go down to the charitable organization and tell them about it," he said. "And if you come in here again, I'll have you locked up."

"O. K., baby," May answered him jauntily, and we turned and walked out.

When we were on the sidewalk she grinned at me.

"Scrummy old bastard, wasn't he?" she asked. "What did you get, Bertha?"

"I don't know what you mean," I said.

She looked up in surprise, meanwhile fumbling in the folds of her dress.

"Do you mean to say you didn't swipe anything from that old bear?" she asked. "Why I got two cakes of soap and a can of tomatoes, and I dunno what this is. . . ."

It turned out to be toothpicks!

We went into another grocery.

"I want a large basket," she said, "because I want to get a number of things. Two pounds of butter, half a dozen cans of condensed milk, five pounds of sugar. . . . And have you got some nice fresh cheese? Put in a pound . . . and I'd better take two dozen eggs. And a bottle of shoe polish . . . black."

The clerk loaded the basket while I looked on in astonishment. May looked all the things over, then turned to
the clerk.

"Now my brother's going to come in the car for these,"
she said, "and he'll pay you when he gets here. Just leave
them in the front of the store."

She looked at me without cracking a smile. Out we
went, and up over a bank to a doctor's office. The doctor
was sitting at his desk writing.

"Hello, doc. Have you any cough medicine?" she asked.

"Tell me what's the matter," he said.

"Oh, there's a bunch of kids out at the camp, and
they're sick and need some cough medicine. We ain't got
any money and you look like a good fellow. Thought
maybe you'd have some samples. . . ." He not only gave
her what she asked for, but some pills and fifty cents. We
thanked him and then went out and found Don.

"There's a basket of groceries right over there by the
door," May told him. "Get them for me."

And he did . . . just walked over to the door at the
right moment, picked up the basket, put it in the car and
drove off.

"Do you think it's right to steal that basket of groceries?" I asked May.

"Do you think it would be all right to let that bunch up
at the camp go hungry?" she countered. But I wasn't very
happy about it.

"I'd feel better if I'd paid for them," I said. "I've got
a little money."

"Don't be a chump," said May.

"Some day I may be a thief, but not now. . . . I don't think my mother or my grandmother would be very happy if I told them I stole the groceries," I continued.

Just as I was about to go ahead and pay for them she stopped me.

"Why don't you go over and pay for all the rides you've stolen from the railroad company?" she asked angrily. "Is it any worse to steal groceries than to steal rides from the railroad?"

I had never thought of it that way. It had never occurred to me that riding freights was stealing from the railroad. May made her point.

"Drive on, Don. Go to the biggest candy store in town. I'm going to get some candy and ice cream for the children," I said. And when I came out I had two quarts of cream and a big box of candy that I had not paid for.

"Which is the worse," asked May, "begging or stealing?"

We had a very happy supper. Old Mrs. Heaton, the cook, prepared a fine meal in at least a dozen pots and kettles. Each of the car owners and a number of the "bundle stiffs" (hoboes who carry their own cooking utensils and a blanket on their backs) had their pans filled. "Gump stew" (stolen chicken) was the chief dish, and it was served on pie tins, and so was most everything else served in tin. I saw only four or five china cups and saucers in the lot. (The usual bundle stiff's outfit for the road is a little frying pan, a stew pan for stew or tea or coffee, a tin cup, and a knife, fork and spoon.)

After supper we girls helped clean the dishes and scour the pots and pans, and then I helped put the children to bed. One mother had four youngsters, two had three each, three had two, and two had one each. All but two of the families had cars of their own, and the motorcycle belonged to a woman and her little twelve-year-old girl. Three couples had shared the truck. One of these had two children. The youngsters were tucked in the cars or on little pallets on the ground. Then we older ones sat down to enjoy the chilly evening around a huge bonfire.

It was a motley crowd. The men were dressed for the road, in overalls and jackets, and the women, most of them, because they were for the moment resting, had on calico dresses, cotton stockings, low rough shoes. Only a few had coats. Three of the men brought out an accordion, a violin, and a fife, and when the music grew lively some of the older children crept out in their nighties to join in the singing and the fun. Cigarettes and tobacco were passed around, and nearly everybody smoked. Three of the women were drawing on corncob pipes, and a short, gray-haired woman about sixty pulled out of her pocket a handful of cigar butts, and chewed on them, passing the largest ones over to her crony, "Sunshine Molly." Molly was a tall, malaria-ridden South Carolinian, traveling with her grown son, Slim. She did not chew her cigar butts, but lit them.

"Mom," begged Slim, "C'n I have the butts when you're finished?"

The talk was largely about the road. The car owners had long tales. Gas was high, the cars they had were pieces of junk, needing everything they couldn't afford.

"When the charities know you've got a car they won't

help you," one of the men wailed. "They always ask, 'Why don't you sell it? You'd get fifty or twenty-five, or at least ten dollars for it.' Well, I've got four kids and all the junk we own in the world is in that car. I couldn't get more'n ten dollars for it . . . and it's our home. You know they wouldn't ask a man to sell his home for ten dollars."

"You see this wrench?" spoke up a young Italian. "I can open any pump in any filling station with it."

"You know how I get gas?" asked a mother with a babe at her breast. "I just drive up in front of the City Hall. I leave my husband and boy in the car. Then I go in with the baby in my arms and find the sheriff or the mayor or the chief of police. I say to them that we're broke, and we need gas and oil, or even a new tire. If they'll give it to us, we'll get right out of town. But if they won't, they'll have to take care of us, 'cause we haven't got a cent. I always tell them we've got some relatives about a hundred miles farther on, if we can only get to them."

Don put in, "That's all right in these little jerkwater towns. But in the big places they send you to the charity officers. And they want your whole life's history."

"My old man and I and the little girl left Muncie for Florida," a square-faced woman of forty broke in, "and we used to stop at the city hall in the small towns and get gas and help. But we tried it in one little place in Kentucky, and they sent us to the Welfare Office. They searched our car and found two quarts of whiskey. They had us arrested, and they said we wasn't fit to take care of the child. They took our baby away from us, kept her in an orphan asylum for awhile, and then sent her back to Indiana. Anybody that's got any sense won't never go to no charity organization or to the police. They don't like the poor, and they never do them no good. I'd rather steal or beg on the street. I find I can most always manage to find a day's work in town."

May got up from the fire and stretched.

"These plutocrats with cars give me a pain," she said. "Let's go over there awhile."

She pointed to another fire nearby where sat five or six young men. The twins, and a girl from Chicago named Sue, a New York Jewess called Helen, and Ena and I joined the new group.

We were welcomed with cigarettes, and, the talk drifting into personalities, Sue told her story.

"I left New York with my sweetheart, Fred Hardy," Sue said. "He was a wonderful person, and before he took sick he worked in a book-store and we got along fine. But he got terribly weak, so he opened a little restaurant and forum called 'The Nail Rack,' and I helped him nights when I got home from my job at the telephone office. He got so sick that I thought Florida would help him so we started out for Miami, riding freights part of the time, and hitch-hiking some. When we got to a little town near Birmingham we had only a dollar. We stopped at a hotel for seventy-five cents, and Fred went out to get a package of cigarettes. In the alley near our hotel a colored man held him up and shot him in the stomach when he resisted. A policeman knocked at my door and I ran out and found

Fred groaning in the street. He was taken to the hospital, but he died three days later."

Her story led off to other stories of love and sex. Many of the unattached hoboes began to edge into our group. They were frankly on the make. Pauline and May sat off to the side with two of the younger boes. Georgia Jim was trying to impress the Jewess by asking her a lot of questions, but she flatly refused to have anything to do with him, saying, "Keep your dirty, poisonous hands off of me." Ena had snuggled up to a blond young Norwegian and didn't seem to hear much of the conversation.

And then, out of the shadows on the roadside of the jungles came two more men. One was tall, handsome, wearing khaki. The other was a short, strong figure. Suddenly my heart leaped wildly and I was on my feet in an instant. The short beard, those shoulders. . . . It could only be Mallettini! I threw myself into his arms.

He was surprised to see me and pleased. And for me the crowd around the fire faded, and my eyes saw only one person—Mallettini. We went for a long walk through the woods, down along the edge of the highway. He had been organizing the Italian cooks and waiters for a strike, and was driving to Miami the next morning, and there would catch a boat a few days later for New York.

"I'll go with you," I said.

He looked at me a little wistfully and hesitantly.

"But I haven't enough money to take you," he told me.

"Never mind . . . We'll get it!" I insisted.

Don drove me to the telegraph office in town early in the morning. I wired both E. A. O., at Seattle, and Lowell

Schroeder in St. Louis. . . . "In great need . . . if possible wire me fifty dollars." By the next evening I had a hundred dollars, and Ena and I took a bus to Miami. When the boat sailed for New York we were on it with Mallettini.

I had looked forward to a beautiful experience with him. I had known him for a long time, and there seemed to be between us a strong and compelling attraction. I knew that I loved him and I felt that I was his so strongly that he must be mine. It was one of the commonest errors human beings make. But, to my surprise, he refused to come to my cabin, nor would he let me come to his. We walked the deck. He was miserably silent.

"Darling," I said. "Why don't you talk to me? Why don't you let me love you? What have you got on your mind? Why are you so unhappy? Life is to live."

"Baby, you don't understand," he said. "I have love for the people, not for myself or for a woman. All over the world people are hungry. Tyrants, kings, dictators, popes, priests, capitalists make slaves of the people. I want to get rid of them. I have nothing left to love a woman with."

But I did understand. When I looked into his eyes and felt his suffering. I felt humble and no longer wanted to intrude my yearnings for his body upon his spirit. I wanted to be a part of his work, and to share his suffering. When he left me at the dock in New York I held his head to my breast and we told each other good-bye. Mallettini was to spend only a few days in New York—busy days, and then would be off to Chicago.

SEVEN

ENA and I took a room in Greenwich Village. I wasn't interested in anything except looking around, but Ena hunted a job, and got one, as a maid for a young woman in a small apartment on Washington Square, and I loafed around the Village. But a week was all I could stand. Mallettini was on my mind. I determined to follow him, even if he did not want me. I had a little money left, and I took a bus to Trenton, where I caught a freight to Chicago. Except for being scolded by a fussy brakeman at Buffalo and having an uneventful night in a hobo camp at Erie, nothing happened until I reached Cleveland.

I had heard the yards were tough there, so I got out of the empty box car in a hurry and made off between the rows of cars. About fifty feet down the tracks a rough looking "dick" stopped me.

"Where are you going?" he asked.

"I'm going home," I answered.

"Now, don't lie to me," he growled. "Where do you live? You know damned well you came in on a freight. I'm going to lock you up."

He took hold of my arm and led me over to a little section hand's shanty and shut the door behind us.

"If I took you over to the police station they'd give you

sixty days," he said. "If you are nice to me I'll let you go and give you a little change besides."

His face was ugly. He was used to getting what he wanted. I had a vision of all the girls on the road running into him and being taken into the same shanty before they could get through Cleveland. I saw red, and I hauled off and slapped him across the face.

"Give me the sixty days," I said.

His face was ugly and red with fury as he reached for a phone and called a patrol wagon. Then he sat and glowered at me while we waited. If looks could kill, we would both have died in that shanty.

They took me off to the station and the next morning I came up before Judge Dan Cull.

"Have you an attorney?" he asked me.

"No."

Then a young lawyer, Martin Eisler, stepped forward and said, "Your Honor, I'll be glad to defend this young lady."

The clerk handed me a Bible.

"I don't want to swear on the Bible," I told him.

"Why not?" asked the Judge.

"Why not?" I repeated it after him vaguely. I wasn't sure. But the Bible put into my hands at that moment made me angry. Words of my free-thought friends came to me, and I used them.

"Because the Bible is a pack of lies. Because it's a lot of bunk to keep the minds of the workers in bondage."

The Judge scowled down at me.

"Go on with the case," he said to the lawyers.

The two railroad dicks swore they had seen me get out of a loaded car of merchandise, and it was quite evident that I had broken the seal of the car to enter. They also said that I had cursed them and used vile language in resisting arrest, and that I had tried to slug them. Mr. Eisler said what he could for me, but it was no use.

"Bertha Thompson, I sentence you to sixty days in the Warrensville Work House. I want to give you plenty of time to read your Bible."

A big bus took seven of us from the Cleveland County jail to Warrensville House of Correction, where all our clothes were taken from us, and we were sent to the regulation shower. When we left the shower room we had to walk a distance of perhaps ten feet stark naked, with our arms raised high, hands wide open and mouths open, too, in full view of the matron. Every orifice of the body, and the spaces between the toes and the hair were examined, to be sure that no dope was being brought in.

In the dressing room we were given our own shoes and stockings and underclothing and clean uniforms. Too late for the regular supper, seven of us they called "fresh fish" were given a meal. Then we were shown our beds in the dormitory and taken to the prison yard, where we were allowed to spend two hours before bedtime.

I looked over my fellow prisoners. No one seemed downcast. The girls were gossiping and laughing. The older women, and fully a third seemed to be over fifty, were sitting quietly on benches, talking. Nearly half of the prisoners were colored.

Big Mamie, a husky Irish woman, greeted me with a wide smile.

"Welcome to our hotel. What are you in for?"

"The Judge said it was vagrancy," I answered. "But my guess is that it was for not handling a man right. What are most of these women in for?"

She shrugged.

"Oh, booze . . . jazz . . . and stealin'. Some of them are dopes."

Franklin Jordan's statement, "All women's actions are motivated by the desire for pleasure, profit and power," popped into my mind.

"Who is that mopey-looking one there?" I indicated a sad-eyed girl who stood pressing her hands together in front of her and mumbling.

"Oh, that's some jane the bulls picked up on the street saying, 'He murdered me . . . he murdered me with his love.' I think she's nuts, but the Judge didn't think so, and he gave her thirty days out here to quiet down. But instead of that she's bawling all night . . . 'he murdered me with his love.'

"That bunch of women over there on that bench are dope fiends." She indicated a haggard looking group. "They make it hard for everybody," she continued. "If they ask you to help them make a connection, don't have anything to do with them. If they want you to let somebody write you a letter for them, say no. A workhouse would be a good place if it wasn't for the dope fiends. On account of them you can't have nothing sent in, no food or clothes or anything to make things a little more pleasant. And say, sister, see those two girls there with the short hair?" She pointed out two girls with boyish bobs. "Keep away from them, too. They're lady lovers. And if you don't look out, they'll try to make you."

Big Mamie, I found out the next day, was my partner on the mangle in the laundry, where I was assigned to work. Her weakness was booze. She had been in Warrensville twenty-three times, and twenty times she had been pinched by the same bull. She had some sort of a complex. Every time she got stewed in a joint called Cassidy's Saloon, she wanted to "clean up" the place. She finished her bit in the workhouse two days after I got there.

My next partner on the mangle was a beautiful grey-eyed girl, Lucille. She was transferred that day from working in Superintendent Burns' residence. She had not been in the laundry more than twenty minutes before the place was alive with buzzing. Being the maid in Superintendent Burns' house was the most coveted job around. There were good eats there and also comparative freedom. The talk was that this job could only be had by a fix from the outside. Some of the girls said that Lucille was kicked out because she was lazy. Others said for using dope. But the older ones, looking at her nice figure, said that the old lady Burns was jealous.

All of us women slept in one room, a large dormitory with sixty beds on each side and a large window between every two beds. The ceiling was high and the place airy. I slept on the cot at the end of the row. Lucille was next to me. The aisle between the rows of beds was fifteen feet wide. The space between the beds three feet.

Lucille and I worked together for almost a week. She was not at all unfriendly or hostile, but she refused to talk about herself. I told her about my box car experience. I asked her questions. She shook her head good naturedly with always the same smile. She seemed absorbed and very quickly I learned it was better not to say anything to her. Her philosophy seemed to be, "I've got sixty days to do. The less I say about it the quicker it will pass by," and I accepted this also.

Periodically the officers of the jail searched the prison. This was known as the "shake." Every prisoner was carefully searched. The bunks and the lockers in which they kept their personal belongings next to their beds were also rummaged. The purpose of the "shake" was to discover whether the prisoners had any contraband objects, weapons, knives, saws, booze, dope, cigarettes, tobacco, matches, clothing stolen from the laundry, extra food. They were especially on the watch for articles which the girls might have stolen from each other.

Most of the prisoners did not fear the "shake" because they had nothing to conceal. It wasn't any special crime for one girl to swipe a lipstick from another, and it was no great offense to steal each other's underwear and handkerchiefs. But it was regarded as grand larceny to steal clothes from the matrons and the officers. I remember one day one of the girls gave me a lovely brassiere. She had two of them. A few days later one of the matrons found it on me and asked me where I got it. I quickly sensed that it was stolen and said I had found it. Good naturedly she said she had been working here for twenty-five years and never found anything, and took the brassiere away from me.

Sunday was general visiting day for all comers. Any other day it was necessary to get a pass from the Director of Public Welfare or from the Superintendent. No one came to see me. No one knew where I was. But Lucille had a number of special visitors.

We only worked half a day on Saturday. Saturday afternoon before our time was up, Sadie, the "runner," came into the dormitory and announced that Lucille had a visitor. While she was out with her visitor, Mr. Burns, with three matrons and two guards, came in and ordered all of us to stand against the wall at the head of our beds. The "shake" was on.

One matron and one male guard, together with two male trusties, carefully examined every bed. They took off the sheets and pillow cases and shook them thoroughly, and felt and punched each mattress. They watched for little rips or any new stitches. Often prisoners made little incisions in the mattresses, hid what they wanted, and sewed them up again. But the "shake" squad was on to nearly all of their tricks. The lockers where the girls kept their combs, rouge, face powder and trinkets were carefully "fine-combed." They squeezed the tooth paste if it belonged to an apparent dope. Every article of clothing was carefully examined, even the bulky seams opened.

The general "shake" had been completed up to Lucille's bed when she returned from her visitor. She was startled. Immediately she turned and asked the matron if she could go to the toilet, but was refused. The window between our

beds was open. I noticed that she was clutching something
in one hand. She shifted about, and finally put her hands
behind her back. Then she attempted to throw whatever
she had out the open window. She miscalculated and the
object hit the ledge of the window, bounced back and fell
on my bed near the pillow. The squad was working at the
other end of the bed but immediately picked up a rubber
finger stall filled with heroin. Burns looked at me.

"You Big Truck Horse, you've fooled us all the time
you've been here."

I felt myself blushing. I turned my gaze to Lucille,
thinking that she would admit ownership, but her face
was expressionless. They took me by the arm and sat me
down in a chair in the middle of the room while they
frisked Lucille's bed and person. Burns went to the telephone, and a half hour later two men came in, members
of the federal narcotic squad.

Burns took me to his office.

"Miss Thompson, these are two federal officers and I
want you to talk to them honestly and fearlessly. You're a
good girl. We don't think you're a dope fiend, and if you
tell the truth we'll let you go. You have only a few days
left here and here's a chance for you to do something for
your government. You love your country, you're a good
citizen and you can help us."

But I said nothing. Then the federal man started.

"Look here, kid, this is no joke. This is a federal offense.
We found this stuff on your bed and if you don't tell us
the truth, we'll send you to the penitentiary for five years.
If you don't want to disgrace your mother and your folks,

you'll tell us the truth. If you didn't put it there, you know who did. This broad Lucille don't mean you any good. She wouldn't give you a quarter to keep you from starving to death. Are you going to be a sucker and go down there for five years for her? You know this Lucille is a dope fiend and we know you've been holding her stuff for her."

"I don't know anything about it," I said, and I repeated it a hundred times. "I'm not a dope fiend. I've never used it in my life. I wouldn't know how."

They coaxed me. They tried to bribe me. They threatened me, shook their fists in my face, shouted at me, abused me. I became so infuriated finally I slapped the matron in the face, and at that point two matrons and three guards dragged and carried me down to the basement and threw me in the "hole," the horrible, dark cell used for solitary confinement.

I fell to the floor exhausted. It must have been hours later when the door opened and the guards threw someone else to the floor. The cell was pitch dark. I heard someone moaning, and then heard Lucille's voice.

"Are you in here, kid?" she asked.

I crept over to her side and put my arms around her. She was in pain, sobbing bitterly.

She said nothing and I felt too miserable to say anything either, and we both sat there on the floor, our arms about each other, sobbing. After awhile we both went to sleep. I don't know how long we slept. I woke to find Lucille holding my head in her lap.

"How do you feel?" she asked. "They told me you

squawked on me but I know you didn't. You're all right. You ought to be doing something better than riding in box cars. You're not going to get yourself any money that way."

"We do those things," I said. "It doesn't seem to matter. Why do you use dope?"

She laughed harshly.

"It's good for my asthma," she said.

Then she became serious.

"Junk neved did anyone good, except peddlers, and if you're not convinced of this now you will be in a couple of days when I start to 'kick my habit.' Thank God, we're both going to be out of this joint Friday morning."

In the next two days I had one of the most harrowing experiences of my whole life, watching a woman taking the "cold turkey" cure, or "kicking" a dope habit. Lucille did everything but die in that cell. First she was irritable and talkative. She walked up and down. Then she kicked and stamped and began to vomit. She complained about pains in her abdomen and muscles. She begged me to rub her legs and arms. She prayed and cursed. We lost track of time for it was always pitch dark there. Lucille became more and more noisy. After hours and hours the guard and the matron, who had evidently been standing in front of the cell for a time, suddenly opened the door.

"Ah, what's the matter—too much heat in here, sister?" the guard asked.

"For Christ's sake, send me a croaker," Lucille begged them. "I'm dying—I'm dying!"

"You know how to get a doctor," they answered her.

"You know the federal officers are the only ones who can help you. Why don't you send for that doctor who came to see you Saturday? They grabbed him off and he's confessed everything."

But between groans Lucille still managed to be defiant.

"If he's confessed anything, he's lying," she said.

The next three days dragged along. Lucille lay exhausted and limp but no longer in pain. Then we tried to make plans. She told me little about herself, but when she asked me where I was going, and I told her that I wanted to go into Chicago, and that I would go by freight, she said, "I never rode in a freight, Box Car, but I'll bet I did something once you never did. I beat my way in the ladies' toilet and got a trip all the way from Omaha to Cedar Rapids, Iowa. I was flat in Omaha. Never mind why. I knew a traveling salesman who made his headquarters at a hotel in Cedar Rapids. I knew if I could get to him he'd fix me up. I got the idea about the toilet from way back when I was a child. My mother and I were in the toilet when the conductor came through and he never came back to take up our tickets. We turned them in after our trip and got our money back.

"I knew it was risky, but I was desperate and willing to try anything. I picked a day coach, and followed along closely behind a bunch of college people taking packages on for a girl going away. Luck was with me. The toilet was unlocked. I waited for over a half hour till the train got under way and the conductor had come through, and then I sauntered out and sat down by the first man who eyed me. He had the little yellow ticket up between the windows, showing he had had his ticket punched. It was night. After awhile everybody slumped down in their seats and took off their shoes like they do. I saw the conductor opening the door to come into our car, so I snuggled down quick and put my head on this bird's shoulder. He had been trying to get his hand on my knee ever since I sat down, so he didn't throw me out."

I asked her where she was going when she got out of the workhouse.

"I'm going to Chicago and I'll pay your fare."

Suddenly I was aware of my lack of clothing. I told her.

"To hell with clothes," she answered me. "They don't mean anything. You're all right with me, kid. If you were good enough to go to the hole for me, you're good enough to ride a pullman with me."

Thursday afternoon I was called out by the federal officers and, in their phraseology, I was given another and a last chance to save myself from the five years if I would admit that I saw Lucille throw that dope on my bed.

"I don't know anything about it," I said. "I don't use dope. I don't want to use dope. I don't know how it got there. I don't want to know anything about it."

They tried to confuse and threaten me, and to the end told me they would be there in the morning to take me to the penitentiary. But they did not take us back to the hole. That night Lucille and I slept in our own beds after we had been given baths and a good supper. Lucille was still unable to eat. She gave me her food and I devoured it as well as my own. After breakfast we were called and "dressed out."

I had eleven cents when I was arrested, and this was returned to me. Lucille signed a receipt for sixty-five dollars. We got on a street car and when we had gone about a mile Lucille saw a taxi. We hailed it and were driven to the Statler, in Cleveland, where Lucille registered and received mail which was waiting for her. We went to the room and Lucille gave me money and sent me out for the daily paper and some oranges.

When I came back, in about fifteen minutes, I found her in finer spirits than I had ever seen her, and I knew she was full of junk, which she had received in her mail. All her woes and days of torture were over. She ordered a meal sent up to the room for us and we ate and laughed and joked as if we hadn't a care in the world.

We took the night train and arrived in Chicago the following morning at eight o'clock and took a taxicab to Lucille's home. It was in a modest enough apartment house but expensively furnished. Anna, Lucille's roommate, welcomed us. From another room came two sleepy looking men, Jake and Jimmie. Jimmie was medium-sized with sallow complexion and dirty brown hair. Jake was very dark and looked like an Italian. Both had been lounging about in B. V. D.'s and trousers. They did not seem to mind newcomers.

Anna gave me a dress and some of her underwear and drew a tub of water for me. I had just bathed and dressed when the bell rang and they admitted a man who was introduced to me as Big Otto and who I quickly learned had just been released from Bordeau Prison, Montreal, after having served a two-year stretch. Later I found it was for being a sneak thief, a "heel" as they called it.

I was struck by the lack of enthusiasm and emotion. No one seemed particularly excited about the fact that Big Otto and Lucille had just been released from jails. Everything was very matter of fact.

Big Otto fascinated me from the beginning. He was tall and powerfully built, and very dark in complexion, in spite of his prison pallor. He looked straight at me with deep-set eyes and said, "How are you, big girl? You look good to me. Can we all have a little drink together?"

I looked well in Anna's dress, and felt especially comfortable and snug in my girdle and brassiere. I had brushed my hair back, and while Anna was helping me to dress, she had insisted that I rouge my lips and she had pencilled my eyebrows. As I looked into the glass I smiled in admiration of myself.

We had a lively lunch. The conversation was purely business. Otto said the French Canadian guards didn't like Americans, especially in jail. There he had a job in the bathroom and met quite a few of his old friends who came in. No one expressed any sympathy or concern over him. They appeared somewhat bored if he spoke of anything in jail. Everybody in the room had been through the same thing. If not in Bordeau it was at Leeds Farm, Kansas City, the Beanery of Chicago, Down Duck at Boston, or on the Island at New York. The conversation quickly switched to the next spot they would grift.

Otto announced that he had to run over to the Sheridan Plaza to deliver a message for Jimmie Doyle whom he had just left in Montreal, and invited me to walk over there with him. When we came near the hotel he asked me to wait in the drug store until he returned. He came back in about fifteen minutes and I asked him if he wouldn't like to walk over towards the lake.

"Not to-day kid. I've got a little business."

We stopped in front of a ladies' specialty shop and he asked me to wait outside for a few minutes while he went in to see someone in there. When he came out, he stopped at the corner drug store and had me wait outside again. When we got back to the apartment he walked over to the table and from somewhere mysteriously brought forth two beautiful teddies, six pairs of hose and a bottle of perfume, some face powder, and a jar of cold cream.

"Here, kid, you may need these. If you don't like them, don't try to exchange them, because the sale was final."

For a moment I didn't know what to say and just looked at the things Otto had given me. I was pretty sure he had stolen them, and I didn't like it, but I hardly felt as though I were in a position to be his moral arbiter, so I thanked him briefly and let it go at that.

"That's all right, kid," he said. "Just forget it and I'll get you some handkerchiefs so you can keep your nose clean."

That night he came into my room after I had gone to bed, and I was glad.

He was a unique lover. He didn't say personal things to me. He avoided all tenderness. But when I woke up in the morning, his arms were around me. His cheeks were sallow and somewhat sunken. There was sorrow in his face. When I kissed him he started, then opened his eyes slowly.

"Is that you, gorgeous?" he asked gently. "Jesus, it's good to wake up and see wallpaper. I've been looking at bars and calcimine for two years."

EIGHT

FOR the next week the little group was very busy. I was so wrapped up in Otto that I didn't know what they were doing. At night Otto showed me that he loved me. But in the daytime he was almost impersonal and avoided any show of affection on my part or any personal talk. About the affairs of the gang he said nothing. Nor did any of them. They came and went with suitcases and handbags. Occasionally a man who, I learned later, was a "fence" came in and they dickered over the price of merchandise which they finally sold to him. I paid little attention to prices. I remember one lovely transparent velvet dress which was tagged eighty-five dollars for which they accepted twenty-five dollars. The "fence" stressed the fact that he had to resell the stuff for a profit and that's why he couldn't pay more. From what I was able to learn, they usually asked one-third of the tag price, but often the buyer gave much less.

After they had grifted for a week in Chicago, they announced we were going on a road trip with Jimmie and Jake, who had their own cars.

The next morning we left Chicago by automobile, Anna and Jake driving together, and Lucille, Jimmie, Otto and I in the other car. We stopped at Bloomington and Springfield, in each of which they lifted merchandise from the stores. At Springfield Otto got me a beautiful bag with a $50 price tag on it. It seemed so easy! They simply went out and came back later with the things. I didn't want to steal myself, but I was glad to see how it was done.

When we got to St. Louis we went to the Statler Hotel and took three rooms on the same floor. The following day was Saturday and everyone was active in the stores from eleven o'clock on. I stayed at the hotel. About three o'clock Lucille came in with three dresses and said that Anna had just been "guzzled," (that is, arrested) in the Famous Barr Store, and that she would have to get busy and telephone to get her out.

We went to a drug store and she called a number and asked for a Mr. Miller and told him Anna was in trouble and to get busy and that his dough would be ready as soon as Anna was on the street.

We went back to the hotel and met the rest of the group. When Lucille told them what had happened, no one seemed upset. They simply got ready to go on with their plans, saying that they could not help the situation by lying around the room, and they could be out making some money in the meantime. I asked Otto if I could go with him. At first he refused, but I pleaded that I didn't want to sit in the room and that I wouldn't interfere and that I just wanted to go along.

"All right, you can come as far as the stores, but don't connect with me at any time regardless of what you see, or what happens," he told me.

He left me at Stix, Baer, Fuller's, and I bought a few postcards at the corner and stepped across into the post office to mail them. When I came out, I crossed the street and saw him coming out of the store and turning towards the hotel. He did not see me, nor did he see two men who followed him out of the store and up the street. I started to catch up with him so I could warn him, but then I remembered his instructions and did not speak, even though we walked into the hotel within two feet of one another.

Otto went immediately into the elevator just as it was leaving the main floor. The two men who were following stopped and spoke to the house detective, and I, taking advantage of the delay, went over to the house telephone, and called Lucille's room. Jimmie answered the telephone.

"There are two men in the hotel tailing Otto," I told her and shut off quickly. When the officers searched our room they found nothing but twenty dollars Jimmie gave them.

Outside the hotel I met all but Otto, who had made a hurried exit, after arranging with Lucille to meet us at Indianapolis, and we drove to the Jefferson Hotel, where we were to meet Miller, the "fix." It was after seven o'clock when he drove up with Anna. Lucille, Anna and Miller went into the restaurant to complete the financial end of Anna's release, and the boys and I remained in the car. We left that night for Indianapolis, arriving very early in the morning, where we found Otto already checked in under a pre-arranged name at the Claypool Hotel.

As we drove through the darkness from St. Louis to Indianapolis, I realized that I was caught in a net. It was an exciting net, and it gave me all the action I wanted and a lover to thrill me. But I found that I didn't like being part of a gang of crooks. Something·in my heart rebelled against it.

When we checked in I found that Otto had thoughtfully registered me in the hotel as his wife. He was sleeping when I got to our room. I woke him up and he said, "Oh, hello, come on in," and turned over and went back to sleep. I wanted to talk with him. I was disappointed and furious and shook him and said, "Otto, aren't you glad to see me?"

"Sure I am, but I'd be glad if you'd go to sleep, too."

I watched him as he slept. His face was more sallow than ever, and strained and worried. I thought as I watched him that I was not very important to him. I wondered whether he was very important to me or whether it was only the novelty of living with a grifter that held me. I went to bed beside him determined to make him stop living the kind of life he was living or to go away from him. But before morning he moved toward me in his sleep and when I took him in my arms I wanted nothing in the world except to hold him away from danger.

"Otto, do you think we ought to go on this way very much longer?" I asked him across the rose-lighted table in the hotel dining room at breakfast.

"What are you beefing about?" he answered me. "Aren't we getting along all right? Haven't you got everything you need? What do you want? If I can't steal it, I'll buy it for you."

"I don't like the way you're living," I protested. "I don't like these narrow escapes."

"Listen, kid, if I can keep on having narrow escapes the rest of my life, I'll be satisfied," he told me grimly. "The narrow escapes don't count. It's the pinches that bother me."

But he was suddenly very dear to me, and I couldn't stop.

"Dear, can't you get a job so you and I can settle down?"

Then he looked at me impersonally, as if I were nothing to him.

"What have you been reading lately . . . *Good Housekeeping?*" he asked scornfully.

The next few days in Indianapolis were but a repetition of former days. But after Otto's rebuff I could not speak to him again of stopping. I sat around the hotels, worrying lest something happen to my man. From Indianapolis we went to Pittsburgh, and from there to New York. And it was here that I first noticed they spoke less about their business before me. Otto surprised me the morning we left by throwing a fur coat at me, and saying, "See if you can get into that." It was my first fur coat, and I was overjoyed until I remembered some woman was going without a coat. When I threw my arms around him, he looked bored.

"Cut that out," he said abruptly. "You've been going to the movies again."

I went with the mob six months. We traveled from coast

to coast and it began to be monotonous. Every few weeks Otto would give me money to send to mother and Ena. But I couldn't tell them how I got it and that depressed me. It was the first time I had ever had to conceal anything from mother. Yet I felt that I had gained a great deal from association with the gang. I had wanted to learn the intimate details of the lives of crooks and now I knew. The books I had read and the professors I had talked to gave the world the impression that professional criminals were entirely different from normal people. They inferred that crooks looked and dressed differently and had a language all their own, but this was not my experience.

When Lucille first introduced me to her friends and later to many of her friends' friends who were in the racket I was thrilled, and made up my mind to learn all I could about this group. My first reaction was one of astonishment. They looked and they dressed like respectable men and women.

Professional thieves, when they are beginners, go in for the gaudy and conspicuous. The women like to wear theatrical-appearing gowns, and some of the jewelry they steal. The amateurs paint and decorate themselves like soda fountain girls, but they soon find, and often by costly experience, that this is not only bad taste but extremely unwise.

If a thief is to operate successfully over any length of time, he or she must be inconspicuous in everything. They find by experience that they always have a market for the gaudy dresses in the vice areas. But in the gang itself there is always feeling against any of the women even owning flashy things.

NINE

AS the weeks passed the discipline of the mob, which required such utter and constant secrecy, came more and more to bore me. I had decided that it was hopeless to try further to make Otto leave his life of crime, and, although I loved him, I knew that I could find no permanent satisfaction in living his way. It wasn't only that I didn't like crime or the uncertain, furtive life of the criminal, but I knew, too, that I would never be satisfied with the casual, impersonal attitude all of the mob took toward their love lives. All of them seemed detached from living and from any intense relationships. I knew they slept together, but it always seemed to me that any sex relationships they might have was incidental to everything else.

After a time I began to realize that they were all probably like Otto. Otto didn't talk sex. In the daytime he looked at me matter-of-factly, as if I had not been in his arms at all in the night. If he discussed women it was always from the angle of their grifting ability or something else that had to do with their accomplishments or sense. I found that I could not help resenting his attitude toward me. We would have a gorgeous night together, and I couldn't always forget it the moment we got up. But he could, and did, and if I mentioned it, he would cut me off short with talk about something else. In the night he loved me as if I were an escape from something else, something to help him forget. But he didn't want to talk about it. Talk of loving appeared to bore him and the others. After I had been with them a few months, I began to wonder if it were not embarrassment which inhibited them. They prided themselves on their nerve and on their hardness. They were afraid to speak of things that were close to them for fear they would go soft.

There were few legal marriages among them. The philosophy was, "If you won't stick without marriage, you won't stick with it."

Just because they didn't practice marriage did not mean they did not believe in loyalty, however. They did. Among their own group the men and women were rigorously faithful to each other. No man in the mob would think of making sexual approaches to his friend's sweetheart. Only occasionally a man would take an excursion, and then with a public prostitute. I only heard of one woman who was associated with a grifter who was promiscuous. Most of the cannons (pickpockets) were married and had wives to whom they sent their money, established in homes in some part of the country. Quite a number of them had children who were kept in ignorance of their father's business. Their social life was confined to their own circles. They had no friends outside, nor did they seek them. They had many acquaintances, of course, among the operators of fake auction rooms, purchases of stolen property, pawnbrokers, lawyers and doctors, all of whom knew their means of livelihood.

I had always wondered what connection professional crooks had with politics. I found they had little. The average thief asks no political favors. When he gets into trouble he gets it "fixed" by paying cash for it. Most of the affiliation of crime with politics in the large cities is carried on by the vice, gambling, liquor interests and labor, with the aid of the local hoodlums. The real professional crook doesn't even know who's mayor and cares less. All that he needs to know is that he has to have a bankroll when he goes to the politicians. And he knows, too, that bankrolls operate as well with Republicans as they do with the Democrats, and that they have done even some good in Socialist Milwaukee and in Farmer-Laborite Minneapolis. A bankroll has even been known to work wonders with reformers. The professionals have learned that when they go to the "fix" nobody asks, "Who did you vote for?" or "How many votes can you get me?" but "Have you got the cash with you?"

The racket people with whom I was associated ate well, but were never gourmands. I realized, with them, that I knew little about food, little about forks and spoons and knives. These folks knew the difference between an oyster and a salad fork. I found they liked good food, and delicacies—alligator pears, caviar, olives, stuffed with anchovies, artichokes.

I was surprised to learn how little they drank. Their's was a hazardous business, and for safety it was essential that they keep sober and not appear at the "meet" with a hangover. I never saw anyone of the grifter group drunk. I was told that gang members who did forget and whoop it up at cabarets usually didn't last very long.

On the other hand, a good many of the grifters I was with and many of the professional groups of pickpockets, shop-lifters, and confidence game people I knew during that time were users of narcotics. I should judge that one in every four was an addict. Anna and Jake smoked "the pipe," (opium). This consisted of a round bowl about three inches in diameter with a bamboo stem eighteen inches long and an inch in diameter. I have seen many variations of the opium pipe, but this particular outfit, or "layout," consisted of six bowls and four stems, three small traveling lamps that burned peanut oil, a dozen yen hoks, (like a crochet hook, but finer and more flexible, used for preparing the opium pill) and three yen shee gows, steel instruments for removing the yen shee or ash from the inside of the bowl.

When they could, Anna and Jake smoked twice a day. There were in the group, however, "three-a-dayers" and "four-a-dayers," and there were parties which included the non-habitual users, those who indulged occasionally merely for the pleasure, companionship, or intimacy which the pipe afforded.

Anyone can learn quickly to snuff cocaine or heroin, or take, under the skin or in the vein, a hypodermic injection of morphine, but it takes expert skill and considerable equipment to prepare the opium pipe. Soon the group got used to me around with them, and went right ahead in front of me or in front of Otto, who did not indulge, either.

Gum opium, in brick or ball form, is bought from dealers, usually for about fifty-five dollars a pound. Anna and Jake paid about eighty-five dollars a month for "stuff." They reduced the gum to "tar," a dangerous process, to be done in private. Opium has an extremely strong, penetrating odor, and the trained nose can detect it at a great distance and for a long time. It is cooked in a double boiler until it is a syrupy mass, then strained through cheesecloth several times. A bit of glycerine is added and the composition poured into a "toy," usually an opaque glass jar. The residue, known as the "dog," consisting of leaves, twigs, and stems from the plants, which remains in the cheesecloth, is thrown away. The opium then looks like tar and is so called.

Although I would not use it myself, I watched the others many times. With the yen hok, a piece the size of a small pea was taken and held over the flame of the lamp, where it changed to a beautiful golden brown color and increased four times in size. This was pressed on the heel of the hand and made solid again. Then, still on the yen hok, it was held over the lamp once more. Next it was "shied" or manipulated into a conical form known as "the pill." This pill was placed over the "bushing" or small opening in the bowl, and the yen hok withdrawn. Then the smoker placed the stem to his mouth, and held the bowl of the pipe over the lamp, where the heat vaporized the opium so it could be inhaled as smoke. A few short puffs and the "chef" got ready another pill, for some one not adept enough to prepare his own.

Anna and Jake and other habitual users smoked the pipe in recumbent position, lying either on the bed or on a mattress on the floor. Before this stage of the procedure they were careful to stuff all keyholes, and to paste adhesive tape over the cracks around the door and to hang wet sheets over the doors and windows.

The actual smoking process was very complicated, and very quick, only about ten seconds to smoke a pill. Anna, whom I watched many times, placed the stem against her lips and inhaled quickly. She took six or eight short deep breaths, and, then, as her lungs filled, one final, prolonged draw to get all of the smoke possible from the pill into her lungs.

For the habitual smoker the desire is to produce a state of self-satisfaction that he must have. Really he smokes not so much for pleasure as to avoid pain and mental anguish which he suffers if free from opium. Anna was a habitual smoker and had a hunger only opium could satisfy. She put it this way:

"I smoke my habit off before going to bed and I smoke my habit off when I wake up in the morning."

To smoke her habit off meant to take enough opium to protect her from pain and anxiety.

With the pleasure smoker who takes the pipe only occasionally, the reaction is quite different. I watched a number of women just learning to smoke. After the first pill they began to experience buoyancy and a sense of well-being. They got talkative. These emotions increased until the fourth pill, and then they became drowsy and quickly fell asleep. Even after eight hours' sleep they retained some of the same buoyant feeling. As far as I could learn, neither the habitual nor the pleasure smoker had any fantastic dreams or illusions of grandeur, nor did they become bold or courageous.

The sex life of a pipe smoker is lessened. Desire is suspended and capacities are extremely weakened. Anna admitted to me that what sex she had meant little to her or to any of them on the regular habit. On the other hand, the pleasure smoker has his desires greatly stimulated by the pipe, although it retards considerably the culmination of the sex act.

Lucille and Jimmie used "white stuff," heroin and morphine, which are the alkaloids of opium. "White stuff" comes in small tablets, cubes, or in powder. It is sold in New York for twenty dollars an ounce, and was shipped out to our group by mail in ten ounce lots. They never kept more than an ounce in their possession at one time. They kept the balance in a safety deposit box in a Chicago bank, and when they were out of town they arranged for a friend to send it to them. Lucille and Jimmie always carried a small heroin "plant," or supply, sewed in their clothing, to be ready in case of emergency, such as an arrest. Heroin was more easily used than morphine, as it could be inhaled.

Lucille told me that her "junk" habit cost her at least thirty-five dollars a month. If anything interfered with their source of supply in New York, they had to pay thirty-five dollars an ounce instead of twenty from a different dealer in Chicago.

I did not know then, but I do now, that very few women hoboes use drugs in any form. The number I have known is not even one percent. In the first place, women of the road are invariably broke, and junk costs money. The same is true of the women who spend much of their time in shelter homes. The only sisters of the road who indulge in it are those whose hoboing is secondary to their racket. Crooks or prostitutes who occasionally hobo their way about sometimes go in for dope. In the south this is much more common than in the north. The specialty there is marajuana cigarettes.

Marajuana is called among the users, "muggles." It is really a form of hasheesh, slightly changed when grown on American soil. It came to this country first from Mexico. New Orleans and all the southern cities are full of it. In New Orleans it is grown commonly in the back yards of the Old Town. It is available also in every northern city. In south Chicago there is a whole field growing wild, which is harvested by Mexicans and various small wholesale dealers.

Marajuana is popular because it is prepared without trouble and because it gives tremendous effect at very low cost. The leaves and blossoms are gathered, dried, and rolled into cigarettes slightly thinner than the ordinary package cigarettes, and twisted together on the ends so that none of the substance may be spilled. In almost every city they may be had as low as twenty-five cents each. In New Orleans they are two for a quarter. One cigarette, if

smoked by those who know the way, will give a thorough
"muggles jag" to at least three persons for an entire night.

Otto was the only one of the grifters I was with who
had ever used marajuana. He stopped, he said, because he
didn't intend to get into the dope habit. Just twice while
I was with him did he make a buy, once in Philadelphia,
where he just walked into a poolroom and secured one
cigarette at the cigar counter, and the other time on a
party down on Dumaine Street in New Orleans.

We had driven down to New Orleans from Savannah
on one of the road trips and the gang had put in three
days grifting, making good hauls. Otto had had a narrow
escape, being pinched the last day and having to pay two
hundred dollars to a fix to get him out. It was summer
and terribly hot. The night was stifling as we walked down
in the little streets of the French quarter. Suddenly he
declared he wanted "a weed" and after asking a few questions of some of the loafers around Tony Vaccaro's saloon, we made a purchase of a half dozen cigarettes in a
little charcoal store on Saint Ann Street. Otto didn't even
wait to get back to the hotel. He lit one right there and
walked out with it. After a few short drags he handed it
to me.

"Try it, kid," he said, already cheering up, "it will kill
the blues. Now don't waste it. Draw the smoke inward in
short drags and hold it in your lungs for a minute and
then let it out very slowly. There . . . there's enough for
a beginning. Did it put on the rose-colored glasses?"

I didn't get much effect at first. The cigarette was
sweetish in flavor. The flat dead smell almost nauseated

me. But after the second drag I began to feel very happy and light-hearted. Otto promptly snubbed out the cigarette carefully in the palm of his hand and put it in his pocket.

"Here's once we save butts, kid," he told me jovially, "that's good to the last shred. Here, smoke a regular cigarette now. That will keep the effect of the other longer."

As we went on down toward the old French market, all the objects in the street suddenly became very vivid. Colors were stronger. Objects and people larger. The lights shone more brightly, and the edges of their flares diffused into reds and greens. We found ourselves very gay and joking. Everything Otto said seemed exceedingly important. People were amusing to us.

My last experience with my criminal friends was the second time we were in Boston. I was window shopping, avoiding Filene's, which I knew they would be working. I was stopped within a few minutes by two plain clothes policemen who said they had seen me in company with police characters, and wanted to know who they were. I denied knowing such persons. Then they demanded to know who I was. Not thinking very fast, I said what I usually said in such cases, the truth, that I was a hobo, just traveling around the country, and that I had just come to town. They looked at me and laughed and took me to the Lagrange Street Station. "Look at the hobo we just picked up," they said to the sergeant, and he laughed too when he looked at my clothes.

They took my purse and found nearly a hundred dollars and the key to the hotel room. My heart sank. Lucille and Otto had warned me repeatedly not to carry a key. I was mugged and finger printed and locked up in a cell.

Sergeant Lake called the hotel and asked who was in that room. Fortunately the call was answered by a clerk who was very friendly to the gang. He had to give the information, of course, but he recognized the police voice, and tipped off Otto, who cleaned the room before the squad got there. They found nothing in the room but my handbag.

Later they wanted to know where the Mr. Smith was who was registered as my husband. I didn't know, I told them. I stayed in jail all night, but I was called out front by Otto's lawyer, who said I would be turned loose, not to worry, and to meet Otto at the Essex Hotel about noon next day. The trial was simple. I pleaded not guilty to whatever they charged me with, and when the judge found that I had no police record, he suggested that I get out of town. They gave me back my purse, from which someone had lifted seventy dollars.

I felt I'd pulled a boner. When I saw Otto's face I was sure of it.

"Well, gorgeous, you finally got yourself in the can and you damned near got us all in with you," he said. "We've talked you over, Bertha, and we think you're too good for this troupe. Your clothes are all packed, and here is a hundred dollar note. I'm afraid you can't stand this city life, kid. Go back to your box car. If you're smart, you'll never leave it!" He said not one personal word of good-bye.

But by that time I knew Otto, and I knew that in

daylight he would never show what he felt. I felt pretty wretched, but I made up my mind not to show it either. And all of my training and experience had made quick and unexpected partings easier for me.

I took the train to Providence and the night boat to New York. Outwardly I was calm. But my heart longed for Otto and I knew that I wanted him as I had never wanted anything else.

TEN

SEVERAL months before mother had learned, from a visitor at Home Colony, that my father, Walker C. Smith, was still in New York, operating a little radical book store, and had sent on his address to me. Suddenly I wanted something that belonged to me. I had never seen him. One morning I rang the bell at his little basement flat on 113th Street, which was both his shop and his home. A short man, middle-aged, rather vague in manner but with intense eyes looking out under shaggy brows, answered the door. He did not ask my errand.

"Won't you come in?" he said pleasantly.

I followed without saying anything and as I entered the room from which he had come, paused, before speaking, to examine it. Everything in the room was dirty and in great disorder. Stacks of old newspapers rose from the floor nearly to the ceiling. Pictures of Ingersoll, Walt Whitman, Charles Darwin, Heckel, Tolstoy, Proudhon, and Voltaire hung on the walls. There was a rack of pamphlets with sale prices on them, ten, twenty-five and fifty cents. When he saw that I was looking at the books, he went back to his writing without saying a word. Finally I came over to him and put a hand on his shoulder.

"Mr. Smith," I asked, "do I look like anybody you know?"

He squinted one eye at me and finished writing a sentence to its end.

"There's something familiar about you," he said, "and something pleasant. But I can't place you. Have you ever been to any of my dinners?" (He was the Secretary of the Rising Sun, a famous dining and discussion club.)

I sat down on the edge of his desk. Then he put aside his pen.

"Don't you know who I am?" I asked. "I'm your daughter. Didn't you ever care if I existed? Why haven't you tried to get in touch with me?"

He looked up at me with mild interest, but no surprise or special enthusiasm, and certainly nothing which remotely resembled embarrassment.

"Your name's Bertha, isn't it?" he asked.

I felt let down by his casual air and answered him shortly.

"Yes. Box Car Bertha."

"Where did you get hold of such a name?"

"Mother told me that when I was a child and couldn't be found anywhere else, she could always find me in a box car. The kids began calling me 'Box Car Bertha,' and the name has just hung to me. Even in school in Seattle they never called me 'Bertha,' but 'Boxie.' "

I paused and tried to pierce the veil of his face to discover what thoughts and feelings were behind it, but so far as I could see he was feeling nothing he would not have felt if any other strange young woman had come and perched herself on his desk. It annoyed me and I began to scold him.

"Tell me why you have never written mother?" I asked. "Why didn't you ever try to find us?"

"I've been too much interested in other people's children," he said. "You didn't need me. They did. Your mother was able to be father and mother to you. Many women are not able to be even a mother. Your mother and I liked the idea of having a child. We had one. That was all there was to it. I wanted to go, so I went."

"But don't you think I need a father as much as I do a mother?" I protested.

He laughed pleasantly.

"All men are your fathers and your brothers," he said, "and all children will be your sons and daughters."

He told me I was welcome to stay with him awhile and I moved in that day and slept on a cot in a stuffy room filled with books and papers. He asked no questions of me. There were two men living in the flat with us. One was Morton Fleming, a man of fifty who was compiling material for a book on the history and use of violence in solving social problems. The other, an Englishman, almost seventy, named Burton, did nothing, so far as I could see, but read. He had been in the English free-thought and labor movement with Annie Besant and Bradlough. My father and these men were bachelors and bibliophiles. They lived in and for books.

I was with them only two weeks, and such a sombre, intellectual, honest, thoughtful, and non-earthly atmosphere I would not have believed existed anywhere. They lived simply and frugally on a hundred dollars a month for the three. Nothing was superficial or vulgar in that flat. Nobody ever wasted a word. There was no smoking nor drinking, no phonographs, no music.

Every Sunday morning, promptly at eight o'clock, a woman named Emma Wayne came to the house to have breakfast with them. She was a thin, worn-out blonde of forty, with a high forehead and light blue eyes, behind thick glasses, and beautiful hands that were always calm. She was a designer for a fashionable dress house.

"And so you're Bertha," she greeted me when introduced. "I have been taking Sunday morning breakfast with your father for almost twenty years."

She took my arrival in the same casual way that my father had. Both were friendly but neither seemed really interested in me as a person. It was obvious that they were lovers and Emma said, "Why, of course," when I asked her. She added, with no embarrassment, that for the last ten years she had been sleeping with Morton, also.

My father and his friends were dreamers. They believed that they could write books that would remedy all the wrongs of the world. They would not let anything disturb them. They seemed to regard sex as purely a physical function. Neither father nor Morton seemed to feel any sense of possessiveness about Emma, nor any jealousy. She was a companion to both of them and filled an important need for them both. Neither seemed at all to mind sharing her with the other. Nor did Emma seem to feel that there was anything strange about living with both of them in this way.

But it seemed strange to me. As much as I believed in freedom, and as much as I practiced it, there was something about the lengths to which the thought of these three went which appalled me and made me feel out of place among them, an intruder.

One day I asked my father whether he had any other children, and he said that he had one, but had completely lost touch with it—that he didn't know where it or its mother was.

"But how do you justify yourself?" I exploded. "How do you and the other 'free' men justify yourselves in having children and then going off and deserting them? Your explanation that you're busy and have more important things to do and your quoting Jesus: Who is my brother and Who are my children, doesn't satisfy me. Suppose I hadn't had such a wonderful mother to look after me? I might have been in an orphan asylum with thousands of other helpless children. Doesn't your creed take in responsibility and family loyalty? How about Emma? She's been serving you men for twenty years, and has to work hard for a living every day. Now she's just worn-out."

"Fathering and supporting children was never my function in life," he answered calmly. "I never felt that it was the thing I wanted to do. I belong to that class of men who are not fathers, and who get no joy in supporting a family. Bernard Shaw says, 'A married man will do anything for the family.' It sounds well but it means nothing. There are fathers, and there are educators. I am an educator. According to Maeder there are two different types of men and women. In women, the uterine or maternal type, those who are mothers, who want to be mothers, and the clitorid or sexual type, those who want men, many men. The men are also of two types, the orchitic and the phallic type. The orchitic type corresponds to the uterine type. This male is a good father. He is the home lover, the monogamist. The phallic type is like Morton and myself. We need women. Any kind of women will do. We do not want a wife or family. It is very difficult to say which type gives most to the world. So far, I don't think any of us have succeeded very well. This last war and the statistics from the criminal, insane, and charity organizations demonstrate that no one should be very proud of what any of us have accomplished."

"But what is your solution, father?" I asked him. "What is your goal?"

"My dear Bertha, there are no solutions to the problems of life. There are no goals. You just go on living and loving and doing the best or the worst you can. I've lived and have had all the women that I've wanted. I've struggled and fought for my principles. When it was necessary I went to jail or starved. I haven't denied myself anything I wanted. As I grow older, I find I want less. I have found that most of the things I used to struggle for were not worthwhile. I've cut down my needs. You see us here living a very simple but comfortable life. There's no goal, no heaven ahead. I've withdrawn from many things. We just enjoy every day, make the most out of every experience. There are no certainties, no eternal verities, no reward. In the past I had joy in struggling and agitating and going to jail. Now I can get more out of life living simply with my friends.

"I've been working all my life, studying and writing. I gave up lecturing ten years ago. I no longer have confidence in the spoken word. A great many people who heard me were moved by what I said. I found out that you can stimulate people to hate, to do stupid things. Audiences, the mobs, can never think straight. Thinking is an individual process. It must be done in silence and humility. You can make wars, incite labor riots, provoke violence and destruction, and drive the mob to lynch by what you say. But no speech ever made a people gentle or honest. There are thousands of sermons and inspirational, political, radical, and revolutionary speeches made daily. They never change the behavior of people.

"I doubt if an oration, no matter how powerful, ever soothed the frenzy of a mob or neutralized the hatred of a group of southerners who are determined to lynch a Negro charged with rape. What could you say to a mob of Georgians to prevent them from lynching a victim? Could you appeal to their pity and say that this man has ten dependent children? Would it do any good to appeal to their patriotism with, 'If you lynch this man you will discredit your state.' Or to say, 'If you kill this man, you'll be labeled murderer.' Do you think it would do any good if we went down to the owners of the department stores and said, 'We have here figures compiled by Columbia University and the Labor Department in Washington. They clearly demonstrate that no woman can live a respectable life and have all of her needs satisfied for less than eighteen dollars a week.'

"You know what their answer would be. Suppose we went to the coal company and the steel mills and said, 'Gentlemen, the men that are working for you have families and children. They need so much a week.' If you spoke with tears in your voice and brought a dozen hungry families with you to prove your statements, would it help? So far, force has always won.

"I like to believe that thinking enough on the subjects of brotherhood and co-operation will eventually bring them about, but we can only hope. Mutual interests and enlightenment only will pave the way for a new society."

I agreed with so much that my father said, yet he, and his thoughts, and the way he lived, left me feeling confused and helpless. I could not accept his complete lack of a sense of responsibility toward his women and his offspring, or his complete impersonality. I felt constantly out of place there and so I decided to go. When I told father I intended to leave, he merely said, "All right. Come and see me any time, except," he smiled at me whimsically, "not on Sunday mornings!"

Without any plan, or any idea of where I would go next, I walked to 59th Street and crossed over Queensboro Bridge. I was delighted by the towering office buildings stretched out in a magnificent sky-line. Tugboats puffed below me in the river like earnest porpoises. Directly below the middle of the bridge I saw Welfare Island with its house of correction and penitentiary, its almshouse, where thousands of old men and women were waiting to die. The Metropolitan Hospital, Hart's Island, with its delinquent boys and girls, Women's Prison, with its prostitutes and dope fiends, were all close by, and seemed to attract me.

I walked slowly back towards Manhattan, wondering where I would spend the night. It had never occurred to my father to ask me that when I left. I walked down First Avenue to 26th Street. There was massive Bellevue Hospital. At the next corner was a group of forlorn looking men and women slowly wending their way down towards the river. I joined the procession. They were old, many of them foreign looking. Some were on crutches. They joined a line at a large seven-story building marked "Municipal Lodging House." Around the corner of the building was a door marked "Entrance for Women."

I took my place in the line.

ELEVEN

THERE were twenty women ahead of me. We moved slowly. No one paid any attention to anyone else. We were like a row of automatons, moving forward to something which held neither interest nor pleasure, nor hope for us. Finally I stood inside before a desk.

"Were you ever here before?" a man at the desk inside asked.

"No," I answered.

"Go upstairs and register," he said shortly, and turned to the next in line.

Upstairs I was asked if I could write, and was told to sit down and fill out a registration card. After I had done so, I handed it to the clerk and she gave me a small blue identification card, also a small metal tag with my bed number on it to be hung around the neck while bathing or sleeping. I followed the line into the dining room and sat down to eat a palatable beef stew, three thick slices of bread, a tin cup of tea with milk, and a dish of stewed apricots. We ate in silence and then sat around in the dining room until our names were called. At the "bundle cage" a matron asked me a number of questions.

"Are you looking for a job? What can you do? Do you want to do housework? We can get you a job."

"No, thank you," I answered her. "I think I can get a job for myself."

"Just leave your purse here."

I handed it over to her. I had paid for my own food while I was with father and had sent some money to mother, so that I had only a little money left. When all had deposited their purses and possessions, the whole line started for the bathroom, as baths were compulsory. Our clothes were placed on hangers and fumigated. We were given nightgowns.

In the bathroom I had a chance to see my fellow guests. The most startling thing was that the bulk of them seemed old women. All about me were sagging, misshapen bodies, stringing grey hair, faces with experience written deeply in them, tired lusterless eyes. The average age, I found out later, was between forty and fifty, but most of the women looked much older. Together they appeared all middle-aged, hard-working housewives. Certainly none of them looked like criminals. The majority were Irish and Irish-American. About ten percent were Negro, and there was a sprinkling of Polish, Lithuanian and English. A few showed signs of drink. A number appeared to be sisters of the road. All bore the marks of poverty. Most of them were talkative and friendly.

Half of them told me they were widows. At least one in four told the same story.

"Our home was broken up . . . my husband lost his job . . . we couldn't pay the rent. My old man's in the men's side, next door."

Some had been there only a few days, others for

months. Most of them came periodically. When they got a job they would leave, and when it failed they came back. Between jobs they looked upon the Municipal Lodging House as a home. I heard no dramatic, tragic stories. They accepted without resentment the fact that they were the product of "the system," a society that hires and fires, of a society in which landlords must have their rent. There were only a few like me who didn't need the place, just tramps on a little excursion.

We slept in double-decked iron cots with comfortable mattresses, clean sheets, blankets and pillows. I didn't sleep much. Many of the women were hacking and coughing, many of them groaning and talking in their sleep. Quite a few were climbing in and out of their bunks and going to the bathroom frequently during the night.

In the morning we were given a breakfast of bread, coffee and cereal. I had to stay in for two hours to help make beds and clean up, and I spent another hour typing cards. Before I left the place, the matron returned my purse and asked if I wanted a job.

"They need a couple of maids over in Bellevue. There's one fairly good job . . ."

"No, thank you," I told her. "I think I can find a job myself."

I left the building with two Irish women, Mary and Martha. They were both over fifty, spent with work and whiskey. Mary was tall, gaunt, with a wide toothless smile and yellow-blue blotches under her eyes from a recent saloon fight. Martha was smaller, with iron-grey hair pinned with only one bone hairpin and therefore slipping down her neck, and with unhealthy high color in her cheeks.

"I need a drink," Mary said. "Let's go over to Devine's and he'll give us one 'on the cuff.' "

We walked up First Avenue to a bootleg joint at the corner of 18th Street, sat down at a table and waited till a big laughing bartender came over.

"How's everything over at the Ritz?" he addressed Mary. "I suppose you'll be wanting a drink and you'll pay me this afternoon. And who's your friend? Also, what'll your daughter have?"

"The same as my friend."

He set a half-pint bottle of whiskey on the table with three glasses and no chaser. Martha filled all three glasses and then drained hers at one gulp. I imitated her. There were five other women sitting around, all guests of the Municipal Lodging House.

"No, I won't give you another drink until you pay me," the bar-keeper scolded good-naturedly when Mary called him back. "You've had an eye opener. Go out and get some money if you want to have anything more to drink."

"Where do you women get the money to buy drinks?" I asked.

"Where does anybody get money?" answered Martha. "We earn it, beg it, steal it, or find it."

"Well, how do you get your money?"

"Well, let me see . . . Yesterday I got ninety cents. My son, Tim, is janitor of a flat building and he gave me fifty cents. I went over and seen Mrs. Cohen that I used to work for and she gave me my lunch and twenty-five cents, and an old man that I know stopped me on the street and gave me fifteen cents."

"And, how did you get your money, Mary?"

"Oh, it was easy. Yesterday was pay-day down at the docks. My old man was a stevedore for fifteen years and the men know me, so I just stood around and some of the boys that worked with my husband gave me some change. I got over two dollars. I thought Devine might give us another one before we have to pay, but since he won't, here goes my last quarter."

She ordered a pint of "moon" and invited us and all the other women to have a drink with her. That batch of women were the most battered and disreputable group I've ever known. Not one of them had ever been on the road or out of New York.

"You want to know where I got my money from?" said a short roly-poly woman that I had noticed making up to all the men in the place. "I earned my money. I always earn my money. Yesterday I worked in a laundry, in the basement, for a Jewish family. They've got seven children. I washed, ironed, and scrubbed and I got a dollar and car fare."

A tall, English woman, in an old suit and with carefully braided blond hair wound around her head, answered next. "A gentleman gave me my money, but not for nothing, girlie. Would you like to meet him?"

Peg-leg Ellen, a heavy, black-eyed, black-haired woman about forty, who had one foot and walked with the aid of a home-made crutch, said, "I got my money, two dollars and a half, on the main stem begging, and it was mostly in pennies and nickels. I had to stay out six hours."

A sad-looking woman over sixty, huddled with an old sweater about her shoulders said, "I didn't get any money. I tried to get a day's work, and they sent me over to the hospital, but I couldn't scrub and clean. I've got such an awful cold."

The last of the five, a buxom chattery woman who had removed, when she came in, a patch from a perfectly normal left eye, said: "I make my money by peddling. I take my matches, collar buttons, and shoe strings and go in restaurants and stores. I can always earn fifty cents to a dollar a day, but the more I earn the more I drink."

Soon we were joined by a group of men, also from the Municipal Lodging House. Old, stiff, dressed in garments that dirt and many fumigations and washings had made all the same color, the color of poverty, they were a motley crew. Some were crippled. Many of them had teeth missing. All of them needed hair cuts. Their old faces were knotted with pain, with disappointment, with weakness. In their eyes was the softness of habitual drinkers. They bought bottles, too, counting out, like the woman, the pennies and dimes and nickels they had secured by begging or by doing a few odd jobs.

I questioned Ida about a pale younger woman, obviously pregnant, who was beginning to rock with merriment at a table with two old wrecks of men. "She's a panhandler, too," I was told. "And she's been pregnant like that for years, but she never has a kid. Wait till she goes to the toilet, and you'll see her come back with her stomacher in her hand. She'll drink till her money is gone, then she'll disappear and put it on again and go out on the street and look pathetic and beg for the sake of her unborn child."

Later I saw many such women on the road, but never have I known so many of them together in one place, off guard, as I did that day in Devine's speakeasy. Some were actually blind (blinkies), some deaf (deafies), some dumb (dummies). The deaf and dumb ones my informer called "D and D's." The armless ones were known as "wingies," the legless as "Peggys," the feeble-minded or insane as "nuts," those with pronounced tremors (drunk-palsied) "shakies," and the epilepsies "fitzies." Those who've had their legs cut off near the hips and who ride around on a low wheel-chair are called "wheels."

"There is a group of professional beggars who imitate practically every type of true handicap so well that only experts can detect them," the English woman told me. "That woman over in the corner with the ugly sores on her arms is a 'blister.' She got the sores by putting acid on her arms. She begs money saying she needs it for a doctor."

She pointed out a normal looking young man drinking at the bar. "He looks O.K., but wait till he gets ready to go on the street. He's a 'tossout.' He throws both elbows and one wrist out of joint and looks like a freak in a museum. There are others who bind back their hands so that they seem not to have them. These are called 'hidden hands.' Those, and the 'floppers,' the ones who pretend being crippled and sit all day before churches and entrances, and the 'ghosts,' who assume pale haggard attitudes and imitate tubercular coughs, make the most money on the street. But none of them have any of it. They spend it right here."

I stayed there and drank continuously until about four o'clock in the afternoon. Then I fell asleep. When I woke up I was in bed, stark naked, with a brutal looking man. His body was dirty. He had kept his socks on and his sodden toes sticking out the ends were as grey as the socks. I sat up.

"Where am I?" I cried in a panic.

"You're with your friends," he leered at me. "Have a drink."

"What's this place?"

"This is on 10th Street near Avenue A."

"How did I get here? Let me get out of here."

My dress and coat were in a mess. I examined my purse and found it empty. Everything, letters, a ten dollar bill which I had hidden away in the lining, and a diary, my most valuable possessions, were gone. I cried and raved and stormed, but the man on the bed only laughed at me. However, when I began to dress, he made no objection, and, despairing of getting any of my things back from him, I dressed and got out as quickly as I could.

Sick and miserable I walked over to Union Square and sat down on a bench, thoroughly ashamed of myself. I had gone a bit too far this time trying to learn about different types of people! I was completely broke now, and had no idea what to do next. I didn't want to go back to the Lodging House, and I was in no shape to face my father. I let my head sink to my hands and sat there, completely desolate. I was called back to my surroundings by a voice.

"It's a chilly evening," said a man I had not noticed sitting at my side.

I glanced up quickly. He looked a decent sort and his remark had evidently been stimulated by sympathy for me.

"Have you got the price of a cup of coffee?" I asked, without looking at him.

"Just about," he answered. "Come along."

I drank two cups of coffee and ate half of a roll. I looked at my benefactor. He was short, bald-headed, dressed in a shabby but spotless grey suit. His mouth was soft, like a woman's, but his speech gruff.

"Where you livin'?" he asked.

"You tell me," I answered, trying to laugh. "Where's a good place to live?"

"Well, I'd take you home with me but my woman would throw us both out. But I know where you can go if you want to. I have an old friend, Edith Adams, who has a flat down in the Village and she always takes hoboes in. Come along down."

I started at the word "hoboes." So it had taken just one day for me to look like a tramp again! I glanced down at the expensive clothes Otto had stolen for me and which had been in good order the day before. They looked as if I'd slept in them in the jungles. One stocking was torn. My face felt stiff with dirt. But I was too miserable to care.

He took my arm and walked me to Christopher Street,

near Washington Square, and introduced me to Edith Adams.

"Edith, I found a hobo over in Union Square. She's on the bum and sick. Can you take care of her to-night?"

"Sure. Are you hungry?"

"No, just let me go to the bathroom and then let me go to sleep. That's all."

I remained in bed for over a week. I was horribly sick, with the most terrible gastro-enteritis for days. I remember being violently cold and almost insane with headaches. Edith Adams and a woman called Christine nursed me day and night. As I grew better I found I was not a complete stranger to them. They had both known mother when she had made speeches in war-time and they were acquainted with my father.

Edith's flat was a combination hobo boarding house, hobo college, hobohemian hangout, and certainly a training school for female roughneck anarchists. She had seven rooms and a huge bathroom that must have been made out of a bedroom. The place was carelessly furnished but had a certain rough charm about it. Edith had a way of sticking up radical posters and of wangling from the artists who came in and out of her house some very decent modern paintings. One thing I'll always remember. Every room in the place, even the bathroom, had a bed or studio couch. When I got to know her better I could see why.

Edith was a large woman. Her face was strongly chiselled and was topped by a bobbed mop of wiry red hair. She was always grinning. She never used cosmetics. She was known to be living with her husband, Mac. He was an engineer on an ocean liner, out of town most of the time, and gave her all of his money.

Edith was born in Kansas in the early eighties. She lived there until she was twenty-three, then went to St. Louis and married a barber. She got to running around to new thought and radical meetings, and became interested in "The Brotherhood of the Daily Life," which was the first organization of Dr. J. Eads How. When How started his hobo meetings, Edith became one of his group and gathered in all the female hoboes in St. Louis. She drifted from socialism to the I. W. W. and then to anarchist groups. For the last quarter of the century she had been a good-natured, whole-hearted, full-fledged, roughneck anarchist. With her the sky was the limit. She disregarded religion and conventionality and whooped it up for the Revolution.

Edith only lived a few years with her first husband in St. Louis. Then she drifted to Chicago and went to live with Lucy Parsons and hobnobbed with the anarchist group. There she became very active with W. C. Foster and Earl Ford, and was with them when they wrote their famous pamphlet on "Syndicalism." Soon after that she went to New York City and located in Greenwich Village. Her house had become one of the most active and popular there. Noted writers, hoboes, poets, sculptors, and propagandists immediately became Edith's friends, among them Emma Goldman, Elizabeth Gurley-Flynn, Mary English, Anna Strunsky Walling, Eve Adams, Margaret Sanger, Romany Marie, Eugene O'Neill, Benn Ben, Sadikichi Hartman, Hippolyte Havel, Jig Cook, Bobby Ed-

wards, and Franklin Jordan. Her Christopher Street flat
was crowded day and night.

She told me:

"The men, artists and spittoon philosophers come in to
chew the fat, rush the can, sleep off a drunk, get away
from their sweethearts, and to make some new woman.
The women come in to take a bath, get away from their
lovers, and find someone to buy them a meal or a drink.
Most of all they like my place because they can be natural here."

Among her cronies was another anarchist of the same
type, the woman called Christine. Christine ran a little tea
shop in the Village, over the Provincetown Playhouse. Her
last name was Ell, but her place was known only as
"Christine's."

Edith and Christine belonged to that rare type of
women which has a special attraction for intellectual hoboes and rebel men and women. Both of these women
had sex appeal, but they had something more valuable, an
understanding and a genuine admiration for men and
women of talent. It was always easy for a poet or an
artist or a writer to tell his plans, dreams, or hopes to
them. They all left Edith's flat believing in themselves.

Not only did the artists, anarchists, free-lovers, and
labor leaders come to Edith, but also quite a few crooks.
The most interesting of the grifters I met there was Mary
Ireland, a much photographed "moll-buzzer." She was
tall, angular, black-haired, with a quiet and aristocratic
face. Her pictures were in all of the "galleries," and all
the store dicks were familiar with them. She specialized

in drawing the contents out of women's pocketbooks while they were busy shopping in department stores.

Mary Ireland was a lady. No question about it. While in New York she had always lived at the Brevoort and other good hotels. She dined and dressed for dinner. And when she was out picking pockets, she always dressed for the part, in a sombre black coat, so that her appearance was that of a widow. When she worked she wore very little rouge.

We were walking one day down Broadway, when I happened to mention that I wanted to get a package of safety pins.

"I'll get them for you," she said quickly.

"Why do you take a chance on stealing a cheap five-cent package of pins?" I asked. "It doesn't make sense to run that risk for a nickel."

"I steal everything," she said. "I enjoy it much more than paying for it."

Mary was thrifty. She had spent almost one-half of her life in jail, in Joliet, Illinois, in Waupon, Wisconsin, in Atlanta, Georgia, in Pittsburgh, Pennsylvania, and in Auburn Prison, New York. When I met her she was out on a ten thousand dollar bond.

"I just got to beat this rap," she said. "I'm a four-timer, and if I am convicted I'll be sent to the penitentiary for life as a habitual offender." Her grifting would make a gross of a hundred thousand dollars, she told me without boasting.

"I've got twenty thousand dollars salted away in first-class bonds and real estate mortgages," she said. "When I get another five grand I'm going to retire."

At least one-half of her grifting proceeds had gone to her attorneys and "fixers." One day she disappeared and I got a little note from her saying "I'm down at the Tombs. Come and see me." She had been picked up at Macy's. I intended to go to see her, but never did, and later heard that she was convicted, was sent to Auburn, for life, as a habitual offender, became unruly there and was transferred to Matteawan, the prison for the criminally insane. But just the other day I met her in Chicago back at her old tricks again.

I stayed at Edith's six months that year. She let me earn my room and board by keeping the place clean. The men and women who came in and out of that house fascinated me, and I was learning every day.

Edith and Christine had a genuine interest in the Revolutionary Labor Movement. If they had any pronounced convictions, it was that they wanted the right to live their lives in their own way. They weren't immoral or unmoral. They paid their way through life. Both were hard workers. Both loved excitement and newcomers. One morning while we were at the breakfast table, in walked Ena, Franklin Jordan and Lizzie Davis.

I had not seen my sister for some time. She had not grown any taller and did not weigh over one hundred pounds. But her face was glowing with life and her figure was willowy and more fully developed than when I had last seen her.

"How are all your sweethearts?" I asked her.

"Grand," she said. "I've had a lot of them since I've seen you last, and the two I have now you'll love. I'll share them with you."

"Thank you, I'll choose my own lovers," I said somewhat testily.

"But you have already chosen one of mine," she said triumphantly. "Franklin Jordan."

Something gripped my heart. How close the currents of life run! First my mother and I had the same lover, and now my sister and I loved the same man, the man I still thought of as the one I would eventually choose to be the father of my child.

Franklin Jordan and I had our reunion at an Anarchists' Mass Meeting in the Bronx. The rooms at Edith's were always crowded and there was no opportunity for personal conversation. He asked me, through Ena, to attend the meeting, where he was the principal speaker. There was to be another speaker, but I didn't know who it was until Jordan told me after I got there. There were four persons on the program ahead of him, and we sat in a little side room of the Labor Lyceum until it was his time to speak.

As I looked at him in that little room while we were waiting for him I felt all of my old desire for him. Suddenly it didn't matter that my little sister had taken him for her lover or that he had loved dozens of other women. I wanted him just as I always had.

"Oh, Jordan," I cried, "I want your baby!"

He smiled. "There's scarcely time to do anything about that just now," he said. "I think you'd better go out in front now. There's a great Italian speaker coming on next, Mallettini."

I started when I heard his name, and for the moment forgot all about wanting Jordan. Leaning over and kissing him swiftly, I ran out and took a seat and almost held my breath while I waited for Mallettini to come out.

He had not changed a bit. The same stern bearded face, the same kind eyes. But now his voice was the wrath of God, stirring the people to frenzy. It was a mixed audience of Jews, Italians, and Americans, but you didn't have to understand Italian to be moved by his voice, any more than you had to understand Italian to enjoy an opera star. He finished amid roaring applause.

Jordan was next. He was calm, professorial, logical, reasoning, argumentative, convincing, provocative, soothing. My mind kept running from the speech to the man. I compared him with my first lover, E. A. O., with Lowell Schroeder, with Big Otto. Whom did I love the best, Mallettini or Jordan? Whom would I ask to take me home? I knew I could see Jordan any time. I chose to go with Mallettini. After the meeting a group, including all the speakers, went to an Italian comrade's house, where we ate and talked. It was two o'clock in the morning when we left.

"You must take me home with you," I whispered to Mallettini.

"Not now. I want to see you some other time," he answered.

I was angry and I turned to Jordan, who had not heard me whisper. He had a little room on the fifth floor of a

13th Street tenement. It was unfurnished except for a low double-bed, a kitchen table, and a bookcase filled with books. A strong-box, back under his bed, was filled with letters, love letters he told me later. There was a large whiskey decanter and six whiskey glasses and a few dishes.

Ena and I often went together to Jordan's room in the afternoon. He asked us never to come without whiskey and we never did. Much as I tried I could never really be jealous of Ena. She never showed that she was jealous of me. And I learned a great deal from him.

"Tell me about lesbians, Jordan," I begged him one day. "They called them 'lady lovers' on the road. There are so many of them here in the Village. What about them? You've had a lot of experience with them. What makes them that way?"

"They are God's step-children," he said. "You know some of them well, Yvonne, the dancer, Mickey Mouse, the prancer, and others. I have had a lot of experience with 'queers' and they always make me unhappy.

"My antipathy toward them is not because they are variants—God knows I do not demand that everyone be cut from the same pattern—but because they are typically anti-social, selfish, and willing to exploit others. So few of them show a desire to earn an honest living. Many of them are willing to get by at the expense of anybody. Outside of dope fiends, I don't know any group which has so many chiselers, racketeers, and petty larceny grafters. Their sins are cheap sins. Their anti-socialness is petty. Few of them have any courage in their love affairs or in their method of procuring a living.

"Homosexuality, as I see it, is largely artificial. Not only the sexual expression of lesbians and male homosexuals, but their walk and talk and entire behavior are artificial. I have known men who, in civil life, were absolutely feminine, and who, in a few months with a group of normal men, or in jail, have lost every vestige of their femininity. Also, I've seen a great many women who were coarse and masculine, with hair on their chests and so on, become very lady-like. Their transversion is, of course, another evidence of their infantilism.

"The worst feature about them is that they are constantly on the make. They are like dope fiends, not content to use dope themselves. They have to proselyte. They have to teach everyone they come in contact with. If they didn't do this it wouldn't matter, for since they do not reproduce themselves, they are not important."

The men and women I knew around Jordan, and those who came to Edith Adams' flat, and the things they said and did, would fill a book. By far the most colorful, fascinating and terrible man who came there was "Sir Thousand Loves," as Edith called him. He was a poet, author, actor, entertainer. Certainly he was an arch lover. He was the author of two books of poetry, several novels, two volumes of essays, and a history of sex worship. He rented Edith's front room. It had an entrance directly on the street.

In appearance he was not much, of average height, rather fragile with fair hair and moustache growing lighter with age. His profile was rather good, but, on full view, his face pouted. However, his eyes were grey-blue and very personal.

Ena had an experience with him and was very proud of it. I hadn't been in his presence more than ten minutes when he started to moan and sigh, claw and weep.

"Don't work so fast, poet," I said. "I'm makeable. You can have me."

"Your number is going to be a thousand one," said Edith, who happened to come in.

"I'm willing," I continued, "but first tell me about the first thousand."

"Sir Thousand Loves is drunk most of the time, and when he's sober, he is colossally egotistical, and as far as I hear has never been loyal to any of his women," Edith said.

"How does he do it?"

"Ask him," she told me as she left us.

"How do you win your women, poet?"

"What women? You're the only woman I ever loved in my life. You're beautiful . . ."

He actually refused to commit himself or acknowledge that he ever had another love in his life.

My experience with Sir Thousand Loves was not worth telling about. He made love to me with words—that was all. Jordan I saw much of. There were a few other men that came and went, but none of them mattered much. I had Mallettini on my mind.

I met him again at the eleventh of November meeting on East Broadway. He was as friendly as ever and as impersonal as ever. But I was determined not to be put off again. I went to him after the meeting.

"I will not let you go," I said. "You must take me home with you."

"I live a long way out in Paterson," he protested.

"I don't care if you live in Philadelphia," I said desperately. "I'm going with you."

I paid my own fare on the train. He did not live in Paterson, but four miles beyond it in an old two-story farmhouse at the end of a little side road. He was silent as we walked in the cool October moonlit night. I clung to his arm and pled with him.

"Talk to me. Tell me you love me," I cried.

He patted my hand as it hung on his arm.

"I'm afraid you do not understand what I am trying to do," he said. "Love, as you use the word, has no place in my life."

"Tell me, what are you trying to do? You made me love you," I said.

He stopped and looked at me. His face was pale and stern.

"I made you love me? What do you mean by that?"

I winced, and was ashamed of that stupid, hypocritical, typically feminine remark.

"I'm sorry," I said. "That was a ridiculous thing for me to say."

Then he smiled. "What do you want from me, Bertha?" he asked.

I was silent. Just what did I want? Surely not sex. Yes, maybe it was. Perhaps I was just amorous. It wasn't a child I wanted from him, for I knew that I wanted a baby by Jordan. I didn't want to have a home with Mallettini, or live with him, either. I was aware that he couldn't or wouldn't support me. What did I want from him? What did I want from all the men to whom I was drawn? They had experience for me. That was it. Instinctively I felt that Mallettini had something for me that no other man in all the world had. But I could not answer him.

"Do you love me, Bertha?" he went on.

"Yes," I said, my voice low, and we walked a dozen steps over the rough road, with the moonlight making queer shadows along the fields before he spoke again.

"Do you love the people, the working class?" he asked.

Like a nun taking a vow, I put my hand on my heart and raised my eyes as I answered.

"I do."

"Then come on with me."

It was six o'clock in the morning when we arrived at the little farmhouse. He introduced me to a woman, her husband, three children and a young man of twenty, all black-eyed Italians.

He talked to them in his own language, apparently convincing them I was a friend. They then smiled at me and gave us breakfast. Later he took me to the barn and up in a hay-loft that was fitted up as a study and a chemical laboratory. Here he told me what he was doing and I felt as though I were being initiated into a secret order as indeed, in effect, I was.

"Bertha," he said solemnly, "I belong to a small group

who are trying to bring about a revolution in Spain, in Italy, and in America. We make progress slowly in America, and do you know why? We have not been able to develop an intelligent, courageous type of female revolutionist. The American women, as I see them, want lovers, companionship, a good time. They can love a man, but not men. Bertha, can you learn to love men, the people, the working class, more than you do a man, or a few men, more than you love your family and more than you love yourself?"

For a moment I did not know how to answer him, how to tell him what I wanted to say in a way that would convince him. Then I took his hand in mine and kissed it.

"Let me help you," I begged. "Let me prove to you that I am loyal and will do anything for the people."

We rested together quietly all day. He told me about his life. He had a wife and four children in Italy. He had been in the revolutionary movement since he was fourteen, more than thirty years. He had been jailed and was now a political exile from Italy. Finally he was convinced that I could be of use to his movement.

"Bertha," he said, "if you really want to serve people, you can. I am going to entrust you with a very important work. You go home and we will come for you next Wednesday afternoon at four o'clock."

Tuesday night I stayed with Ena and we talked over our plans. She read a number of letters from mother who was out from Home Colony on a prison reform crusade. Frank and Margaret were in St. Louis working. Mother said she was tired of traveling and wanted to go back to the soil. She hoped to buy a little ranch in North Dakota. "I want to have a place where my children can come when they get tired," she wrote.

I told Ena that I was going to Chicago the next day with Mallettini on an important mission. She begged me to share my secret with her.

"If you are going to do anything really serious, Bertha, I want to be with you and we should tell mother about it."

But I told her I must go alone.

The next morning I went back to Edith's and made preparation to go. Mallettini was to come at four. Sir Thousand Loves, Jordan, and a group of women hoboes came in earlier, however, and we started to drink. I had drunk very little since my unpleasant experience with the Municipal Lodging House women, but this day I started in heavily. By four o'clock I had passed out of the picture, I guess, and was lying on the bed with Thousand Loves and Jordan when Mallettini came. He shook me gently. I got out of bed, bleary-eyed, staggering, sick. I mumbled. He stood there quietly watching me. Even in my drunken state I could see the disappointment and pain in his face. Then he left.

And suddenly my head cleared as though someone had struck me a blow with a wet towel. I looked at the bed and saw Jordan and Thousand Loves sleeping. Their drunken faces were hideous. In a sudden fury I picked up a reading lamp, tore it from its socket and struck Jordan over the head with it. Beside myself I began to beat Thousand Loves with my fists.

"You miserable, vile drunken creatures. See what you've made me do," I screamed.

Three days later I picked up the New York *Times* and read on the front page, "Thirty prominent citizens poisoned at a banquet at the College Club of Chicago. Distinguished Catholic laymen and Archbishop poisoned at a $7.00-a-plate dinner.

"The first on the menu was a cocktail, then an appetizer; the third was soup. A few minutes after the guests ate the soup a hundred of them showed symptoms of acute poisoning. Police suspect a young anarchist called Jeans. He disappeared immediately after the soup had been prepared. Police find in his locker letters from Mallettini, who is suspected of engineering the plot."

And I remembered, "You do not understand. . . ."

Now I understood.

The next day I had a three word letter from Otto in San Francisco, "Hellow Beautiful. Otto." Enclosed were three hundred dollar bills.

Suddenly I knew I wanted to be out of New York. Hitch-hiking or riding in a freight car wouldn't take me away fast enough, and I bought some clothes and a first-class ticket to Chicago, to what or whom I did not know.

TWELVE

I WAS glad to be back in Chicago. I was fed up with Greenwich Village and its intellectuals and drunkards. I needed a change. I had enough money to do it, and I went to a north shore hotel, a big one, which I knew was a hangout for racket people. Soon I was aware that there were a number of prostitutes living there with their pimps. None of them hustled in that particular hotel, however. In fact, most girls who hustle in a joint live some place else.

The room right across from mine was occupied by a pretty little blonde called Ethel. She was a "baboon," always on the go, always talking and quarreling with her man, Bill Steward. When the transoms were open I could hear them. Bill would always start it.

"Now, listen, baby," he would say, truculently, "try and get more money. You know I got those notes on the car, and I want to put away a double saw-buck every week so that we can get out of the racket and buy a little hotel of our own."

Then Ethel's voice would rise in a high, scornful crescendo.

"You're a liar. You're giving my jack to these other broads of yours!"

157

They argued and they cursed, but the sessions always ended by Ethel giving Bill her money.

I liked Ethel. She was small and wiry in build, with platinum-blonde hair and washy blue eyes. Her face was thin. She had plenty to say about everything. She was raised in Duluth, a police lieutenant's daughter, and like so many other girls I have known in one racket or another, she had earlier hitch-hiked her way from this place and that until she got to Chicago. Just got tired of high school, she said, and went off in a friend's car as far as St. Paul, where she managed to pick up rides from acquaintances of friends the rest of the way. She stayed straight all that time, she said, and got a job as a stenographer in the Loop and lived at the near north side "Y." Here she met another girl who took her along on parties. Everybody drank too much. One morning she woke up in a room with Bill. Later she learned that she was pregnant. He got her out of that. And, by that time, she did what he wanted her to do, hustle for him.

She told me plenty about Bill. So did his other girls. I had all their stories, and finally got Bill's own story from him.

He was twenty-nine, lean, sallow, quietly and beautifully dressed. When he was fourteen he got into trouble in Pennsylvania, where he was born, and did a bit in the pen for a hoist (theft). About five years before I knew him he had drifted into Chicago and got to hanging around the gamblers and the racket men on Twenty-Sixth and State Streets. He picked up a little waitress there, and soon she was hustling for him. In five years he had thirty different women. When I knew him he had four, Ethel, Josephine, Mary and Barbara. He collected their money from them every day and spent about a night a week with each girl.

When I chided Ethel about living with a pimp and giving him her money she said, "What is money for? To make a man you want happy. These other bitches are just hustling for Bill. I'm his heart. He loves me, and when he gets a bankroll he'll give them the kick, and then we'll get married and have a home."

I knew that in her heart she doubted what she was saying and that she said it vehemently to reassure herself. The truth was that she was madly in love with Bill and was one of those queer women who get their satisfaction by degrading themselves in order to be slaves to the men they love. I wondered whether Josephine and Mary and Barbara said the same things about their relationships to Bill. Later I found out.

First I met Josephine. She was tall, a brunette, rather furtive in manner, with rich full lips which she always painted with lipstick too orange for her complexion. She had finished grammar school in Quincy, Illinois, she told me, and married and had a child by a bootlegger. Her husband killed a man. They had partly owned their home, and she spent everything she could get on it trying to defend him. When he went to the pen she took her child and hitch-hiked to Cleveland. She said she had no trouble at all getting rides, as everyone took pity on the little girl. One night one man paid for a room for them, and tried to come in and sleep with her, but she managed to get out of it by reminding him of his own children.

She used to grin over this story when she told it, laughing at her "fussiness" in her earlier days. She thought she would get a job in Cleveland, but didn't, and finally left the child with relatives and went on, again by the road, to New York. She had a fair singing voice and finally managed to sign up in a cheap night club chorus, and came on to Chicago. She made barely enough to live on, and after several unhappy, cheap love affairs, began taking a little money from men. She met Bill in one of the cabarets where she sang. He told her she was crazy to waste her time making a living with her voice. After the other men she had known in the joint, Bill seemed considerate. He took her out and let her talk about her child. The night before he slept with her he gave her fifteen dollars to send to the relatives keeping the child. It took him just two weeks to get her to hustle for him.

I asked her why, in the name of common sense, she lived with a man who had three other women and gave him all her money. She answered, "I'm his heart, and these other foolish broads are working for me. I'll get most of the money they earn."

Later on I met Barbara. She was short, squat in figure, dark in complexion. She kept her hair so waved that it looked like molded metal. She avoided looking at anyone directly when she talked. But she had plenty to say in a twangy southern voice, especially about Bill. She was the only one of Bill's girls who had ever ridden in a box car. She said she and a barber "lay up" in one the first time

she took a man, down in Atlanta, and before they knew
it the train was moving and they didn't get off till they
got to Nashville. She had had several men while she
worked in a restaurant, and then had married Willy
Barnes, a gangster who was killed by a policeman during
a filling station holdup.

Barbara had a queer twist in her. Willy Barnes was
crosseyed. After Willy died she went off with "Bad Eye,"
another gangster, and had hitch-hiked with him, hiding
out in jungles, all the way up to Chicago. When he went
to Joliet for holding up a Chicago filling station, she
took up with "Goggles," an auto thief. He had only one
eye. When he got caught in the district attorney's drag-
net for changing auto plates, she went with "One-Eyed
Jim." She said that for years and years all the sweethearts
she had finally went to jail, and all had bad eyes. She
could never see what made her fall for them. She was
quite sure that the reason she fell for Bill, when he found
her sick trying to hustle on the street, was that he had
such wonderful eyes, straight ones.

After I got to know her a little I asked Barbara the
same question I'd asked the others.

"Tell me, why do you hustle for a man that doesn't
love you and that has other women?"

She looked at me straight, with defiance in her eyes and
scorn for the other women.

"Bill loves me. I'm his heart. He's my child and I've
got to take care of him. He's promised me that he's going
to get rid of all the other women just as soon as he has
ten thousand dollars, and we are going to Duluth and start

a legitimate business. I've been with Bill four years and I'm the only woman he really loves."

I had only one more to check up on now, so I cultivated Mary. She was almost as tall and heavy as I am, with big thick arms and thighs. She had started hustling after her husband caught her with a salesman in Cincinnati, and had met Bill in Chicago on a party she was on with a man who was born in Ohio who was attracted to her when he heard somebody in a night club call her "Cincinnati." She didn't seem to take her hustling very seriously, though she complained quite a bit about not having enough clothes. I asked her, as I had the others, what in the world she was doing living with a pimp who took all her money.

"Bill loves me, I'm his heart . . ." she began.

I stopped her, my patience at an end, and exploded.

"For Christ's sake, don't tell me you're Bill's heart and that all these other women are working for you. That's what each one of them says. Bill is a louse and a liar and a bum. He's had thirty women in the last five years and he's told them all the same story. He's as low and as crooked as a man can be. What does he have that makes you women fall for him? I wouldn't wipe my feet on the man. I don't believe in law or jail, but hanging is too good for such a creature. Why one of you don't kill him I can't understand."

But she only smiled quietly and tolerantly.

"You don't know Bill," she said, and something in her eyes disturbed me and made me tremble. And suddenly I thought of Jordan. To be sure he wasn't a pimp. He had never asked any woman to hustle for him. But he had had dozens of women. He had my own sister and me at the same time, yet I always wanted him. I left Mary thinking about Bill and feeling shaken.

After that I used to see Bill around the hotel nearly every day. He always smiled at me and had a friendly greeting. And I found myself half trying to avoid him and half looking forward to seeing him. One night Ethel was too drunk to go to work and Bill beat her. She screamed and I rushed across the hall and, finding the door unlocked, pushed it open.

"You dirty brute," I screamed, "isn't it enough that you take your slave's life blood and money and ruin her?"

He answered calmly.

"Listen, my dear young lady. This little bitch belongs to me. I'm her man. She was a no-account clappy little chippy when I found her. She didn't have a rag to her back. I got her well. I dressed her. I taught her to get money for what she was giving away. She's having the best time of her life now. She even sends a little money home to her family. I make ladies of all my women. I make money-makers out of them. They wouldn't amount to a snowball in hell without me."

But Ethel, with swollen face, sobbing on the bed, seemed a different story to me, and I let loose on him.

"You dirty bastard! Ethel isn't over nineteen. She comes of a nice family. If it wasn't for you and your likes she could get married and be a decent woman. She ought to kill you. She's do society a favor."

Very wobbly, very drunk, Ethel got up from the bed,

and, casting a drunken, scornful look at me, went over and put her arms around Bill.

"Daddy, forgive me for hollering. I deserve worse than you gave me. I love you. Kiss me."

Bill turned to me coolly.

"Take a look, kid," he said. "And get a load of this—just because you thought you had to butt in here and tell me off, I'm going to have you in my stable one of these days!"

I grunted with what I thought was disgust.

"Me in your stable!" I yelled. I picked up a book-end and threw it at him. It struck him in the neck. Then Ethel flew across the room at me, arms and claws flung out to attack me.

"You big dirty cow!" she screamed. "Get out of my room or I'll kill you!"

In my own room I threw myself on the bed trembling and cried, cried for Ethel and the rest of Bill's girls. Cried for myself, feeling suddenly completely alone, cried because I knew girls like Ethel and the others did what they did because they felt they were alone.

After awhile there was a gentle knock at the door and a bellboy handed me a vase of flowers and a note.

"Dear fighting Bertha," it read. "I like your style. I like 'em rough. My car will be down in front at four o'clock. Let me take you for a ride.—Bill."

I held the note in trembling fingers. How well Bill knows women, I thought. I remembered, "I'll have you in my stable," and prayed, "No, it must not be," but found myself pressing his roses to my breast. I was suddenly afraid.

I had a little money left, and I walked all the way to the Northwestern Station and bought a ticket to the first place I could think of, Milwaukee. While I was waiting in the train for it to pull out I began to get nervous. I remembered, "God help me to succumb to my temptation quickly." Bill, I suddenly knew, had something I wanted. It didn't make any sense, but it was true. Just as the train began to move I jumped off and went back to the hotel. It was just four o'clock. In front of the entrance Bill opened the door of his car and I got in. Neither of us said a word.

We drove through Lincoln Park and out Sheridan Road and then we began to talk.

He talked about the weather, about trees, about books. His voice was soft and persuasive. He looked straight at me and through me. I began to tingle. I loathed him. I despised him. I knew that in my heart. But I found my body wanting to be close to him.

"Thank you for sending me the roses," I finally managed. "Tell me, Bill, how does it feel to be a Bluebeard and murder your victims?"

"Bertha, I'll tell you. It doesn't feel very pleasant. I like music and books. I like lectures. I'm interested in movements, radical movements. I want a system in which there'll be no more whores, no more wage slaves. Now, if you think it's a cinch taking care of and satisfying women, you're mistaken. They're always sick, always getting pinched, always fighting. I have plenty of grief every day. I spend all of my time looking after these girls. Now, if I had an intelligent woman like you to work with, someone that could help me, that would really love me, I could do something. I used to be a union man and make sixty-five fifty a week, more than I make now. I once ran a gambling joint. Knew something about politics. I don't need these broads any more than you need a dozen men. I need a boss, a woman who can keep me straight. These girls of mine pull me down. They're all rotten and degraded. Bertha, if you will love me, if you'll help me . . ."

We had dinner at the Edgewater Beach Hotel. He was gentle. We danced.

"You're beautiful, Box Car!" he whispered to me. "Please, may I come to your room to-night?"

I did not answer. But I knew. And he knew. I knew all he had said to me were lies. It did not matter.

Back in my room I put on my pajamas with one of Bill's roses in my bosom. He came with a bottle of Old Crow. We had a highball.

What a night! Bill knew women. It must have been that, for he was not much to look at, only about five feet seven and weighing probably not more than one hundred and thirty pounds. His complexion was sallow. He was burned out. But his touch was that of a master. His fingers on my throat sent me into ecstasy. I let myself go. I was completely magnetized, not to passion, but to sacrifice. When, at length, he took me in his arms, I was at peace. I felt mother, child, and lover, all in one.

"Bill, Bill, what have you done to me?"

"What do you want me to do?"

"Bill," I begged him, "you don't need me to hustle for you. There are many other women. I want to do something in the world. I want to help people, the poor, the thieves, the crooks. How could I do this if I became a whore. I might catch a disease. Please don't make me hustle!"

I heard my own voice in a whine. I knew his answer before it came.

"Now listen, baby. You're my heart. I love you. These other broads don't mean anything to me. They're working for you. I don't want a nickel you earn. Every cent you get we'll put in the bank and we'll get a little business. And if you want to start a hobo college or a mission, you can do it. Now, Bertha, I just want you to work a week or so and help me out. I've got a note on my car. I've got a lot of debts. Now, baby, if you love me, you'll do this thing for me."

The identical words he had used to win his other women! A drug he poured into me. My body stirred luxuriously in his arms. I was his woman. One of his women! Judgment whispered to me, "It's dangerous," but everything in me surrendered to him and I felt almost exalted that now I knew completely how women all the years had felt when they surrender to "I love you—and if you love me, you will."

In the morning I walked along the lake in front of the hotel. It was a wild day and the waves were rough. My mind was tumultuous as the waves. The spray cooled me. My brain became clear. How silly it was. I was going to be a whore and give my money to a pimp! I thought of my grandfather who had worked for women's emancipation. I thought of my mother who was free and honest and who had taken her lovers with a clean heart. I thought of E. A. O. who said I had something to me, of Lowell Schroeder, of the men and women I had known in the co-operative colony in Arkansas and in Home Colony in Washington. Free men and women! I was no longer under Bill Steward's spell. I could think clearly, but I knew I was not going to renege. Thousands, millions of men the world over pay women for a few minutes of contact. Why do these men go to such women? What have these women to give them? I wanted to know. For a long time I had wanted to know.

Was I a chameleon taking on the conditions of every new environment? I was. I recalled that when I was in I. W. W. hall I thought and talked like a wobbly. When I was in Greenwich Village with Franklin Jordan I felt like a highbrow. When I was living with Schroeder I felt like a wife. Was it true, then, what Jordan had said, that we are all products of environment? Had I the power to choose whether I was to become Bill's slave? And then I knew that being a prostitute was no new idea of mine. Even as a little girl in Bismarck, watching the hustling girls, I had wanted to be one with them. Bill was only my excuse, the opening wedge.

Ethel was asleep when I got back. I shook her.

"What do you think? I've fallen in love with that bastard pimp of yours and I'm going to start to hustle for him in the morning. But I'm different from the rest of you. I'm going to get something out of this experience. I'm going to learn why women let their feelings make slaves of them."

"The hell you are," Ethel said crossly, turning over to go to sleep again. "You're just another damn fool."

Bill slept with me again that night. In spite of all my thinking during the day, all of me waited for his fingers and his lips, and by morning there was no decision in me, one way or the other.

At six a call came from Pollack, manager of the Globe, a house of prostitution. Bill answered it.

"Sure—I've got a new doll. What does she need?"

He turned to me.

"Have you a nice teddy?" he asked.

"No," I said weakly.

"All right. I'll get you some. Get up and dress. They want you over at the Globe at seven o'clock."

He went to Ethel's room and came back with a heavily fringed and embroidered georgette teddy, and sat on the edge of the bed while I dressed.

"If you're a smart girl you'll come home with a nice bank roll to-night," he said. "The maid, or one of the broads will tell you what to do. Don't let them put anything over on you, but try to get along with them. It's a good spot. Stop downstairs and get a cup of coffee. I'll call a cab for you."

He kissed me, only matter-of-factly, but I was so thrilled at the thought of this new experience that I did not mind.

THIRTEEN

THE cab stopped in front of the Globe, an old three-story brick building on Erie Street near Clark. It had once been run as a man's lodging house. I walked up the steps and was met by the clerk at the desk.

"Are you Bill's broad?"

I nodded affirmation and he pressed a button back of the desk and a door opened. The inside man, Rudy, a pock-marked individual with over-hanging brows and an unhealthy odor about his feet, appeared.

"Right this way. Take your clothes off in this room. Did you bring a teddy with you? Take your drugs out of your pocket-book, and your make-up. Put your clothes in a bundle. Don't keep any money on you."

I took the things out of my purse Bill had provided for me the night before—a small tube of vaseline, a bar of germicidal soap, a small bottle of antiseptic, and my lipstick, rouge, powder and comb. Rudy took my bundle and put it in a small room called the get-away room, a secret escape leading to the outside. One of the wainscoting panels was on hinges, and led to a small opening between the floors which gave a passage to the roof. The girls could walk along this roof to a ladder that led up to another roof, on top of which was a cupola where they could hide until the police had gone.

After Rudy had explained the get-away he took me back and introduced Margaret, the colored maid, a high-yellow in her early thirties. She asked me my name, and I told her "Bertha."

"Now, honey, we's already got a Bertha, so we'll call you Dottie," she told me. "We work in turns 'til every girl 'breaks luck,' and then it's choice. You'll take the next man that comes in, unless he's someone's friend. Sit down."

We were in a large room, the parlor, a room full of mirrors, with a linoleum floor. It was well lighted. There were no chairs, but it had benches on three sides. There were six girls waiting. The other three were busy, and I met them later.

"This is Edna, and she is going to show you how we does business here."

Edna, or French Edna, as the girls called her, broke in most of the new girls. She was a bleached blonde, weighing about two hundred and fifteen pounds. I was glad to see someone larger than myself.

Edna did more business than any of the others, but she did not make the most money, for she was strictly a two-dollar woman. The next girl was Lorraine, the broad of Pollack, the manager. She was tall, nicely formed, red-haired. She always "topped the house," that is, made the most money.

Next to her sat Jackie, a little girl with a hooked nose that made her look like a guinea pig. She was a "nigger lover." Her pimp was a colored man. She was a mediocre hustler, and was known as a "three-way broad." She had the best street clothes of any girl there.

Irene was a thin, dark little woman of about thirty. She didn't have so many tricks but was a hard worker and made pretty good money. Chickie, a bleached blonde, didn't look very young, and had a mousey face. She was the mother of two kids, and her man was a gambler. In the corner sat Dolly and June, who looked, both of them, like statues, with hair combed back and expressionless faces. "They're French, and lady lovers," Edna whispered. "They both live with Earl Walker, a 'jigaboo' pimp from the south side."

Katherine was a mature, thoughtful-looking girl of about thirty, always reading a book when she wasn't busy. Her pimp, Scotty, was a guard at the county jail.

"And so," she greeted me, "you want to be a two-dollar whore, huh? I congratulate you. If you stay here more than sixty days, you belong here. Anybody can get into one of these joints accidentally, but the girl who remains here was born for the job."

Peggy, a peppy, bleached blonde, was like a young panther. She had a great line of bull and would say to most any man who looked like he had money, "Daddy, you're wonderful! Oh, you're such a fine lover. Won't you please take me out of here? If you'll let me have twenty dollars, I'll pay my debts to this gang and I'll meet you on the outside." Sol Rubenstein was her pimp, and he came for her every evening in a big Lincoln.

The last girl I met the first day was Alabama, a thin

brunette who looked as though she might be tubercular. She was a comedienne, singing and telling stories and playing jokes, half-drunk most of the time, although it was against the rules of the house for the girls to drink much. She was a good money-maker. All the customers liked her. She had two pimps, one a married man, a cab driver with two kids, that she was supporting, and the other a bartender named Kelly, in a Loop hotel. Katherine said, "She told Kelly that the cab driver was her husband. He knows she's a liar, but he's satisfied as long as she slips him most of the money."

The turn-over in girls was very large, Margaret told me. All of the girls had pimps. I found out that the Globe was a syndicate joint, bossed by a mysterious personage that I never saw. They called him "the old man." He never came to the joint, but the girls said they met him occasionally at his cabaret.

The manager of the house was Pollack, a big-nosed, syphilitic, squint-eyed, bald-headed man known affectionately as "the slaver-driver." Besides being paid for his job, he was kept by four women, one in our place, Lorraine, and one in each of the other three syndicate joints. Next in authority was Rudy, the inside man. And then came Pork Chops, an Italian with a lowering countenance and a greasy vest, who stood on the corner and watched for the cops. When they were coming he gave us the "Air-loft," or warning to get away. The "roper," who stood in front and solicited business was Bad Eye, a tall, goofy kid of about twenty who had lost his eye from a gonococci infection picked up on a towel carelessly tossed in his mother's bathroom. Bad eye was the only man working there who did not have a girl of his own, but was constantly, "on the make." The last man was Chew-Tobacco Rocky, a big Italian with a cud constantly in his mouth. He ran errands for the girls and carried messages from one joint to another. He was Irene's man, and the girls called him a "coffee and" pimp, because Irene just gave him a dollar a day.

The person we girls had the most to do with was Margaret, the maid. When a "John," or customer, came in he was ushered into the parlor where half a dozen girls sat around. He would take his choice and they would go to a room. The girl asked him for the money as soon as they were alone. Although this house was known as a two-dollar joint, when a stranger came in the girls would hustle him for more money and get all they could. We were taught to say to strangers, "We'll give you a good time for five dollars." If they hesitated, we were to say, "Give me three dollars, and I'll take off all my clothes."

When a cab load came the maid would always say, before the men came into the parlor, "Portier," which meant to get as much as you could, because the cab driver would have to be paid a commission, four dollars out of ten, two out of five, and one dollar out of three. We weren't supposed to take less than five dollars from each man in the cab load. There were exceptions. If a "good man," one who had plenty of money to spend, came in, the maid would say "Friday." If he was a five-dollar trick, she said, "Holiday," and if he was a ten-dollar trick, "Double Holiday." In this way strange girls would never cheapen the good trade. It was Margaret's duty to remember every customer, and what he spent.

Just as soon as we got the money from the customer we went out and bought aluminum checks from Margaret, similar to the old-time brass beer checks. A two-dollar check was marked "Five Cents in Trade," and a three-dollar check was a little larger and said, "Ten Cents in Trade." If there was a ten-dollar trick, she'd give us two threes and two deuces.

As soon as Margaret had a bank of a hundred dollars she passed it on to Pollack, who later gave it to the collector, Solly, who came twice a day with a little handbag and two heavily armed guards; Boyle, an ex-police sergeant and another called "The Indian." They took the money from there to the Newland Hotel belonging to The Old Man. He had charge of about thirty joints, houses of prostitution and gambling joints, and was then Chief of the North Side Syndicate. None of the joints was owned by him or his partners.

It was easy to start a joint, I learned. An old hotel was taken on commission and the former owner of the hotel might be kept right on to run the place. All the old man did was to conduct his business for him, furnish him the girls, a staff and police protection. The original owner or manager of the hotel got anywhere from twenty-five to fifty per cent of the old man's share of the day's receipts. The girls were told that police protection cost ten percent. But Pollack, who had been in the game for twenty years, said that the police got very little. The old man had an "in" at the City Hall. He contributed heavily to every campaign fund, Democratic or Republican. He donated to all the politicians, was good to the poor and divided about two hundred dollars a week for each joint to the police. The captain, harness bulls and squad men got the most of it.

The day and night crew of the Globe consisted of twenty girls. Each girl made on an average of thirty dollars a day for the house. When we were "going good," it wasn't unusual for the house to clear as their end four thousand or five thousand dollars a week.

I had thought a house of prostitution would be very exciting. I was surprised to learn how quiet it was. Edna showed me how to put the footpad on the bed. No man ever took off his shoes, and a piece of blanket was laid on to protect the spread. Then she showed me how to examine a man, and told me not to take him if he showed any signs of disease.

Before Edna was through breaking me in, I had a definite feeling of having to make good on my job, just as I have felt when I started a new typing job anywhere. I felt she and the other girls knew more than I did and that they expected me to keep up with them.

My first trick was a bit of a shock to me, however, a big Hunky, a man of about fifty with a handle-bar moustache. He was clumsy and rough. He put his hands under my teddy and pinched me. I didn't mind the roughness, but his fingernails were filthy and he had a vile garlic breath.

The next dozen men were fairly easy. Then an old smooth-faced man of about seventy came in. All his manhood had left him, but he wanted me to pet him and kiss him, and do things. I tried but failed completely. I found myself sorry for him and wishing that I could help him, but it was impossible.

Toward evening a big roughneck came in. The minute I looked at him I knew he would be trouble. I made my first mistake by asking him to spend five dollars, and my second by insisting that he spend an extra dollar to see me take off my teddy. He wasn't going to wait for anything. He wouldn't let me examine him. He handed me two dollars, and picked me up and threw me on the bed. I protested, but he fought with me and wouldn't let me up. I called for Margaret, and he began abusing her. Margaret pushed the buzzer for Rudy, the bouncer.

He came in with Pollack right behind him, and while Rudy pulled the fellow off, Pollack said, "Let him have it!" Rudy hit him over the head with a "sap," a soft blackjack with shot in the end of it. While he was unconscious they dragged him down the back steps and put him into a car, took him a few blocks away and dumped him into an alley under the "L" tracks.

Some of the men were embarrassed. They chose a girl quickly without hardly looking at her. Or they pretended to be tough and tried rough jokes. One well-dressed man with a long thoughtful face picked me out by coming over and putting a hand on my shoulder. Then, and when we were alone, he never said a single word. I let him rest a few minutes in my arms when he was through, and when he went out he gave me a look like you've seen on the face of a hungry dog after you've fed it. Another one, just a youngster really, a little drunk, cried after he was satisfied and said he'd never been in a place like that before. But most of them seemed old customers and used to the joint.

During the course of the day at least half of my customers asked me if I were French. I said "No." Some of them coaxed, some of them threatened to get someone else, but no one made any serious trouble, until a young stubnosed Italian came in, and when I flatly refused, he went out to Margaret and said, "I want a French broad. I don't have to come here for the regular. I can get that at home."

Margaret said something to Rudy, and he came in and sat beside me, gave me a cigarette and lit one.

"Kid, a notch house is a place of business and the customer must be satisfied. Nowadays few men want it straight. They want it half and half. Don't blame me. I didn't invent human nature. We're in the business, and if you're going to hustle in any kind of a joint you're got to learn to be French, and maybe Greek. Now don't be a damned fool. You get on to the tricks, and it will be easier that way than any other."

I learned quickly. The rest of the girls thought nothing of it. Enda said, "The big money is in the 'queer' guys. And what freaks some of 'em are! But that's the way nature made them and what are you going to do about it?"

At the end of the day I had forty tricks, forty sex-hungry men that I had satisfied.

In common with all the girls, I kept track of all my tricks in a little notebook. Here is an account of my first day's work as a prostitute:

20 men at $2.00 each	. . . .	$ 40.00
10 men " 3.00	. . . .	30.00
5 men " 5.00	. . . .	25.00
2 men " 4.00	. . . .	8.00
3 men " 10.00	. . . .	30.00
Total	. . . .	$133.00

At half-past six Margaret sent me into the office to cash in. I had a hundred and thirty-three checks and naturally thought I was to get half that much, or $66.50. Instead Pollack and Rudy counted my checks and handed me $40.

"Why only $40?" I asked. "I gave you $133. Where I went to school in North Dakota half of $133 is $66.50."

"Don't you know how we do business here?" Pollack answered me. And he took a pencil and showed me.

Tricks	. . . .	$133.00
50% for the house	. . . .	66.50
		66.50
10% for protection	. . . .	6.50
		$60.00

"You see, kid, if there's a pinch we take care of you. You don't have to worry about a thing. We get you bondsmen and everything."

"Well, that still leaves twenty dollars unaccounted for," I protested.

"What the hell difference does it make, as long as you don't have anything to worry about? And we took three dollars off for the maid. She's supposed to get fifty cents on every sixteen checks, but we only took three dollars from you to-night because you're new and you haven't many friends. We gave Bad Eye two bucks for bringing in the business. How would you make any money if it wasn't for the roper? You've got to give Chew-Tobacco a buck for getting your cigarettes, your java, and your eats. We took off two bucks for towels. You used about four dozen, and it costs two bits a dozen to get 'em laundered. If you'd like to bring your own towels from home, you can. Then we bought you a teddy, and four pairs of stockings . . . that cost twelve dollars. So there you are."

Protection	$ 6.50
Teddy and stockings	12.00
Maid	3.00
Roper	2.00
The Runner	1.00
Towels	2.00
	$26.50

"Now, do you understand? How long have you been hustling? You'll get along better if you don't ask so many questions."

My spirits somewhat dampened, I accepted the forty dollars without further question, and went wearily back to my hotel. I didn't feel that anything had changed in me because I had become a prostitute. I just felt completely worn-out, as though I'd finished an unusually hard day's work.

Bill came into my room that night just long enough to

order up my supper and say, "Good girl," and "How's tricks?" and to take my money. He took all but two dollars. I was too tired to protest. All I wanted was to bathe and sleep. I remember thinking as I dozed off how easily I had fallen into Bill's system. Only one day, and I was a full-fledged prostitute. That's the way it happened to women. The routine of every day after that would carry them on, just like it does in an office or factory. When their day was over they would be too tired to think.

Bill didn't offer to sleep with me. I couldn't have let him touch me, then. He knew enough to know that. I tried to remember, lying there, how he had felt to me when he took me in his arms, but I couldn't. Instead, I kept seeing the faces of the men who had come in to me that day. And I knew I would go back again and again until I had learned what I wanted to know about them and about the girls who received them.

FOURTEEN

I GOT fairly well acquainted with most of the girls at the Globe. During the day we'd go window shopping, and, although our pimps bought our clothes and toilet articles, we got a few little things for ourselves, mostly at the five-and-ten.

Many of them had started out by hoboing. I mentioned one day when we were all sitting around in the parlor before the trade began to come that my name was "Box Car" and told them where I got it. And immediately they all started telling their stories of flipping freights and hitch-hiking. It seems like most of them started off by running away and being on the loose on the road for awhile.

In spite of the fact that all the girls at the Globe made good money, they never had any. They were constantly trying to short-change their pimps. It may sound unbelievable but it was true that we had to account for every dollar we earned. Pollack usually told our pimps how much money we got and unless we slipped him a little, he would let our men know exactly how much we ought to turn over to them. If Pollack didn't tell on us, one of the girls would tell her pimp, and he would tell the injured man, so we were pretty well checked up.

Sometimes, when we'd have a good trick, he'd slip us five dollars, and say, "Girlie, you tell the maid you only got two." Or, sometimes we'd get a dollar tip and not mention it. But it was uncanny the way our men and the employees in the house could check on us. We took our money behind closed doors, but very few girls cheated the management or the pimps successfully very long. If you cheated the house you were fired. If you robbed the customer and split with the house you were praised. If you held out on your pimp and got away with it, you were lucky. If you didn't get away with it, he beat you up . . . and that was just your tough luck. Even so, the girls were always trying to cheat and lie to their pimps, and the pimps were constantly lying to and bulldozing their women.

Some of the girls who had children to support would be given five or maybe ten dollars a week of their own money, for their kids. Once in a while a girl would be allowed to send a few dollars to her mother.

It was almost impossible to believe that here were a group of apparently intelligent women earning anywhere from fifty to two hundred dollars a week, and having indigent parents and children in institutions and elsewhere, and not sending them a cent.

One afternoon when "the heat was on," and the police ordered the joint closed for a few hours, and they had locked the doors, a bunch of us girls were sitting around discussing pimps. Marie maintained that her only reason for keeping one was because she liked to wake up in the morning with someone who was lower than she was.

"I'll tell you why I have one," said Lorraine. "I know that Pollack doesn't love me, but he's good to me and he takes care of me. If I get in a pinch, or I'm sick, I don't have to work. I was one of the pavement pounders and hustled on the street for a year without a man. What did I get out of it? I was always gettin' pinched, and some lawyer or fix, or some bull always got my money. There was always somebody trying to make me and worry me. I tell you, a hustling girl is up against it unless she's got a pimp to protect her. Pollack buys my clothes, and if I need a little money to send home, he gives it to me. I haven't got a damn worry in the world."

I suppose that's the way all the girls felt about it.

When I had been at the Globe about two months things began to get hot. I was on the night shift. Every day it was getting worse. The town was clamoring for the enforcement of vice restrictions. We used to close between one and four o'clock in the morning when the vice squad was on the street. Many times we had to take the air-loft, but there was no actual raid until the last Saturday I was there.

About six o'clock we got the buzz. Pork Chops had seen the vice squad coming around the corner in their Cadillac, heading for our place. All the lights went out. Someone grabbed me by the hand and said, "Make for the get-away, kid." Each of us grabbed her bundle of clothes as we went along, through the get-away, up the short incline to the roof, across the roof, up the ladder and across another roof to the cupola. Rudy followed us in and closed the trap door.

The vice squad, twelve men in all, had to break down the front door to get in the joint, but they found only four or five men in different stages of undress, hiding in closets and under beds. Everybody else was out except Pollack, and, of course, Margaret. But one of the rules of the game is that a maid or servant in a joint is never bothered by the police. They could see, though, from the men being around, and the disorder in the rooms, that we were not very far away. They determined to find us. One of the "Johns" told them what general direction we had disappeared, and after chopping around in the walls for awhile, and not finding the get-away, they went out on the roof. Neighbors next door had heard us cross, and we couldn't have got out except through their building. On the second roof from the hotel the squad found our ladder which we had not had time to pull up after us. Then they knew they had us. The only place we could have gone to from there was the cupola.

This little cupola was a space four by six feet, and there were nine of us girls and Rudy in it. We were nearly suffocated and when the police began chopping on it Rudy saw there was no use, so he called to the cops and said we'd come out.

We climbed down out of the cupola with our bundles of clothes in our hands. We went back to the joint and put them on. The squad was very friendly and kidded us, and in the confusion four of the girls and Pollack escaped. But the police didn't seem to mind. Five made a good showing.

The local police and the squads think it unwise to have

more than four or five girls arrested in any one place, I learned. If they do they have to explain why a house could do so much business without them knowing about it.

The five of us were taken to the Hudson Avenue Police Station where we found fifteen other girls who had been arrested in the same district. We were taken to Police Headquarters. Bill came over at eleven o'clock and brought me sandwiches and cigarettes.

"Don't worry, girlie," he said, "everything's fixed. I spoke to the pudge myself just before I came here, and the States Attorney is a friend of mine."

He lied about this, of course, as he did about everything else.

For three weeks prior to my arrest I had been completely alienated from him. I learned very soon that if I complained of my lot or got temperamental that his manner would grow very tender with me and he would sleep with me and take me out to dinner. Only when I threatened to stop was he really considerate. He didn't care if I had fifty men in a day just so I brought him the money. He'd pet me and try to make me think he was trying to save up enough jack so that he could get me out of the business. But I had his number. I had refused to give him any more money and he threatened to beat me up. I was too big a woman for him to beat, and he knew it, but he kept on talking about it just the same.

"I don't know why I don't knock your head off and take your money from you," he said one night.

"Bill," I answered him, wondering if there was any sense left in him to reason with. "You're just an experience

with me. I needed some excuse to be a whore. I just hypno-
tized myself into believing that you were my man. You
were never my man, nor any woman's man. I wonder why
pimps with so much charm and power to thrill women use
it only to degrade them and themselves. And I wonder
why I go on with it now. I suppose it's just inertia. I suppose it will take something new to jar me out of it."

But I hadn't counted on quite such a series of jars as
that which began with my arrest.

We had a wild time in the police station. There were
several drunken women who kept us awake most all night.
In the morning, Sunday, at nine o'clock we were taken to
the Venereal Disease Clinic in the Police Building at
Eleventh and State Streets.

There were forty-five of us girls waiting to be examined.
Health Department regulations were that every woman
arrested for prostitution was to be taken to the Social
Hygiene division and examined for active venereal disease.
If she was found free from infection, she was admitted to
bail, usually about twenty-five dollars. Those found to be
infected were sent to the Health Department Venereal
Hospital known as Lawndale.

Half of the girls waiting to be examined were colored.
All of us were nervous and excited. The pinch didn't seem
to mean anything to the girls. The worst thing that could
happen in the court was to get a ten or a twenty-five dollar fine. It was only occasionally that a girl was sent to
the House of Correction. But the thing that bothered most
of them was the fear that they might be diseased. That

would mean a month or six weeks in the hospital, and they all dreaded this.

It had never occurred to me that I might possibly become infected. But when the police matron began to call the girls from the Globe, something gripped my heart, and I had a weird apprehension that something was going to happen to me. I envied the Catholic girls who were nervously handling their beads and saying a prayer. One of the girls was saying, "Oh, Mary . . . Mother of God . . . help me!"

"Dottie Mack!" That was the name Rudy had told me to give. It sounded as if the Devil were calling the roll.

The matron and the nurse led me to the table, and Dr. Joseph Sonnenschein, the physician in charge, looked tired and bored, but was courteous and kind. He examined me and took smears for microscopic analysis, then told me to wait, and I began to feel the choking sensation of nameless fear.

We sat around for about two hours waiting for our results. Finally the reports came and the matron called the names of thirty-seven girls who were negative, or apparently free from active venereal disease. The eight of us whose names were not called were left sitting in the little room, a depressed, silent, fearsome group. Dr. Sonnenschein called me into his office.

"Miss Mack, I want to talk to you. Tell me, when did you menstruate last?"

"Oh, about six or seven weeks ago, I guess. I don't know. I didn't pay much attention to it. Why, is there anything the matter with me?" My voice was trembling and I was afraid to look at him.

He put his hand on my shoulder and his voice was kindly as he told me.

"You're a sick girl, Dottie," he said. "But don't worry too much about it. We'll get you well. You have syphilis and an active gonorrhea—and you're probably pregnant."

For a moment all of the training my mother had given me in the technique of taking whatever came deserted me. I felt limp and faint and was grateful for the doctor's steadying hand on my shoulder.

Me? Bertha Thompson, Mother Thompson's daughter? Ena and Margaret's sister? Me, to whom E. A. O. had said that nothing terrible could happen? Me, that Lowell Schroeder had said was destined to do big things in the world? I couldn't have syphilis! I couldn't be pregnant! I knew about birth control. E. A. O. had taught me. I had watched myself carefully. Why, when I wanted a child, I was going to choose as his father Franklin Jordan, and have a Christ-like child like How. The doctor must be mistaken. I couldn't have gonorrhea! This must be a joke, I told myself. I'm Box Car Bertha! I've lived through everything. I'm not a whore. I'm not the kind of woman to whom these things happen!

The patrol wagon carted us to Lawndale Hospital. I went in a daze. I tried to think of my mother's face. I tried to repeat over and over her words, "There are no tragedies in this household."

Katherine, my pal from the Globe, put her arm around me and said "Buck up, kid. We'll live through it. This is the third time I've been to Lawndale, and I never had to stay out there over two weeks."

I patted her hand gratefully, but I couldn't talk.

The matrons at Lawndale Hospital registered us, told us to bathe and gave us uniforms. We were permitted to keep our cosmetics, shoes, and stockings. I was placed in an isolation ward with five other women who had active syphilis. We were given a good dinner and I lay down on my cot and soon fell into a troubled sleep.

Twice that day I was given local treatment and three times took douches. The next morning I had another dark field taken and another blood test. The dark field was positive, and the blood test, I was told, was only one plus. The doctor, June Edmundson, tried to reassure me.

"You're very fortunate, Dottie, that you were arrested. Your syphilis is only in the primary stage and your blood test was just beginning to get positive. One plus is not at all bad. If you had waited for another three or four weeks, you might have had a four plus and secondary eruptions all over your body. You're a strong girl and I'm going to push the treatment. It will be comparatively easy to get you well. You can have a perfectly healthy child. There's nothing to worry about. If you take your treatment regularly, the probabilities are that this disease won't affect your offspring."

I was amazed that there was so little pain connected with my diseases. By the end of a month the gonorrhea was reported cured. As to the syphilis, only the first two Wassermann tests were positive, one plus. The next five weekly blood tests all proved negative.

The six weeks in Lawndale Hospital sped along. The matron let me help with the clerical work so I was busy and cheerful. One would suppose that a venereal disease hospital would be a very sad place. The opposite was true. We danced and played dominoes and checkers. We had all kinds of books and magazines and newspapers. There was plenty to smoke and every day large bundles of food were sent in to the girls. We were not allowed to have visitors, but all our pimps drove up in their cars and stood on the sidewalk and waved to us. Most all of the girls received and wrote letters. A number of the girls were illiterate and I wrote and read their letters. I kept copies of the letters the girls sent out and received.

I never tried to correct them, but took them just like they wrote them so their pimps and their friends would find them natural. All of the girls wanted to get out of Lawndale. All were worried about what their pimps were doing in their absence. All showed they were afraid of losing their men.

FIFTEEN

THE Sunday night before I left I stood at one of the dormitory windows just as the sun was beginning to set against the factory stacks. I felt well. I had gained nine pounds.

I thought of "the things that were" and the lines of Kipling came to me, "God, what things are there I haven't done?" I looked up at the top of the hospital. I seemed to see the large banner floating from the top of the building, and I wanted to inscribe mother's words on it: "There is no tragedy in our household."

"I'm going to have my greatest experience now," I thought. "I'm going to have a baby. A child . . . and who is his father?" How many different men had I stayed with when I was at the Globe? I had worked there two months, twenty-five days a month, and averaged thirty men a day —fifteen hundred men! Anyone of fifteen hundred men!

When I left Lawndale the next day I did not take to the road or ride a box car. In the last few weeks at the Globe, while I was on the outs with Bill, two of the girls had taught me a sure "knockdown" system, and I had succeeded in laying aside five or ten dollars a day. I had a roll of over three hundred dollars in a safety deposit vault. With this I got myself a new front, a smart black traveling dress and a hat to match. Then I bought a ticket with a Pullman on the Northern Pacific Limited train for Seattle.

I made myself comfortable in the seat, determining not to talk to anyone, but trying to think straight about my new problem. It was strange but very pleasant to think about a baby. I had always wanted a child, I reminded myself. Then I corrected that to what was more nearly the truth, that I had always taken it for granted that I would have children. I thought about my parents. My mother, certainly, had been always the mother type. But my father? He had said he was a male, not a father. What was it I really wanted? Actually, it seemed to me, what I wanted was the experience of being a mother. I had a certain curiosity about it. My body, inside my sleek traveling dress, felt good to me. The world going by between the telephone wires was green and cool. The earth was a good earth. Contentedly I looked at the people about me.

The train was crowded. The upper berth that night was occupied by a man fifty or sixty years old. He was not the type of man I had ever known much about. His reddish hair was thinning and greying. He had a spiked greying beard. He wore glasses. He sat opposite me in the daytime with his long legs wrapped around each other. His luggage contained a brief case and a typewriter.

He spoke to me several times, offered me cigarettes. I refused to talk, although I wanted to. I thought I should be planning what I was going to do about my baby. Once, when he left his seat, I saw his name, Harry Fredericks, on his brief case. On the seat he had left the papers he had been reading and marking with a pencil. They were "The Suicide Record" and the "Cancer Record." The term "consulting statistician" caught my eye. I wondered what a consulting statistician was.

By next noon my curiosity got the better of me, and I asked him if he minded if we ate together, and he acceded cordially. I found him a gold mine of information. Franklin Jordan had been well-informed. To me he had seemed highly intellectual. My father was a philosopher and thinker. I had met many well-educated, informed men. But this man knew everything. He was like an encyclopedia. For every opinion of mine he had a correction or something to show me I was right. And every time he had the figures to prove it. In the two short days he gave me a new poetry, the poetry of figures. He knew the death and birth rates, the age and sex and number of Negroes in America. He knew the number of murderers and rapes and suicides and cancers in every one-hundred-thousand population. He showed me that everything could be reduced to mathematics, and how it was possible to estimate the number of persons passing Forty-Second Street and Broadway at any given hour, or the number of persons that will die in a year and the probable causes of their deaths. Among other things, he told me that out of every one thousand births in the City of Chicago that year that there were one hundred and twenty-nine illegitimate children, and of those 79.7 were Negro.

From his figures we went on to very interesting discussions, for although he always used his figures as a basis of his talk, he seemed to have all kinds of scientific knowledge you didn't see in books or hear in lectures. He warned me that many of his assertions were only opinions, but they sounded so logical that I put them down, and I remember them to this day. He said, for instance, that there were very few prostitutes of the correct weight for their height. They are all overweight or underweight, with few exceptions, he said. The heavy ones are probably most popular, he said, backing up what I knew. He gave as the reason for this the fact that many men have never gotten over a feeling for their mothers and need the sense of physical comfort they knew as children. The heavyweights among the prostitutes are very often victims of glandular disease, he said, and the same disease made them less emotional and therefore able to go into the job without being squeamish about it.

Many prostitutes, he reminded me, are unusually thin. The first cause of this is venereal disease. The second is probably the drinking that usually goes along with the job. But the third cause, one I had never thought of, probably because my body was strong, is that the job itself is a terribly strenuous job, making for unusual physical exhaustion, and often results in such diseases as tuberculosis which thrives upon exhaustion.

Of course, I kept my experiences at the Globe very carefully concealed while I talked to Mr. Fredericks. I know he thought I just had a scientific interest in what he was saying. When he got on the subject of prostitutes and pregnancy I was not only amused but deeply interested. He said that all figures proved that very few prostitutes get pregnant, and if they do it is always in the first few months. The reason for this, he told me, was because "on a path often trod no grass grows." He explained this by saying that when exposed to various sperm the ova did not respond, and also by the fact that the constant douching with high-powered antiseptics indulged in by most prostitutes almost always made for sterility.

He said that he had just completed what he called "speculative statistics" for a doctor in Chicago on a study of Chicago prostitutes and female immorals and the number of pimps they utilize. I was so interested in this that he let me use his portable typewriter and I made a copy of the tables he had compiled. Here they are, with me right among them, I suppose!

A CLASSIFICATION OF PROSTITUTES AND FEMALE IMMORALS AND THE NUMBER OF PIMPS THEY UTILIZE

	Estimated No. in Chicago	Estimated Contacts Per Week Each	Total Contacts Per Week	No. of Pimps Utilized
1. "Juvenile" Prostitutes (Children from ten to fifteen years of age, many of whom appear in Juvenile Court, used by perverted men and young boys.)	1,000	2	2,000	100
2. "Potential" Prostitutes .... (Girls with a high sex urge and low restraining power who give themselves for love, daring, or out of obligation for a	10,000	2	20,000	5,000

	Estimated No. in Chicago	Estimated Contacts Per Week Each	Total Contacts Per Week	No. of Pimps Utilized
"good time," but are always ready to accept remuneration.)				
3. "Amateur" Prostitutes .... (Girls of all classes, but particularly those who give themselves to men for gain, but work or live at home.)	10,000	3	30,000	6,000
4. "Young Professional" Prostitutes ...... (Girls who have entered the field recently, operating as recruits in houses of prostitution.)	1,000	50	50,000	700
5. "Old Professional" Prostitutes ...... (The old established prostitutes who operate in houses of prostitution.)	800	75	60,000	700
6. "Field Workers" ... (These include street walkers and cheap hotel girls who pick up their men on the street, dance halls, etc.)	5,000	30	150,000	4,000
7. "Bats" .... (These are aged or worn-out prostitutes, drunkards, dope fiends, sought by bums and odd types.)	1,000	5	5,000	400
8. "Gold Diggers" .... (So - called "Boulevard"	10,000	5	50,000	5,000

	Estimated No. in Chicago	Estimated Contacts Per Week Each	Total Contacts Per Week	No. of Pimps Utilized
women who are "high-toned," keep expensive flats in residence districts and wear fine clothes.)				
9. "Kept Women" .... (Women in various grades of life who are "kept" by one man as a "private snap," but who often "cheat" and pick up extra money.)	10,000	2	20,000	3,000
10. "L o o s e" Married Women .... ("Lonesome" m a r r i e d women whose husbands travel, or who simply "cheat" more or less regularly. "Lonesome" widows and "fly" divorcees. An estimate of 6 percent of 560,000 married women and 15 percent of 110,000 widows and 9,000 divorced women in Chicago —many of these women take money from their husbands to give to their pimps.)	50,000	1	50,000	500
11. "Call Girls" .... (Working girls who take pay for the pleasure they give and are subject to telephone calls by hotel keepers and others.)	1,000	6	6,000	500
Total	99,800	..	443,000	25,900

From this study it appears that about 100,000 females are required to satisfy the sex needs of 500,000 men.

It is of interest to note that every pimp has from one to five or more women whom he exploits.

Just before we got to Seattle Mr. Fredericks took my address (mother's) and said that he would send me literature and have me placed on the mailing list of the United States Census Bureau and of the United States Department of Labor. For this I have always been grateful to him, for whenever I have been very much excited by something I have heard in a public address, I know how to look up the figures on it and see if it is correct. Because of the Globe experience I shall always watch the statistics on prostitutes with particular interest.

Mother and A. E. O. met me and drove me to a home on Washington Street. Mother had given up her house and was staying with a friend, Bessie Levin, and had a lovely sunny room. Mother was just as she had always been, a little greyer perhaps and a little stouter, but with the same warm interest in people and ideas and with the same ability not to ask too many questions. A. E. O. looked me over carefully, rather speculatively, I felt. I was glad my body was lovely just then. But I was careful not to let him think he could touch me. He and mother seemed more devoted than ever, as if there was some quiet understanding between them. That I did not want to spoil. Besides, I had too much else to think about.

I told them about the baby. They seemed pleased. They did not ask me how I had become pregnant, but they did not hesitate to let any of their friends know that I was.

But I was not to stay with them long. A letter from Chicago suddenly made me turn my face east again, to go back to the city I had so recently left.

SIXTEEN

BIG OTTO had written me a number of letters, but I hadn't heard from him for some time when a letter came from the Cook County Jail, in Chicago.

"I think I am settled and there is no need of your worrying about me any longer," he wrote. "I have reformed and will never steal again. If you want to see me this side of Hell, you had better come to Chicago before February 13th. Invitations are already out for my 'neck tie party.'"

I felt as though a cold hand had suddenly been laid on my heart! Otto a murderer! The neck about which my arms had been so many times—could it be possible that it was about to feel the choking clutch of a rope?

Without waiting for any preliminaries, I caught a Northern Pacific midnight freight with four men I made friends with at hobo college. They took good care of me. Mother fixed us a big batch of sandwiches. While we were rolling along through Idaho one of them pulled a candle out of his pocket, lit it and stuck it in the floor in the front end of the car and boiled coffee for me in a big cup. We had an army canteen with us. None of those men tried to make love to me. None of them mentioned the obvious fact that I was going to have a baby. Twice, once in Montana and once in Dakota, when the train hands started to get tough, they walked away as soon as they saw my condition.

The four men were going to Minneapolis to an employment agency that had called for hands in a biscuit factory. We slid out of our box car in the western yards there, and each one soberly chipped in a dollar and handed the money to me as they put me on another freight car later, on the Chicago and Northwestern. The next morning I climbed out in the Kedzie yards and went into the city on a street car.

It was then February 11th. Otto was to be hanged on the thirteenth. He was already in the death cell. They would not allow anyone to see him but his relatives. I pleaded without success with the warden and the sheriff. A young newspaper man by the name of Hennessy heard me begging. He said, "Sister, you come with me and I think I can make arrangements for you to see him."

We sat in a little restaurant on Clark Street near Grand Avenue.

"What is Otto to you, and why are you so anxious to see him?" he asked me. "Are you in the family way? Is it Otto?"

"He was formerly a very dear friend of mine," I told him, non-committally.

"You mean he was your sweetheart and the father of your child and you are engaged to marry him. Now, you let me write the story just as I want it and I'll get you a pass to see him. I'll even do better than that. I'll get you a pass to see him hanged."

"Jesus!—Me see Otto hanged!" I felt as though I had

been hit with a hammer, yet I knew that, if the man kept his word, I would go.

In less than an hour Hennessy came back with a pass and took me to the jail. We were admitted through a large iron gate and I was taken to the jailer's office and searched. The assistant jailer, a matron, and Hennessy walked in front of me as we passed through an iron door into the bundle cage. Then we went through another iron door along the first tier up a flight of iron steps into a big corridor, and to a large room at the front of the building.

"Just sit here, Miss Thompson. We'll call him."

They brought Otto from the death cell, handcuffed, with a guard on either side of him. As he entered the room I held out my hand to greet him. He looked just the same as ever, except that his hair was a little greyer, and he was very pale. He spoke:

"Hello, beautiful. How are you?"

"Just hold that pose," said the photographer.

"Hurry up and snap it," said Hennessy. "I want to get a picture of Otto holding Miss Thompson in his arms."

I was too shocked to protest. The newspaper photographer snapped a picture of us shaking hands, of me embracing him, and then of him kissing me. I did everything Hennessy asked of me. None of it mattered.

"Box Car, tell me, how've you been getting on?" Otto asked me, trying to be offhand about it. "What's your sister doing now? Do you ever see any of the old mob?"

But I could not talk to him of ordinary matters.

"Otto, aren't you afraid to die?" I found myself saying. "Doesn't the thought of being hanged bother you?"

"Well, I ain't hanged yet," he came back at me. "I've beat every rap so far. My lawyers are going to take this thing up to the Supreme Court, and I think the Governor will give me a stay of execution. You never say 'die' until you're dead, Bertha. I've been slated for an exit lots of times, but so far I've beaten every rap. In this game, the crooked live by faith."

Then his voice dropped to a whisper.

"On the level, Bertha, are you going to have a kid?" he asked. Then he added, "Say it's mine, will you?"

Tears sprang to my eyes as I heard him. Fifteen hundred lonely men! And now one man who might have been father to a child of mine, a man who was about to die, was pleading with me to say that the nameless child within me was his. How could anyone ever explain the troubled hearts of men? How could any woman ever hope to give them peace?

But I wanted to talk about him.

"Tell me, Otto, what happened? I've hardly read the papers. How did you get into such a jam? I never thought you were a burglar or a highway robber. I always thought you were a first-class, gentle sneak-thief."

The guards, with an unusual show of consideration, had stepped away leaving us, for a moment, in a little world of our own.

"I was," he said, "but I got overly ambitious. If I had stuck to the trade my father taught me, I'd have been all right. You see, Bertha, even in our racket we have our ups and downs. And ever since you left me I haven't amounted to much. I lost the courage to steal. I didn't have the training to work. I never dreamed, Bertha, that a woman could take so much out of a man when she left him as you did. Jesus, kid, I loved you. You're the only thing I ever loved in my life. I didn't want to live after you left me. I joined a cheap phoney mob of amateur hoodlums just because I thought I'd get croaked or the rope. You see, beautiful, you queered me. You made it impossible for me to be happy about stealing. There's nothing to it, Bertha; it was just a cheap cowboy drunken stunt.

"I was staying at a flop house, over on West Madison Street, and these other guys in the mob were taking a bath in a couple of gallons of Dago Red. One of them had been a bus-boy at the Drake Hotel. That's all they were, just cheap-skate, petty-larceny bus-boys. None of them had ever stolen anything more than an umbrella or a door mat in their lives. One of the guys said, and he was half stewed and the rest of us were soused, 'I'll tell you how we can make a touch for fifteen grand. It'll be a cinch. I used to work over in the Drake Hotel, and the fifth and twentieth they pay. The payroll is fifteen thousand dollars. All we need is five men. It'll be a cinch.' I don't know how the hell I ever got mixed up with those punks, but we got hold of a couple of gats, and stewed to the gills, we went over there like we was Jesse James. We killed the cashier. Two of our mob were killed. One got away. Woods and I were caught before we left the hotel. There's nothing to it, but it made a good newspaper story, and just another testimony for Dago Red."

Otto kept looking at me as if his eyes could never see

enough of me. And when I had to go he whispered again, "Tell me, is it true you're going to have a kid? Please, beautiful, say it's mine."

Hennessy arranged that I was to see Otto an hour before the execution and also got me a press card admission to the hanging. An hour before the State took Otto's life, I stood before the door of the death cell and held his hand. I was half crazy with wanting to say something that would help, wanting to do something, and I didn't want Otto to see how scared I was.

"How's the weather out, Bertha?"

He seemed to be listening for something.

"Otto, I want you to do something for me," I said, to divert him. "Will you?"

"Sure, beautiful, anything I can."

"All right, then. In about forty minutes you're going to say 'Good morning, God.' Otto, when you do that, how about asking Him something? First tell Him I loved you and that it's terrible the State hanged you and that it's awful that you killed a working man. Then ask Him if He can't do something to stop men killing each other. Ask Him if He won't fix things so it will be easier to go straight than crooked."

He was hearing me but his face was listening for something else, too. I tried to kid him, tried to keep him from thinking about the next few minutes.

"Otto, do you think it's true that from the world to which you're going you will be able to send back thoughts and inspirations? Will you think of me, will you try to tell me how to understand people like you, how to help them?"

But it was no use. Suddenly I was throwing my body against the bar close to his body, crying out to him to kiss me, to hurt me. I heard my own voice without any control, crying: "Bite me. Hurt me. Make me feel you after you're gone!"

He looked at me then, with pity and affection in his eyes, and tried to give me strength.

"Take it easy, kid," he said. "It ain't you that's goin'."

Then the guards came and took me away.

Promptly at 7:00 A.M. a hundred and fifty of us were allowed to file into the ground floor of the jail. A temporary gallows had been erected in the bull pen. All the cells that faced the gallows had been emptied and the prisoners taken to the other side of the prison.

"Here they come."

We knew almost before we heard them.

With their heads erect, cigarettes in their mouths and their hands manacled behind them, the men about to die walked to the scaffold. Otto looked quickly through the crowd, quickly recognized me, nodded, and twisted his lips into a ghastly smile. His face was still listening. I knew what he was thinking. His eyes turned back toward the door. Every second he was expecting the telegraph boy to come in with a reprieve. He had beaten every rap in life so far. He had been in the Army for over a year and in the front line trenches for six months. German bullets and bombs and gas had missed him. He had been shot at by police and watchmen a dozen times. In drunken brawls he had been shot and stabbed, but had always escaped serious injury. By the look in his eye, I knew that he felt that he was going to beat this rap, also. He was still listening when the guards tied a rope around his feet; placed a white hood over his head that extended to the middle of his body, put a rope around his neck so that the knot came at the back. Everything was peaceful, orderly.

Flop!

The floor under him dropped and he was swinging in the air. Otto swinging in the air. I tried to make myself remember him as I had been with him. I tried to remember his face before the hood was tied on. But I could not. Into my mind came only one thing, the lines of Oscar Wilde's, over and over again:

> *It is sweet to dance to violins*
> *When love and life are fair;*
> *To dance to flutes, to dance to lutes*
> *Is delicate and rare.*
> *But it is not sweet with nimble feet*
> *To dance upon the air.*

Then, there in the grey prison room with the white shrouded figures swinging slowly and more slowly, I felt deep within my body the first movements of my baby.

SEVENTEEN

IT was Hennessy, the reporter, who led me away from that horrible death chamber, and I was so dazed and so alone that I would have been grateful for the companionship of anyone. He wasted no words of sympathy nor indulged in any sentiment, but under his brusqueness there was genuine gentleness.

"Come along, Miss Thompson," he said. "I want you to come over to the newspaper office and help me write this story."

He rented a little room for me on North Dearborn Street, near Bughouse Square. That afternoon the newspapers were full of the hanging of the Drake Hotel bandits and Big Otto's unmarried wife and her expected baby. The next day I began to get letters—flocks of them, including twenty-one offers of marriage.

Hennessy was very kind to me, and took me to many places, including the Press Club. The men of that club were a wild group, delightful, reckless. Some of the boys suggested that I try to get a job as a reporter, but I declined.

"Not now," I said. "Maybe after the baby comes."

I had a number of offers of jobs and lectures. One day Hennessy introduced me to a shaggy-haired individual,

Jack Jones, the impresario of the Dill Pickle Club. He looked wild but he had an air of sincerity about him that won me.

"Box Car Bertha, we want you to come over to the Dill Pickle Club and make a talk," he said. "I'd like to have you talk about, 'What shall an unmarried mother do? Have a child, an abortion, or commit suicide?' I know, Bertha, that you're not thinking about an abortion, or suicide. But there are a lot of women in your condition who are. I know your mother, and something about you. Your old friend, Franklin Jordan, is a pal of mine. We've been in many a strike and jail together. You've got a story to tell. You've had experience. You don't have a husband and you're going to have a baby. How do you feel about it?

"At the Dill Pickle we've had Yellow Kid Weil tell how it feels to be a 'con' man. Lizzie Davis told her experience as a panhandler. We've had the guy called Theda Bara talk about his life as a homosexual. We like to have speakers who've had experiences tell about them at the Dill Pickle. There's no married woman or obstetrician who can tell your story. Some people may object and raise hell. Will you come down and talk?"

I didn't much like the idea of displaying myself and a child not yet born, like that, but I finally consented. Hennessy went with me. The place was crowded. A man by the name of Roxy was announced as the chairman. He began his introduction of me by reading from Voltairine De Cleyre's poem, "Bastard Born."

Why do you clothe me with scarlet of shame?
Why do you point with your finger of scorn?
What is the crime that you hissingly name
When you sneer in my ears "Thou bastard born?"

Roxy read only these first four lines of the poem. Then there was a terrible commotion, a shower of eggs, vegetables, and brickbats, and the meeting broke up in a riot. In the middle of it stood John Burns, half-drunk with whiskey, half-mad with Catholic indignation, thundering maledictions on the heads of everyone.

"This Dill Pickle Club has had enough of infamous speakers and subjects!" he shouted. "We've discussed queers and crooks, but this is too much, even for me, to take a woman about to become a mother and drag her through a lot of talk about it.

"The audience came because they like vulgarity. They don't want to learn anything. They don't care whether Box Car Bertha lives, whether she commits suicide, or becomes a prostitute. I've helped to build up the Dill Pickle, but I'll be damned if I'm going to let it be disgraced by a lot of cheap notoriety seekers. I don't know anything about Box Car Bertha, but Jones and Roxy and the rest of these cheap-skates who try to exploit misery and suffering ought to be thrown in the lake."

The police came and cleared the hall, and I was relieved to get back to my room. Hennessy and one of his friends came along. They seemed interested in what I was going to do about my baby and the friend suggested that I go to the Polyclinic Hospital for my confinement. As a result of this I went to see Dr. Charles Bacon, the attending obstetrician at Polyclinic. Remembering what the doctor at Lawndale had told me, I told Dr. Bacon all about my infection and the fact that I might need treatment before the baby was born. He was courteous and friendly, and I felt better as soon as he began to talk to me.

"What are you doing now?" he asked. "If you'd like to come and work at the hospital, I think we can give you a position and you can get your treatment and perhaps earn a little money. I think you'd like to feel that your baby paid his board and did not begin its life as a charity-seeker."

Then he introduced me to Professor Maxmilian Herzog, who was at the head of the Polyclinic Pathological laboratory. He was short, stout, pompous, with a great shock of red hair.

"We need a girl in the laboratory to clean up," he said. "The last boy who was there did so well he's now studying medicine. I want some one who can clean up and shut up. That boy talked all the time. You'll get your board and room and six dollars a week. When your baby comes, Dr. Bacon will take care of you and you can go down in the clinic every other day and take treatments."

Dr. Herzog was gruff and matter of fact, but neither he nor Dr. Bacon showed in anything he said or did that he thought there was anything unusual about my pregnancy or illness, or that I had anything to be ashamed of. I was overjoyed! I felt suddenly as though I had been given a new lease on life and my baby a better start than I had hoped he would get.

The Polyclinic was a post-graduate school where country doctors came to take special work. Dr. Herzog taught laboratory technique. My task was to clean the laboratory and act as a general assistant. From the first hour in the laboratory I loved it. I learned the technique of staining gonorrhea and tuberculosis slides and how to make a dark-field examination and to mount histological and pathological specimens. Dr. Herzog said I was born for the laboratory, and in a month I became very useful to him. There were a good many doctors from the country attending the courses, and one of them, Dr. A. H. Wight from New Hampton, Iowa, who had known mother and who invited me to visit his wife in their home.

Dr. Herzog gave a course in elementary laboratory work, dealing with the examination of blood, discharges, and tissue. I had heard him deliver the lectures six different times, and took notes. One morning when he came to the laboratory at eight o'clock and the students were all assembled and waiting for his lecture, he arrived a little late, started hurriedly for his office, fumbling in his pockets, and suddenly stopped in annoyance.

"Dunervetter!" he cried. "I have forgotten my keys!" He could not get into his private office where the microscopes were kept and had to go back home, a distance of two miles.

The other doctors talked awhile and then began to fidget impatiently. Laughing at something one of the other men had said to him, Dr. Wight called out to me.

"Bertha, why don't you give us a lecture. You know as much about it as he does."

I hesitated for a moment, and then saw that they

wanted entertainment. Why not? I had entertained plenty of men in more difficult ways than this. I turned to my notes, found as many long words as I could, put on a solemn expression, and began.

"Gentlemen, the neutro-phile-poly-morpho-nuclear-leucocyte reaches out its pseudopodia and engulfs the bacteria."

There was a roar of laughter, which was interrupted by an opening door and Dr. Herzog burst in. Looking about him wildly, he rushed up to the platform and motioned for me to be silent.

"Gentlemen," he thundered, "don't believe her at all. She's only my *diench maedchen!*"

While I was at Polyclinic I seldom went out, but I did get to attend a wake and a christening, and had an invitation to a party.

One evening after a long day in the laboratory, while I was walking along the lake front, an automobile honked. I looked up and was delighted to see my old friend, Katherine, of the Globe, and her new pimp, Johnny Mangates. Johnny's father had died and they were going to the wake, so they took me along. Katherine and I sat in the back seat so we could talk.

"My old pimp, Scotty, who was guard over at the County Jail, got pinched for carrying some junk in to a prisoner, and he's down at Atlanta for five years," she told me. "I've been with Johnny for five months. He's a swell guy and gives me everything I want."

I looked at her worn, cheap clothes, and felt sorry for her. Hers was such an old story!

The auto stopped in front of a newly painted frame house in the heart of the Italian district at Fourteenth Street and Racine Avenue. Johnny led the way up the stairs. The place was crowded with relatives and neighbors. Father Nick Mangates was lying in his coffin in the parlor. He appeared to be sixty and looked serene and stately. He had come to America thirty-eight years before and had worked thirty-five years as a laborer for the Crane Company. He had married and fathered twelve children. Johnny was the eleventh.

On the sofa sat Mary Mangates. She had lived with Nick for more than thirty years, had raised their twelve children, bringing up a dozen boys and girls in the heart of Chicago's slums, in the district the sociologists call "one of the largest juvenile delinquency, crime and homicide areas in all America."

Eleven of their twelve children had made good, were honest, decent working men and women. Johnny was the only bad egg in the family. He had lost his left arm when he was ten, when a chunk of ice from a wagon on which he was sneaking a ride, fell on him.

The truant officer came often to his house. Before he was twelve he was in Juvenile Court. The only real schooling he had was in Pontiac Reformatory, where he spent three years. He went from pickpocketing to petty larceny, to house-breaking. He had taken a post-graduate course at Joliet Penitentiary. His parents always stood by him. The Racine Avenue house that took old man Mangates a quarter of a century to pay for, had been up for Johnny's bond a dozen times.

After Johnny's bit in the Big House, he reformed. After all, the Mangates were conservative. Johnny went to work in a gambling house. When the town got hot and he lost his job, he got another good job as a "roper" for the West Side Vice Syndicate. When Katherine's guard went "south for his holiday," Johnny moved in with her.

Angelo, Johnny's brother, who lived in Boston, came in while we were there, kissed his mother devotedly, then walked over to his father, and kissed his forehead reverently. Then he knelt on the floor beside the coffin. One by one, all the children came and knelt beside their eldest brother. Katherine came and knelt beside Johnny at the front of the coffin. Someone started to sob aloud and then all of us made brief articulate. I knelt with them. I heard Katherine whisper, "Johnny, Johnny, please don't ever let me hustle again!"

But, of course, before the week was over, she was hustling in the same old way and giving Johnny her money.

Going through the ward of the hospital one day, I ran into Edna. Her sister's baby had been born the day before and they were going to have the christening in a week. A lot of the old gang I knew would be there. She asked me over.

"Im going to adopt the baby," she told me. "Bennett, her man won't let her keep it. He was awful sore because she didn't get rid of it."

Edna had four sisters and one brother. Three sisters were hustling.

"You know, it's the damndest thing the way things run in our family," she said. "Even before I broke into the

racket, and that's over ten years ago, I was chasing around
while I was working over in the factory, and I got caught.
When my kid was born, my folks threw me out of the
house and I had to give my baby away.

"Then Pat broke me in and we started a little joint on
Blue Island Avenue, and my sister, Toots, saw I was hustling and she came to work in the flat with me. We all got
pinched and when they found out that Sis wasn't eighteen,
they gave me a year for contributing to the delinquency
of a minor. Toots had a kid while I was locked up, and she
gave it way to be adopted. The folks threw her out of the
house, too.

"When I got out of the 'can' I went to work in Gary.
My second sister, Evelyn, used to come out and see me.
I'd give her a little money to take home to the folks.
One day she told me she was going to have a child. The
old folks got onto it and kicked her out. We put her in a
Catholic hospital. She had her baby and the sisters got
someone to adopt it.

"My mother and dad have kicked us all out, but it's our
hustling that supports them now.

"They ain't going to get this kid, however. I'm going
to adopt it legally and I'm going to hold onto it. No pimp
or no man in the world is ever going to take it way from
me. I'm going to have a kid for myself, to take care of,
just like you are."

I thought savagely of my own child and how I, too,
would hold onto it—against the world if necessary. I
thought of how my father had left me, and told myself

that nothing would take me away from my child once it was born. Then I asked Edna more about the christening.

"I thought they had christenings in churches," I said.

"Maybe they do, but this christening is going to be in Rosita's flat, and there ain't going to be any priests, or preachers, parole officers or adoption officers there. We're going to baptize this kid like they do a battleship, with a bottle of champagne. I paid ten bucks for a bottle of Mum's."

Polish Rosita's flat was a small "house" on North Avenue. Rosita had three girls working for her. Saturday night was always a good night in a joint, but Rosita turned all business away that night. I didn't think so many people could get into a six-room flat, but fully two hundred men and women and children came in. They were all racket people, even the kids, and some were babes in arms, belonging to prostitutes and pimps and thieves.

Little Shirley (that was the name they'd given the baby) got enough tiny dresses and shoes and socks to last her ten years, for the boosters, as Edna called the shoplifters, had had a lot of fun in lifting baby clothes for her. And they left the price tags on the presents, for it is a mark of distinction, always, for them to know how to steal valuable material. Among other things, there were four baby carriages.

"They're always a cinch to swipe," one of the women confided to me. "You just go into any of these neighborhood stores and just push one of them along out onto the sidewalk, and there you are."

In spite of the fact that half the crowd were grifters,

there was very little talk about grifting. A few references were made to absent friends in jail, but generally the talk was as ordinary as that of a Sunday School picnic. Not one vulgar story was told. Not one person was over-familiar. There was a modesty and a sanity about the place that pleased me. It was nothing like the wild, drunken parties at Edith Adams' or the fierce orgies at Tobey's.

Grifters always dress modestly and somberly, both at work and in public, but this night they were at home with their friends, and if there was anything gaudy or showy or loud in the wardrobes of the girls, they wore it to Shirley's christening.

The ceremony of the baptism was performed by a genuine clergyman, the Reverend Archibald Smith. He had been in the Baptist ministry. Later he got mixed up with some crooked real estate deals and was working with a mob of con men and using thirty grains of morphine a day. He had the complete clergyman's outfit, including a plug hat. For the ceremony, he was loaded to the gills, lit up like a sky-rocket.

Holding the champagne bottle on his shoulder, he said, "Friends, we've gathered together tonight to celebrate the arrival of Shirley, Big Edna's pride and joy. While anticipating philoprogenetiveness . . ."

At that moment someone let out a yell.

"The fuzz (the squad)! Ditch the fireworks!"

And suddenly hands jammed into pockets and Shirley's presents were thrown madly into drawers. I saw two of the girls put their dope syringes in the top of the piano.

"Those bastards!" said Rosita. "What right have they

got to come to my house? I'm a respectable woman, giving a party."

Lieutenant Daniels, of the Vice Squad, and Sergeant Johnson, from the Bureau, and three plain clothes men who were well known to everybody, came in. The lieutenant pulled out his gun.

"Don't anybody move here," he said. "I've got a search warrant and I want to see if she's here."

Their faces were stern and we all held our breaths. They all walked over to Big Edna, who was holding the baby. Lieutenant Daniels with his gun in his hand turned to one of the men.

"Is that the party?" he asked sternly.

"Yes."

"What's the kid's name?"

"Shirley."

"Well, Shirley," said Lieutenant Daniels, solemnly, "you might as well give up now. You're starting early! Here's a bank book for you with one hundred dollars that Mr. Myers of the Cosmopolitan Bank is giving you. Now, everybody have a drink on us. Mike's bringing two cases up the stairs."

EIGHTEEN

A GOOD many hustling girls came to the Polyclinic for treatment. Professor Taylor, who had charge of the tuberculosis clinic, one day asked me to go over to a flat on Goethe and Dearborn Streets to get a specimen of sputum from a girl who was too sick to come down to the clinic. I did so, and found it was the home of a group of lesbian dope fiend hustlers, who, in all the experience I have ever had were the most abject, pathetic, forsaken humans I had ever encountered.

The basement flat can only be described in Oscar Wilde's words. In it things were done "that sons of God nor sons of men never should look upon." The women were emaciated, decrepit, and though young in years, all of them were old. They had syphilis, tuberculosis, ulcers, and boils. They were half-blind, and lame, and yet, when they had their make-up on and were out hustling, they were able to appear attractive to many men. The house was poverty-stricken. There was nothing in the place that could be sold or pawned. And yet those seven women and three men who lived there never spent less than twenty-five dollars a day.

The sick girl, Polly, was in the last stages of consumption, and was taking forty grains of morphine a day. Four of the other women were thin and looked as if they, too, might have been tuberculous. One, Peggy, was a tall large woman with straight black hair, a heavy jaw, and deep-set brown eyes. Another, a stout girl of twenty, had a prominent goiter.

I took the specimen, and Helen said to me, "Won't you come over Sunday night? We're going to have a party."

"What kind of a party are you going to have?"

"I'm giving the party," said Peggy. "I'm the proud father of a child."

"You think she's kidding," said the sick girl, "but she really is."

"I'm intelligent," I told them. "I'll listen. Tell me about it."

"I can't, but I'll let Slim tell you."

A tall, thin, dopish-looking fellow of about thirty, came over yawning from a sofa.

"What do you girls want now? Got a cigarette? No, I don't want that. Have you got a weed?" He smoked the muggle leisurely and began to brighten up.

"Slim," said the sick girl, "tell this girl from the Polyclinic about our party and how Peggy happened to be the father of Beatrice Fairfax's baby. Slim used to be a doctor, and a good one, before he got on the junk."

"Is there any of that gin left?"

"No."

"Anybody got any money? Have you got four bits, sister? We want to get a bottle."

I gave one of the girls the money and received great returns for my investment. I learned that they were constantly raided by the police, exchanging sweethearts, and carrying on all sorts of practices. Half a pint of gin and three marajuana cigarettes made a great clinician out of Slim.

"You understand, my dear young lady, that the story I'm about to relate to you is not unusual," he said. "It has been well known by veterinarians that you could impregnate a cow without having a bull present. The 'test tube method' of impregnation has been used for years by stock breeders. And it follows also that it is altogether within the range of reason that a lesbian can make another woman pregnant.

"I have just written the complete story. I haven't decided whether to send my story to *The Ladies' Home Journal*, *The Christian Science Monitor*, or to *The New Era*.

"With your kind indulgence, I submit the following for your consideration, knowing full well that if you are pleased with my humble efforts you will purchase another bottle of the liquid that helps us see the world as it is not."

He read:

"The door of Slim's home opened inward for the peculiar ladies of the North Side and the cross puzzles of their love lives. Accommodating Slim offered food, drink, advice, sympathetic understanding and a bed, with or without personal service.

"Of course, the basement on La Salle Street was not an ideal home, and the one at Goethe and Dearborn Streets had an odor not unlike that of the monkey house in Lincoln Park Zoo on a murky morning, but even though the place smelled like the breath of a hippopotamus with halitosis, and Molly, the family cat, cast reflections upon the atmosphere when she used a basement across the street as a birthplace and nursery for her kittens, the generosity and philosophy of Slim attracted the girls.

"Slim was a physician, author, actor, and a self-acknowledged wit. He had a long course of development, and acquired his big-hearted and broad-minded views during a long trail of successive marriage and catch-as-catch-can affairs. Slim married Jessie, the wardrobe mistress with a burlesque show, and then promptly fell in love with Patsy, the pony who led the front row.

"When Patsy threatened to return to her old act as a trapeze artist, Slim offered his heart and attempted suicide by cutting his wrists at her bedroom door as a sacrifice to keep her on the ground. Patsy took to the air. Slim returned to Jessie, joined a carnival, fell madly in love with Goldie, who posed in bronze, offered to marry her to break her affair with Polly, the cootch dancer, and wound up his carnival career in Gary, Indiana, sitting on the bed of Toots, the magician and broken-heartedly confessing the kid's queer, and in love with Polly.'

"One night after supper a week later Slim opened the door of Peggy's apartment and Peggy tearfully told him that her sweetheart, Beatrice Fairfax, must have been unfaithful and was pregnant. Slim leapt into the breach and offered a biological explanation which convinced Peggy that she was the father of the baby. Slim said that it was quite possible that Peggy, as a practitioner, might have acquired the life-giving plasm while carrying on a modification of the orthodox technique, and that it was altogether possible for her to have involuntarily retained a remnant of her masculine contact and conveyed it to Beatrice."

He handed me the paper and said:

"You see Peggy before you. Was man ever more honored and proud? In the medical archives such cases have been reported down through the ages, but in the annals of the East Chicago Avenue Police Station, this is the first authentic case on record, and when Beatrice Fairfax and her baby return from the hospital Sunday, we are throwing a party and Peggy is setting up the 'hop' for the pipe. As usual, Peggy will continue to support Beatrice. She has had a dozen sweethearts, all lesbian, and has always supported them. You will honor us with your presence Sunday night?"

Suddenly I was very tired, and I shook my head and said, "I wanted to learn everything about life, especially about the underworld. I think there are some things to learn that I'll put off for awhile. Thank you, I won't be here Sunday night."

Often, while I was in the clinic, I saw some of the girls and many of the patrons I had known at the Globe. I continued to work in the laboratory until the day before my child was delivered. I always wore a big, wide gown, and my condition was unnoticed. I was so engrossed in the laboratory that I hardly knew that I was about to have a child.

But on July 26th I remembered it when a sudden stab

of agony smote my viscera. I called up Dr. Bacon. "I think I am having pains," I said.

He had me placed in a four-bed ward. As they washed, scrubbed, and prepared me, I became suddenly conscious of my responsibility. I didn't even have a layette. Where would I take the baby? Mother had told me to let her know when my time came, for she wanted to be with me, but I had neglected to do so. In the absorption of my work I had forgotten to make plans. Twenty-four hours later I was taken to the delivery room where the doctors and nurses loomed suddenly in white. Everybody had gauze over their mouths.

"Now, Bertha, we want to give you a little anesthetic," said a woman doctor, who was preparing to put a gas mask over my face.

"What for?" I asked.

"So you won't have much pain."

"Take it away," I found myself saying violently. "Why shouldn't I have pain? What right have you got to spare me the pain that nature gives me? I want to know how it feels to have a baby. I want all the pain there is. I want to be awake. I've seen my lover hanged. Now I want to see my baby born."

Dr. Bacon said gently, "All right. Now take a deep breath."

The pains came oftener and were more violent. I couldn't call it pain exactly. I felt as if I were sitting on a volcano that was trying to erupt.

"Now, take a deep breath, here it comes," they told me.

"Raise my head so I can see. Is it a boy?" I asked.

"I don't know." Dr. Bacon's voice came from far away. "We've only got his head so far."

I relaxed for a second.

"Now breathe hard, and press down."

"Is it a boy?"

"I don't know, we've just got his right shoulder. Now, press down, breathe hard! That's fine! We've got both of his shoulders now."

"Is it a boy?"

"Now, Bertha, just once more! Press down and—here it comes."

"Is is a boy?"

"It's a girl."

"Now, you can put me to sleep."

Two days later the interne stood beside me with a paper and pencil. "I want to get a little information from you," he said. "I want to fill out the baby's certificate. What was the father's name?"

"What did you say?"

"We want to know the name and age and nationality of the father. Who was he?"

"The baby hasn't any father. I'm her mother and her father."

"The baby must have a father. We've got to put down some kind of a name. Surely you must know. You look like a respectable girl, and Dr. Maximilian Herzog tells me that you're a fine laboratory worker and have a future in medicine. Who do you think her father was?"

"Her father was fifteen hundred men," I cried hopelessly. "Fifteen hundred lonely men. But if you must have a name for the father, call him "Big Otto."

"Otto what?"

"Just Big Otto. Age forty. Born in New York City. Dead. Hanged. Be sure you put 'hanged' after the cause of baby's father's death."

"What do you want to name the baby?"

"I don't know yet. For the present just call her Baby Dear. All babies are supposed to be dear to their mothers."

And suddenly I stopped aghast at the sound of my own voice. Why had I said that? Wasn't this baby dear to me? Hadn't I counted on it, after the first shock of knowledge had passed? Wasn't I glad? For the first time there entered my mind a doubt as to whether I had ever really wanted a baby.

When Baby Dear was seven days old the nurse came to announce visitors.

"There's a gang of men outside, and they want to see you," she said.

There were Jack Jones; Birdie Weber, a short squat Dill Pickle poet, blond with a big nose; Eddie Clasby, black-haired Bostonian, from the Seven Arts Club; a Yogi teacher, a Hindoo called Pandin; a thick-lipped colored socialist, Harrison; Ed Hammon, a fellow who was organizer for the painters' union; and a thin fairy called Hazel.

Clasby was the spokesman.

"Box Car Bertha, we came over here to judge for ourselves who was the father of your baby. And to tell you that we're all prepared to marry you, according to the rites of the Catholic, Jewish, Hindoo or free-thought church. You can have anyone of us for a common-law husband, or if you like, you can claim the bunch of us as father for your child. We want you to accept this little bunch of clothes and these flowers, and we are all going to kiss you."

I laughed, and thanked them, and kissed them all, and told them that I intended to go right on being the father of my child.

Dr. Herzog and Dr. Bacon insisted that I stay at the hospital for six months. At the end of ten days, I moved from the hospital ward to the servants' headquarters, and in less than three weeks after Baby was born, I was back at work in the laboratory. Every few hours I nursed Baby. I wanted to keep her in the laboratory but Dr. Herzog said it was too dangerous.

Baby Dear was the loveliest, strangest, most fascinating creature in all the world. She had bright blue eyes, fuzzy red hair, a perfect body with the biggest hands and feet. She weighed seven pounds and ten ounces and quickly continued to gain weight. Everybody loved her, and quite a number wanted to adopt her.

At the end of six months I decided to take Baby home to mother, and thinking about it, I suddenly made up my mind that her first ride would be in her mother's favorite conveyance—a box car.

NINETEEN

JUST before I left I spent an evening at Martha Biegler's boarding house, and there were a lot of women hoboes who came in and out that evening. Most of them had been on the road, some riding box cars, but most of them hitch-hiking. Sarah Jones, a tall, gawky woman of thirty, had spent ten years bumming around the country, just to see things, she said. When she got in a place she liked, she took housework jobs until she got money enough to loaf again. When one of the other girls told how hard it was to hitch-hike without "coming across" to the men who gave the rides, Sarah sniffed and said, "If you're lazy, that's true. But if you're willing to work you don't have to take nothing off nobody. I never go on the road till I have money ahead, and when I run out I stop and earn some more. You can talk about unemployment all you want to, but if a girl can bake and cook and will get down on her knees and scrub floors she can always get a job, at least enough to do to give her meals and lodging and a couple dollars to lay by for another trip."

It was Sarah who suggested that I take a man with me on the road. "There's only one way that the shacks and the dicks will always let a hobo alone, and that is when he's got a woman and a baby with him. If a man and a woman are together, the average tough guy won't hesitate to take the hobo's woman from him."

"Thank you, Sarah," I said. "I'm going to take Baby Dear on her first hobo trip alone."

"It'll be a cinch for you," said Sarah. "Nobody will pass up a woman with a small baby and a bag. But keep away from the charity organizations or they'll take the baby away from you."

Hennessy the reporter was interested and made me promise to write him a record of each day's experiences. I shipped the few belongings I had by parcel post and took only one small satchel of the baby's things. Hennessy drove me out beyond Wheaton and put me down on the Lincoln Highway early one morning and gave me a five-dollar bill. Before he was out of sight a big Lincoln car with a middle-aged man and woman in it stopped and took me in. They made Omaha before supper-time, driving like mad, each taking turns, and eating sandwiches as they went so they would not have to take time out. They said almost nothing to each other. They didn't ask me a question except to be sure that I was going west. In Omaha I said I wanted to get out at a Y. W. C. A. and they delivered me at the door and wished me luck and tore off again at great speed. They had a New York license and were without any baggage whatever. Both were expensively dressed.

The next morning the papers had both their pictures all over the front page. They had been captured ten miles north of Omaha, when their car smashed into another. They were wanted for a murder in Cleveland. I knew then that I had been taken into their car to make them inconspicuous. But I had a good start on my trip!

Baby Dear took to the road as if she had been born to it. Next day I rode a street car to the west end of Omaha and started out again. A furniture truck picked me up and I stayed three days with it, sitting alongside the driver, a husky Kentucky boy who wouldn't believe my story that I was an unmarried mother. He took me in for meals on every stop, and worked up a lot of affection for the baby, and said he had had six like her, before he left his wife in the mountains after she went squirrel hunting with his neighbor.

He didn't ask me where I was going to stay at night, but just got an extra room for us wherever we stopped, and then, after we were in bed, came into my room. He had a load to deliver to a little town near Denver, and turned off the main road about ten miles east of Cheyenne. He wanted me to keep on going with him, and sulked like a child when I wouldn't, but finally kissed me and Baby Dear and put us down on the highway. Though I didn't let him know it, I was sorry to see him drive off. He was my first man since having the baby, and he made me feel all alive and intelligent again.

A bunch of punks picked me up next, four boys riding through to Salt Lake City. When they found I didn't have any money they told me to come on and "jungle up" with them in a camp they knew beyond Cheyenne. We bought some bread and a hunk of stew meat for fifty-two cents in Cheyenne and got directions to the jungle from one of the railroad hands along the Union Pacific tracks.

The jungle was about a mile and half straight west from the depot, beyond the freight yards, down in a gully, hidden behind a clump of trees. There had been a settlement there at one time, apparently, for there were four or five wrecks of houses left, and several chimneys and fireplaces out in the open. Along the side tin cans and old cars were dumped. An abandoned hydrant furnished water. After I had looked around a few minutes, the place showed possibilities.

There were boilers for washing clothes hanging along the side of one shack, and there was firewood. Four or five groups were cooking food. They greeted us with interest, and camaraderie. The next morning, when I took a walk along the tracks we saw Indians, one a woman in regulation cowboy outfit, riding on the front end of a blind baggage. Railroad men always let Indians ride on the blind baggage free.

But that jungle held plenty of interesting women. Two I remember particularly. Sunshine Nellie was about forty-five years old, battered, shapeless, but an excellent cook and able to laugh with anyone. She came from a little town in Minnesota, where she had lived with a husband for twenty years and brought up three children. Two years before she had gotten fed up with the regularity of meals and Saturday night band concerts, and going to church, and had started out hitch-hiking. She was very domestic, however, and admitted she stayed sometimes a month in a jungle if enough men brought in food for her to cook. She was not particularly attractive, but her cooking was good, and she was accommodating, if not very interested, in whatever else the men needed. The second day we were there she spent a whole morning baking biscuits on a big piece of tin she found in the dump yard. By turning them over she got them brown on both sides. While we ate them, she told about her white enamel stove in Minnesota.

Truck Horse May was a different type. She was like Sarah Jones. When she got to a town she did a day's work and earned enough to go on. She was strapping in size, looked competent, and said she always could get housework jobs, but that she wouldn't stay on the premises, because she couldn't take any men home with her. She liked her men rough. If they were dirty she didn't mind. But sometimes she took a motherly interest in their cleanliness. The last morning we were in the jungle she came out of one of the shacks with a red-faced hobo she had been sleeping with, and made a great to-do over him, scolding him roundly, and scrubbing his neck and ears as if he were a ten-year-old. When we left at noon he was still tagging her about while she washed out his shirts and her underwear.

Both of these woman, I found, had lived in railroad division towns. Many of the men had also. And that I have always found on the road. The trains going in and out to places as they grew up gave them the wanderlust. "Red Martin," a small wiry grey-haired old woman in that same jungle, boasted that she had been thirty years on the road and had never paid a dollar for transportation in her life.

The four boys I was with took me out on the road toward Pocatello from Salt Lake City, and waited a distance down the road till they saw me and the baby get picked up by a Mexican in a Ford.

Near Boise we got a lift from two women driving to Spokane. Baby Dear had a little colic on that trip and they were so concerned about her that they made me go on to Spokane with them and paid for a doctor. The doctor told them he had never seen a healthier child, and made them so mad that they didn't even bother to get me a place to stay.

I got a room over a bakery. The baker's wife got worried because I was hitch-hiking with a baby, and next morning she introduced me to a cigar salesman who said that if I'd ride down to Walla Walla with him, he would take us into Seattle before the week was over. I did, and he introduced me to his mother and family. They all fell in love with Baby Dear and suddenly, without warning, began to urge me to marry Charlie, the salesman. I was surprised to learn that an unmarried mother with a baby gets more proposals than the average virtuous young woman.

Mother, my brother Frank, sister Margaret and Professor E. A. Orr met us in Seattle and we had a grand reunion. Mother was older and greyer and asked no questions. E. A. O. was still devoted to her. After a few days with mother, I went to Home Colony, Washington, and lived at the home of J. Ryan, who had a wonderful comrade, Agnes Ryan. They had four fine children. Ryan never referred to Mrs. Ryan as his wife—always his comrade. No one in the Colony ever asked any couples living together if they had ever been legally married. They took it for granted that they were not. There were no legitimate or illegitimate children in Home Colony. There were only healthy, happy, welcome children. And Baby Dear became a part of a group of children who enjoyed fresh air, love, consideration and freedom.

I stayed there a year. After six months I went up to the Health Department Venereal Disease Clinic in Seattle and took treatments, although my blood Wasserman tests were negative, as were the baby's. I spent most of my time hiking and fishing, and helping the Ryan's on their chicken ranch. I read a great deal, wrote many letters.

Occasionally I used to go up to Tacoma to help Comrade Leon get out a monthly paper, *The Agitator*. He was a large, stout man, bigger and more powerful than Lowell Schroeder. He had clear, blue eyes, and was a perfect Adonis. We fell in love with each other at once, but although I would have been glad to stay with him the first time I saw him, there were difficulties in the way.

He was living with Mary. They had a child about a year and a half old and another one was expected in a few weeks. He also had a sweetheart, an Italian woman, Angelina. She was a most motherly type of a woman, and was the widow of an Italian who had died in an Illinois payroll robbery. Angelina was also seven months pregnant. And, although this will seem impossible or at least fantastic to some people, Leon had a third sweetheart who was pregnant, Luba, a Russian woman.

But these women were not the difficulties. They all thought I was sleeping with Leon and they didn't mind. In fact, Angelina asked me one night, in the most friendly sort of way, whether I were not pregnant by Leon also, and was surprised when I told her that I hadn't had the opportunity to assume that honor. This was not strictly true for Leon had offered to make me pregnant, but had refused to be my lover unless I would consent to bear his child.

"Sex is a sacred, precious experience," he said, "and no man and woman ought to every stay together unless they want a child. The class of people who are going to control society are those who have the most children. We radicals and revolutionists should have a lot of children, and we should teach them to hate capitalism and exploitation. We should teach them to fight for liberty and justice. Our radical women are cheapening themselves and disgracing the movement by practicing birth control and having abortions. Love is for children."

I told Leon that I'd had the experience of being a mother and for the time being once was enough. For already I was restless and finding the call of the road stronger than that of my child—just as my father had before me.

TWENTY

THERE were two letters which made me decide to go back on the road again. One was from Franklin Jordan, who urged me to meet him in Washington, to which thousands of ex-service men were on their way to demand the payment of the bonus.

The other was from Eileen O'Connor, the president of the I. U. W. W. A., commonly called the "Women Itinerants' Hobo Union," or "Sisters of the Road." She urged me to come to the Women Hoboes Convention, which was to be held in Webster Hall, New York City, in June.

I thought of my baby and how I had said that I would never leave her. I thought of my condemnation of my own father for having left me. But I thought, too, of Franklin Jordan, and of his words, "Where there is a free-speech or labor fight or unemployed demonstration, there's where I belong," and I decided to go to Washington and New York.

The women at Home Colony gave me a little going-away party. There were ten of them. All of them had some experience on the road. Eight of these ten women were mothers. Several of them had been married but they disregarded marriage ties. All of them lived in a state of free love with their men. The children in Home Colony were

healthy, strong, happy children. Baby Dear came down
with the other children to see me off. Half the folks from
the Colony were on the dock. They were all happy that I
was going to Washington to take part in the Bonus Army
encampment and to the Women's Hobo Convention. I
asked no one to look after Baby Dear. The Colonists said
nothing about it. She was a part of the Colony and everybody felt that they had an interest in her. Here was a
genuine co-operative Colony. Most of the anarchists
worked and shared alike. The children were accustomed
to go to any house to eat and sleep. I knew Baby Dear was
in good hands. My friends, my comrades, wafted their
blessings to me, and the boat paddled up the beautiful
Sound.

The next few days were unforgettable. I hitch-hiked
most of the way to Washington, being picked up beyond
Pittsburgh by three veterans in an old Buick and taken in
to the Bonus Camp, where I met Jordan. The rebellion and
the gayety and the misery of that camp were beyond de-
scription. I had a feeling of America, torn and striving
America, being represented there with absolute veracity. I
went from tent to tent doing what I could, washing
clothes, writing letters, nursing the sick, encouraging the
weak not to break up the Camp until they got their
bonus. Into my ears they poured their stories of frustra-
tion and unemployment. In the confusion and the hatred
of the forced breaking up of that camp, all the early teachings I had had against government and against politicians
struck me with new and bitter force.

Most of the women, wives and sweethearts and trailers

of that camp, many of them new to the road, but some of them old-time hoboes, hitch-hiked to New York, with me, for the Women Hoboes' Convention. The slogan of that convention was "A home and a job for every man and woman," and the result of it were plans for the Women's Hobo College, which would set up service stations, information bureaus, and schools of social pathology.

Every station, for women of the road, we planned, should have cleaning and repair rooms for clothing, complete with service machines, patching material, dyes, shoe repairing tools and all washing and dry cleaning facilities, including the mechanical devices for quick drying. There should be cooking ranges, dishes, and dining room set-up for individual and collective feeding, and adequate places where women of the road, able in some fashion to procure their own food, could cook it for themselves. There should be also, we planned, a room with all facilities for writing letters and receiving mail, including typewriters, in case letters of application for jobs were to be sent. There should be a library, too, with books and magazines particularly specializing in the problems of women.

One of the most extensive plans made was for a personal hygiene room, one complete in bathing facilities and in safeguarding prophylactic equipment, inasmuch as most of the disease common to women of the road is due to inability to carry preventive medical equipment. There was to be in each station a personal counselor, to give friendly advice in problems of love and economics and birth control and pregnancy. There should also be a legal advisor. Sisters of the road are in need of good legal advice. Many of them are divorced or have grounds for divorce and alimony. Not a few are bigamists. A considerable number have either deserted their husbands, often with children, or have themselves been deserted. There are many lamsters—those who have either jumped their bonds or who have run away from orphan asylums or penal institutions. There are some women on the road who are entitled to legacies.

In addition to this, recreation rooms for games, meetings, arts and crafts were to be provided.

The information bureau of each college was to make a specialty of getting odd jobs, and jobs in exchange for board and room and personal necessities. They were to keep lists of cheap, comfortable lodgings, places of free lodgings, free meals, and the latest information on federal and state and municipal and private relief organizations. They were to be able to direct women to free medical clinics and to give advice on methods of free or cheap transportation.

Eileen O'Connor, thirty years old, with slender Irish face alight with enthusiasm and vision for more free and courageous women on the road and for making provisions for their welfare, inspired all of us. When we broke up, I helped her send recommendations for federal and state relief organizations, and have watched with interest since, the adoption of many of our plans in transient bureaus the country over.

Probably the most important thing, next to governmental relief, that was accomplished there was the dissemination of birth control propaganda and information on venereal disease prophylaxis. The tremendous decline in the birth rate, venereal disease and abortions that has been seen in America the last few years is partly the outcome of that convention.

I moved into a little room in Washington Square with Franklin Jordan. Intelligent as he was, he was not unlike Bill Steward in that he divided his time between several women. The nights with him were precious, however, and I was glad whenever he stayed with me. We did a great deal of drinking together. New York was a lonely place for me. I lost myself in the street crowds. I could not bear to mingle with the Village poets or any of the crowd I had known there before.

As I was walking down the Bowery one evening, I stopped in front of the Bowery Mission near Grand Street. I saw a crowd of forlorn men and a few women going in. There was a sign in the window, "Coffee and sandwiches served free." I went in. The place was crowded, and before eight o'clock they locked the door. At least a dozen men and women got up in the meeting and testified that they had been drunkards and thieves and prostitutes, and "through the blood of the Lord Jesus Christ" they had been saved. How does Jesus Christ's blood save a man from sin? What were these people saved from? Could Otto, Katherine and Lefty have been saved the same way? It wasn't clear to me. As I passed out of the hall an elderly lady stopped me.

"Can I give you a lift home?" she asked. "My car is waiting for me."

I stepped into her car, but instead of taking me to my

room, she took me to her own home, where we had a long talk, as a result of which I got, through her influence, a job at Mercy Shelter, a mission which was conducted in a four-story brick building on East Nineteenth Street. No sisters of the road fell into the hands of the Home Missionary Society. The home was exclusively for penniless women of Protestant churches.

The day I was hired, Mrs. Amber, the superintendent, told me about their restrictions.

"We're very particular who we take here," she said. "We do not take any drunks or prostitutes, and positively no one with social diseases. There are plenty of hospitals for them. Now, Miss Thompson, you understand that this is a Christian home, and although Mrs. Robinson said you were not an active Christian, she believes that you are fitted for this position. We need someone who understands women and who can be helpful to them. You'll get twenty-five dollars a month, your board and washing, and we'll furnish the uniforms."

I was happy in my new position, pleased with the women who worked in Mercy Home, and with the Board of Trustees. Everybody seemed honest and anxious to help, although some of the old ladies on the Board of Trustees didn't know what it was all about. Mercy was a temporary shelter. We housed forty women. They slept two in a room. The meals were fine. The only work the guests did around the house was to help to keep it clean, and serve the meals. I was the assistant superintendent, and took the records of the girls, tried to find them jobs, and urged them to keep in touch with their families. No one was supposed to stay in the Shelter over two weeks, and usually we were able to find some sort of a position or get the girl back to her parents in less time than that.

During the nine months that I was there I took the records of over two hundred girls and had got acquainted with most of the social agencies. I joined the Social Service club and weekly met with the representatives of the agencies working with homeless women.

I loved my job and the girls. I read letters from their parents and from their lovers. I helped them write letters. I dreamed some day of having a big institution of my own.

Then something happened. I don't know yet what it was. My jinx, which had been keeping its distance, caught up with me and tripped me. It was on a Friday afternoon, after the Board of Trustees had had their tea. Mrs. Adams, the chairman of the board, came to me, her face solemn and stern, and I knew something was wrong, though I didn't know what it was until she spoke.

"Miss Thompson," she said, "we're very sorry to tell you that we must ask you to resign at once. We all knew that you had had some experience in the underworld and we felt that this would help you to understand the women who come here. But we have just learned from a reliable source that you have been diseased. You know perfectly well we wouldn't admit anybody else who had such terrible diseases."

There was nothing I could say, for, of course, what she said was perfectly true. I could only feel lost and at loose ends again.

The day I was kicked out of Mercy Home, I went to

the Social Service Exchange Register and learned that there was a position open in Alabama at the Women's Municipal Relief Station. I applied for the position and got it. Jordan wanted to go south anyway, so, in a week, we were on the way.

The Alabama Female Service Bureau for Transient Women was located in the same building with a dozen other relief organizations. I began as a case taker. Our applicants were wandering colored and white women. Daily I interviewed from twelve to twenty-five women.

The applicants were the end-product of unemployment. Day after day I heard the same story. "My man lost his job." "I lost my job." "We want to get to Nashville where my mother is." "We was on relief in Florida and they cut us off and I'm going to Chicago." "Ah lived on that plantation for twenty-five years and Mistah Jones tried hard to keep me, but they foreclosed the mortgage on it and put us all out." "The longer Ah worked the more Ah went in debt." "Ah owe everybody money." "Lost my insurance and pawned everything."

Many of these women had children with them and had come in box cars or had hitch-hiked. Many of them had walked all the way. Quite a number had driven in their own cars, mostly dilapidated Fords. When I first came, the organization refused to give them gas, but soon I convinced them of the advantage of giving gas, along with a few days' board and room and the clothes they needed. The procession seemed endless. I was happy at Mercy Home, but here at the Women's Service Bureau I was transported to a peace and joy that I had never had before. I was giving service to my own kind, sisters of the road.

Franklin Jordan was a poetic lover. He loved me with words more than he did with his body. It was a joy to have him all to myself. We had two adjoining rooms in a clean rooming house. He made no attempt to work. I paid the bills. He spent his time at Labor Union Hall, and at the Library.

In less than six months I had complete charge of the Transient Bureau, and was doing some public speaking at conferences and in churches. Life was joyous and crowded. I had forgotten my past.

"I'm so very happy," I told Jordan one night.

"Look out," he warned me. "God takes care that the trees don't grow into the sky."

One day when I looked over the line of the men's waiting room, I recognized Lefty, the pickpocket, I had known with Big Otto. I walked over to him and shook hands and asked him what I could do for him.

"I just did a 'Sixer' on a chain gang in Mississippi, and I'm on the bum," he explained. "I want to get transportation back to New York. I'm afraid of these southern bulls. I can't get in touch with any of the old mob."

I took him in to the case worker and said, "This is an old friend of mine. I hope you will look after him."

Next day the director of the bureau said to me, "We're sorry, Miss Thompson, but we must ask you to resign. You have a criminal record, we find, and in your application you said nothing about it. You've been doing splendid work here, and you helped build up our organization so that it is a credit to the South, but what would we do if some newspaper got hold of this and said that the chief of the Female Transient Bureau had been a jailbird, an associate of thieves? We like you and appreciate your work but we just must let you go. Please understand that we have nothing personal against you and if we were just individuals it would be all right. But this is a government organization and anything that would discredit this organization would bring shame upon the government."

So Lefty had double-crossed me! Smarting still with the dislike he had felt for me when I had been a part of the gang, he had taken this opportunity to undermine the foundation I had built under myself.

It leaked out among the men and women who were living in the relief station that I had been fired for having a record. They all drew up a petition. The newspapers said later that one transient wrecked a passenger train in revenge for the organization firing me. Two days later, in the men's shelter house, a fire broke out, said to be a protest against the organization for letting me go. But Jordan and I were meanwhile on our way to California, riding in a box car.

I had drunk very little for the past two years, and had cut out smoking entirely, but when we got under way we had two flasks of whiskey.

"Cut it, Box Car," Jordan told me. "Booze will floor you. You don't need that much liquor." But I drank and insisted that he should drink.

We took our time, and in twelve days reached the outskirts of Los Angeles. We were both drunk most of the time. Coming into the S. P. yards, at Los Angeles, we rode on the bumpers of a freight. A railroad Dick saw us and hollered and caught the car behind us. He climbed up on the car and stood right above us and yelled down at us.

"Don't you get off until we stop," he commanded. "You're under arrest."

It isn't clear to me just what happened in the next few seconds. Jordan and I looked at each other questioningly, deciding whether to jump for it or not, and then I felt myself going and reaching out—whether to save Jordan or to be saved by him, I don't know. And then the track came up to meet us and I felt a terrific jolt which dazed me as I hit the cinders. I was conscious of the rumbling wheels of the freight train as they passed on and on endlessly close to my ears, over my head, terrifying and surrounding me with their rumbling—conscious of the fact that I was holding onto Jordan's hands, which felt strange and heavy and lifeless save for an intermittent twitching. Then I became suddenly acutely aware of things again and saw that half of Jordan's body was on the right of way beside me, and half was under the train. I tugged at him with all my strength, but knew, as I did so, that it was too late. Already the wheels of more than a score of cars had passed over his legs near his hips. As the last car went by I collapsed on the track, holding the hands of a legless, lifeless man—my lover.

TWENTY-ONE

IT took me months to get back to any sort of reality. I stayed with a family named Geralds whom I had met at I. W. W. headquarters and they were very kind to me. Slowly my health and strength came back to me. I had not realized how much of a hold drink had had on me. One day, almost twelve months after Jordan was killed, I found myself wondering about women I had known on the road. I remembered Andrew Nelson, whom I had met in New York and who had offered me a job in a social research bureau. Suddenly I wanted to be working among women, for women.

I made the trip easily, hitch-hiking as far as Chicago, and got in just in time to join the big hunger march on Saturday, November 24th. This was in 1934. Harry Hopkins had come out to confer with all the relief heads at the Stevens Hotel. It was just after the Illinois Emergency Relief Commission had cut the amount of relief beyond endurance. I had stayed my first night in Chicago at the Mary Dawes Shelter, where they gave us food and let us wash our clothes and gave us lists of possible places to look for jobs. The shelter was overcrowded, the rooms shabby and not too clean, the women mostly middle-aged, broken down, without heart to start in living again. I felt a tremendous urge toward them, but had been dazed too long to formulate plans. I wanted to see Chicago again, just the sky-line and the lake.

I came out on Michigan Avenue unexpectedly into the middle of the hunger march. And what a sight it was! Miles and miles of human beings, twenty to twenty-five in a line, carrying banners, shouting demands, singing songs, marching by, their faces set, their worn clothes hanging bedraggled.

A deep sickening pain took hold of me. I saw banners of the Chicago Workers Committee on Unemployment, the A. F. of L. Trade Union Committee for Unemployment Insurance, the Federation of Fraternal Organization for Social Insurance, the Federation of Architects, Engineers, Chemists, and Technicians; the Interprofessional Association for Social Insurance, the Small Home and Land Owners Federation of Illinois, the Unemployment Council of Cook County, the Federation of Jewish Trade Unions, the American Consolidated Trade Council, the Federation of Social Service Employees, and the Polish Workers Alliance. Slogans against discrimination, against race hatred, against Tom Mooney's imprisonment. Protests because the single unemployed were forced to labor two days a week for fifty cents and lodging in filthy flop houses. Slogans for cash relief, for a public works program with jobs at union wages. Slogans for clothing, blankets, coal.

Women among them. Half of them women. Single women, old, young, stalwart, limping. Women with children trotting beside them. Marching, marching, moving together under the common misery of facing the winter without adequate employment or relief.

They poured by in an unending stream, a grey sombre smear down Michigan Boulevard's smooth pavement. With hundreds of others I found myself walking along parallel to them on the sidewalk, falling into their heavy rhythm, unconsciously adding my burden to theirs. The sidewalks were marching along with the street. Down past the Chicago Athletic Club, down past the Congress and the Auditorium Hotels where well-dressed men and women stepped back in startled alarm when they came out past the doormen from expensive luncheons and liquors. Isolated men and women coming out of expensive doorways, men and women with fear struck into their faces. And below, on the sidewalks, in the street, with me a part, a solid stream, twenty to thirty in a row, marching, marching, till I was overwhelmed by a dull but definite and thrilling sense of power. I fell in line behind the column headed by a banner bearing the name of Unemployment Council No. 1.

It was an unforgettable day, and a day from which much relief procedure changed, especially that for transients, as I have learned during these last months.

I went on hitch-hiking east, purposely stopping at shelters, and I found that a great army of women had taken to the road, young women mostly, gay, gallant, sure that their sex would win them a way about, far too discontented to settle down in any one place. Their stories were very much the same—no work, a whole family on relief, no prospects of marriage, the need for a lark, the need for freedom of sex and of living, and the great urge to know what other women were doing. They took the shelters for granted. They lied when they had to. They gave whatever records about themselves suited their purposes.

I got a ride out of Chicago beyond Gary with a truck driver I met in a gas station when I left the hunger march. The next truck took me to Toledo, Ohio. I had very little money so that when the driver was friendly I let him buy me my meals. In Toledo I stayed in a mission shelter two days, cleaning my clothes and talking with the women there. Among them was a girl called Skip Annie. She could not have been over fifteen. She boasted that she had stayed at all the transient bureaus between El Paso and Toledo. She was plump, short, with black hair and big breasts and a pimply complexion. She laughed a great deal and appeared to take great pleasure in the way she had fooled the social workers.

"They always spot me as a juvenile," she told me, "and try to get in touch with my folks. They always fit me out in clothes. I give them a different name and different relatives each place, and before they get their answers back from their letters, I beat it to the next place."

In Chicago she had been afraid of the transient shelters, she said, as she had heard down in Kansas City that they put girls in jail for beating the Chicago transient bureau. She was pretty broken when she reached the big city, and told a friendly cabby of her predicament. He introduced her to his brother, who seduced her and turned out to be a pimp and infected her with gonorrhea. He took her to a doctor to get her cured and was going to put her in a house to work for him, but she beat it as soon as the doctor told her that the tests were negative.

When I left Toledo, an old couple with a dog picked me up and took me on into Erie. In the shelter there I found two more juveniles who lied about their ages and gave phoney names. The morning I left one of them was crying bitterly because, while she slept, the superintendent had searched her purse and found a letter from her real mother in Alabama and wired Alabama authorities.

"My family is on relief down there and I'll never get away from it if they send me back," she wailed. But they sent her back just the same.

Near Westfield, New York, I stayed at a tourist camp. Next I caught a ride with a man who was an agent for lumber buyers. An old man in a rickety Ford picked me up next and took me to Jamestown. A newspaper route man carried me on to Steamville and bought me my lunch. Almost never did I have to wait for many cars to go by. Men invariably pick up a woman alone on the road. My next stop was Olean, where I was taken by a man driving over on a real estate deal from Salamanca. He propositioned me, but made no trouble when I refused him, and bought me two packages of cigarettes.

I had a break on the next pick-up, two Italians in a Dodge. I rode in the back seat among the vegetables they were taking to relatives in Jersey right close to the Holland Tunnel to New York City, and in a half hour I called Andrew Nelson and almost immediately had a job with him handling statistics and sorting and classifying case histories.

"They won't look up your record on statistics," he told me, "and you can have the job as long as you want it."

My new work was a sort of sanctuary to me. I had no time to think about myself. I had known women and men on the road for years; had watched and felt with criminals and the unemployed. Now I was learning about them and had figures on them. By Christmas Mr. Nelson was working on the New York end of statistics for a federal survey of transients and let me help on this. By February all figures were in from a special study of thirteen important transient centers, with the result that for men hoboes and sisters of the road the conclusion could be drawn that ninety-five percent of the transients in the three months studied were employable, that is, between the ages of sixteen and sixty-five and able and willing to work. The number of transients, men and women, in camps for the whole country in those three months were respectively 393,610, 361,459, and 293,818. Two percent, about 8,000, were women, roaming the country, making their way about on the road, using the government camps for their own convenience.

Three-fourths of the transients, men and women, started migrating to seek work, according to a compilation made from a random sample of 932 cases taken in thirteen cities—Boston, Philadelphia, Memphis, Jackson, New Orleans, Kansas City, Chicago, Minneapolis, Denver, Phoenix, Dallas, Los Angeles, Seattle.

Four percent only gave desire for adventure as their reasons. Only four percent appeared, also, to be habitual hoboes. A new order, certainly, from that of the old hardboiled sister of the road who chose the road for adventure and freedom in living and loving!

"To hell with such a society," Mr. Nelson said to me one day after we had drawn up the results of these figures. "We must, somehow, destroy it, if we have to be thieves, crooks, weaklings and slaves just to exist! Who can remain quiet and peace-loving and be content just to vote. Even now in these deadly days of depression, all we have out of the chaos is the rich growing richer and more powerful and more arrogant and the bulk of the poor growing more submissive and adapting themselves by force to a lower scale of living! The only hope I see left is the refusal of the transient type to take what is given them. You and your kind are the only ones left with a real sense of freedom in America."

Among transients furnished transportation to points where stability seemed favorable, another survey from twenty-two cities showed us that eleven percent of the unattached transients and twenty-five percent of the heads of family groups were women, a much higher percent than the two percent registered in transient camps. The greatest number of these women were between twenty-five and thirty-four years of age, whereas the greatest number of men transients were between the ages of sixteen and nineteen.

The study showed that 15.73 percent of transient women were Negro, and 83.27 percent white. (The figures for males were 10.38 percent Negro as against 86.89 percent white.) And in the nationality count, the native-born women as well as the native-born men far over-topped all other nationalities!

Is it, I wondered, that they only, the third and fourth generation in America, have given up hope of peaceful homes and remunerative employment? Our foreign-born still cling to their old footholds. Only the native-born seek frontiers, moving on foot and bumming freights and hitch-hiking, back and forth across the land.

In March I heard Harry Hopkins, relief administrator, in a speech before New York relief authorities, state that there were 34,500 persons who had "wintered" in California sunshine at the expense of taxpayers. The transients in California, almost 2,000 of them, came from Illinois, he said. Another 1,728 came all the way from New York. Another 2,500 came from Texas, and a similar number from Oklahoma. Certainly our hoboes and our sisters of the road need a place in the sun, I wanted to tell him. Why shouldn't they follow it back and forth across the land? Why should they not hunt out the most pleasant spot for sojourn if employment is not available?

TWENTY-TWO

EVEN to hear Mr. Hopkins talk about this great army of men and women moving about the country made me restless. My work was fascinating. I heard regularly from Home Colony and mother. Baby Dear was well and flourishing. Now and then I was able to make a little contribution to the colony. I was earning my own living. But the old wanderlust was upon me. It was spring.

I told Mr. Nelson how I felt.

"Go ahead," he said laughingly. "You wouldn't be any good to me at all unless you were just like this. Go on out and see what you find. Then come back and help me write about it. And here's something I want. Bring me back material on transient women who get into the courts, who have records. There aren't any statistics on those, because prison authorities aren't interested in the wanderlust in relation to crime and because social workers aren't smart enough to get any racket details out of the transients. You go see what you can find."

I spent the next two years in New York, with occasional trips on the road, my journeys repetitions of other trips I had had, nice, friendly casual relations, sordid, stimulating, exciting experiences. But all over the country I stayed in transient camps, finding them more and more comfortable, having better facilities for the quick use of transient women, and having more human and intelligent direction. But still they had a long way to go! Would they ever learn to handle the grifter and the liar and the cheat? Would they ever understand restlessness? Would they ever stop trying to make, without homes, home bodies of women who want freedom?

There were hundreds of petty thieves and "ex-con" women in the comparative safety of the women's shelters throughout the country. I got story after story from them. Being a government-kept transient was far easier than running the risk of jail, they told me. They were getting all the adventure they needed off the road.

There were some, of course, that would always be in one racket or another, who just used the transient facilities "to sober up on," they said.

State Street Blondie was one of them. I had worked my way around down to St. Louis. I met State Street Blondie in a shelter there. For her sake I would never dare tell you which shelter it was because she might be traced down. She had far too much publicity in the Chicago papers last year. She was actually what we would call a criminal hobo. She had a little bug for writing, and one day, as we were washing our clothes together in the laundry and she said she was getting restless, I suggested she write the story of her life. And here it is, as she did it for me:

"I was born in Wisconsin. My parents were farmers. Mother bought me a pair of shoes once a year, usually in the fall. She said, 'These shoes must last till spring,' and in the spring I went without until the next fall. When I was twelve, father bought me a dress and told me that that was the last money that would be spent on me. I was old enough to take care of myself.

"My first hobo trip was when I was thirteen. I rode from Tomah to Milwaukee, Wisconsin, on the blinds, after a boy I knew had seduced me. I was afraid of my father and went off with an older man who had been a hobo all his life. I was married just five days after I was fourteen in St. Paul. My husband was twenty-four. He seldom worked and soon after I was married I got a job as a waitress. Then I supported him. Occasionally he would make a little money by playing pool or hustling.

"After we had been married about two years, we came to Chicago and decided to take a hobo trip to California. We started out on the highway from Chicago to Kansas City. From Kansas City we took the Southern Pacific passenger train. My husband and I rode on the blinds all the way to El Paso, Texas, where we were taken off by the railroad dicks. We were taken to the police station. The police questioned me and discovered that I was seven months pregnant. They took me over to the charitable organization and got a ticket for my husband and me to San Diego.

"My baby was born in San Diego—a beautiful eight-pound boy. We had a very hard time after the baby was born. My husband couldn't find a job and I got most of my money by begging from strangers on the street. This was my first panhandling.

"When the baby was three months old, we left San Diego to go to Milwaukee. We started out hitch-hiking. We got as far as Needles, California, where we were stranded. We didn't have a cent for any food. We were in desperate straits. We walked out into the desert until we couldn't walk any further, and had got about twenty miles out when the heat became so terrible that I became dizzy and faint and we couldn't go any further. We were there two days, from Thursday until Saturday afternoon, when we were picked up by a judge. He took us to Albuquerque, New Mexico. He provided us with food, bought me a pair of shoes, and gave us ten dollars to eat on.

"The next day a salesman picked us up who was going to Denver. When we arrived in Denver we had three dollars left. I worked in Denver for awhile. Three weeks later we hitch-hiked to Milwaukee. At that time autos were plentiful on the road, but very few would pick people up.

"For the next three years we didn't stay very long in any one place. We hoboed from Chicago to New York, to Baltimore, Maryland, to Maine, to Annapolis, to Springfield, Massachusetts, to Boston. The year and a half we were east we had a free and easy time. Sometimes I worked, but often we were just broke and I would panhandle.

"My husband was never content to stay in any place very long. He would get tired of any town, and so we were constantly on the move.

"In 1925 my husband was killed in an automobile accident. We were riding on the highway in a friend's car and a large car came off a side road and side-swiped us. He died three hours later. I had both legs fractured. The driver was one of those called hit-and-run.

"After my husband died, I went to Portage, Wisconsin, where I tried to obtain steady employment to keep my child. I was unable to find a job. I got acquainted with a girl and two men. One day we were dining in a restaurant and the police came in and arrested all of us. I learned that one of the men was a forger. The police tride to get me mixed up in it, but I knew nothing about the case and because I couldn't give any information, they took my child away from me and put him in an orphan asylum. They gave me ten days in jail.

"When I got out of jail, I hoboed my way to Sparta to see my baby. Then I hoboed back to Chicago. Things were kind of tough, and before I knew it I was in the racket. While I was rustling around Chicago trying to make a living the best I could, I got acquainted with a group of men who were known as jack-rollers and strong arm men. They told me how easy it would be for me to make big money, and then I started in to work with the gang.

"I'd be walking down the street and some man would accost me and ask if I didn't want to go to a room. I would say, 'Yes, but I want to go to my house first. Come along with me.'

"Then I would take him to the rear of an apartment building. I'd take him in, and 'put the arm on him,' holding him tight around his neck while my pals would go to it and rob him. We never had any weapons. I'm a very strong woman and usually when I put my arm around a man's neck, I can choke the wind out of him and make him fall unconscious. When I was unable to do this, my pals would give the man a couple of hard blows in the stomach, which would usually knock him out.

"Any dough we took from the victims we usually split

three ways. I saved with the desire to get my baby out of the orphan asylum. In nine months I had saved five hundred dollars and gave it to a lawyer to get my boy out. He was unable to do anything. The principal of the State School where my child was locked up, told me that if I would give him a thousand dollars he would let my boy go to a boarding school. I gave him seven hundred dollars, and I was to pay the people five dollars a week for boarding him, which I did for two weeks. He was placed with a family near my home town, Tomah, Wisconsin. After the child had been there one week, I asked a friend of mine in Chicago to drive me up to Tomah and gave him twenty-five dollars and his gas and asked him to help me get my child.

"My son, Clifton, was ten years old. The arrangement with the State Institution was that I could see the child once a week for three hours and take him to a nearby town. I just told the folks that I was going to take the boy out for three hours. I brought him to Chicago and the first thing I did was to buy him two complete new outfits.

"I was afraid to keep him in Chicago and felt it was wise to get out of town. We started on a hobo trip. I tried to get him to ride the blinds on a passenger, but he was too frightened to get on and we had to hitch-hike. We went to Sioux City, Iowa, to my brother, where I left him.

"Soon after, I came back to Chicago and got in with the old mob. Down on South State Street there was a restaurant where we all hung out. There were all kinds of chiselers, muscle men, and racketeers. I made my money by panhandling, strong-arming, hyping, and by various kinds of chiseling. I never was very much of a crook, and although my friends asked me to join them in burglary and all sorts of things, I always refused.

"I had only one bad 'fall' and one conviction. We were going strong-arming in a house over on the North Side and the police got wise and pinched me. I refused to squeal on my pals and they took me to the Bureau and took my fingernails practically off trying to make me talk. I refused to implicate my pals. Although we had a 'fixer' and gave the bulls and everybody else money, they gave me ninety days and one hundred dollars and costs. The newspapers took my pictures and ran them for four days. I refused to have my picture taken, but the police compelled me and held me while I posed for the newspaper men.

"I've been picked up by the police at least twenty-five times, mostly for vagrancy and on suspicion. I've had only one conviction, but I've had to hand dough to the bulls a good many times.

"When I came back to Chicago later with my boy, I tried to square it. I wanted to bring my son up to be an honest man and religious and decent. I tried very hard to earn a living and I took all kinds of jobs, housework and everything. Last winter things got so hard we had to stay in the Chicago Women's Shelter at Adams and Ashland. We stayed there for five days. This is the only shelter I ever stayed in in my life. While at the shelter, my boy always complained of being hungry and I'd go down to the restaurants and ask them if I could do any work to get the child something to eat.

"While I was at the shelter, I got one day's housework at two dollars. The superintendent knew it and tried to take the money from me. I refused to give it to her and took my son away with me.

"The night we left the shelter a man in an automobile picked us up and when he learned that we were hungry and broke, he fed us and said he would take us to a hotel belonging to a friend of his. We went to sleep at the hotel and at about two o'clock in the morning my supposed benefactor broke into the room. He asked me if I thought I was going to have room and board for nothing. He said if I didn't want to sleep with him, we could get out of the hotel, which I did, but first I broke a chair over his head!

"I took my son to a girl friend and asked her to look after him and said I'd soon have some money. I was desperate. I realized that the charities would not help me and I could not get a job and I wasn't going to stand by and let my boy starve. I wanted to be an honest, decent, hardworking mother, but I couldn't make the grade. So then I went back into the racket again. I do the best I can. When I can get a job, I take it. When I can't I stay at a shelter until I do enough panhandling to start out again. I'm not going to sit idly by and see my son starve.

"I'd love to have my son with me. I want to see him grow up healthy, but I have so much heat (police record) that the bulls are constantly stopping me and often they take me down to the Bureau. Recently I was held in the county jail for five days. I decided that it was best to send my son somewheres where he'd be looked after. He is now with some of my relatives, going to school. I have to send him five dollars a week for his board and buy him clothes. This is not easy. I have to be very careful of what I do. My ambition in life is to give my boy a good education. I'd like to see him become a doctor or a good musician.

"Since my husband died, eight years ago, I have had two sweethearts. I went with one four years. I've knocked around with racketeers, crooks, and chiselers for nine years and I've had all kinds of propositions. Men have offered me all kinds of money, as high as fifty dollars a night, in the old days, and I never would sell my body because I always thought that was the lowest thing in the world and I'd rather do anything else. I haven't any grudge against a girl that hustles. I just feel sorry for her. I think they're very weak. When I love a man I think a great deal of him.

"I've met a good many 'queer' women (lesbians). Sometimes they've tried to be friendly and make me, but I never have had anything to do with them. I never tried to strong-arm any of them, or any woman. When I'm out working the racket, I usually get a well-dressed elderly man. The average money I get from a guy is about three to eight dollars, and that's a three-way split. The last five men we made we got fifty-five dollars from one, eighty cents from another (very well dressed), five dollars and thirty cents from another, and the last one four dollars and twenty cents, or a total of sixty-seven dollars and ten cents. This had to be split three ways. My end was twenty-two dollars and thirty-seven cents. I spent the money in the following way: The pinch cost twenty-five. I put up ten and my friends put up fifteen dollars. While I was in the station it cost me eight dollars for food and cigarettes for the other women prisoners and myself. I sent my boy five dollars.

"I'm broke now. I pick up a little change on the street. But I'm not satisfied or happy to be in the racket. I just drifted into it. I used to walk down State Street and go into Thompson's Restaurant on Van Buren Street. I met a bunch of young hoodlums there and got acquainted with them. All my life I have been attracted towards rough-necks and hoodlums. They always come to me. I always play big sister to them. The boys all respect me. One day there was a little argument in the restaurant and I knocked a big man down. Ever since then the boys call me, 'Big Sister.' At first some of the guys would try to make me, but they soon found out there was nothing doing and they left me alone and they are glad to work with me as a pal.

"I'm not satisfied in the racket and I'm always trying to get away, but for some reason or other every man I ever loved was a racket guy. One of my sweethearts is now in Joliet Prison doing fifteen to thirty-five years for bank robbery. I write him every week and send him cigarette money.

"I'm not very religious. I never read my Bible until my boy came back two years ago. I read it to him. I sometimes take him to church. I take him to the Catholic Church.

"The Reds, the socialists and the communists and the I. W. W. never appealed to me. I sometimes have listened to the soap-boxers in Bughouse Square, but they never interested me.

"I don't drink and I never did drink. And I don't smoke and I never have in my life. But I've bought a lot of drinks and cigarettes for the boys. My favorite recreation is to dress in men's clothes and to shoot pool. I play pool and billiards fairly well. I often dress in men's clothes when I am out hustling. Most of the time I was hoboing I dressed in men's clothes. When dressed as a boy they think I am about twenty-one years old. I am twenty-nine now. I never sleep in a nightgown, always wear pajamas—preferably men's pajamas. When I was a kid I always used to play with the boys and loved rough games. To-day I like a rough fight. I had a fight just about a week ago. Some man insulted a friend of mine and I gave him a punch in the jaw, knocked him down, and they had to take him to a doctor's office and put eight stitches in his head.

"I haven't had much of an education. I finished eighth grade when I was twelve years old. I don't read very much. My favorite books are Zane Grey's. I don't read any movie or any other kind of magazine. I always read the newspapers. The only kind of pictures I like to see are the gangster pictures.

"I don't know what's going to happen to me if things don't pick up soon. I'm either going to give my boy an education, or else spend the rest of my life behind bars. I'm depending on my oldest brother to take care of the boy if anything happens to me. I don't think I can continue in the racket very long in Chicago. That's why I'm laying low now down here in a shelter. I plan to go to Florida within the next week. I expect to continue to do some strong-arming there. I'm going with three of my pals.

"I know it's wrong to rob people, but I can't get work. When my boy was with me for two years, I went to the employment agency every day trying to obtain work.

"Surely society has a right to defend itself. Society has the right to send me to jail if they get the goods on me. But I've got to eat and sleep and my child has to have his board money. I don't justify myself. I know I'm wrong. I know my example is bad. But I'm so short on funds I have to. There's one thing about the police, they'll take blood money, but they won't give you a break when you haven't got that money.

"I'll never go back to the regular charities again. The shelters I don't mind. Everybody's so busy they don't bother you much if you behave. I've been to fifty factories in the last two months and I can't get work. There's nothing left for me to do but stay in the racket and if I go to jail or get shot, I'll know I had it coming and I won't kick about it!"

While I was working with Andrew Nelson, State Street Blondie blew in to see me in New York. Nelson was to lecture at a Boys' Brotherhood Republic that night and we took Blondie's son, Clifton, along. Nelson told the story of Clifton and asked the Boys' Brotherhood what they could do to help him. The president of the organization took him home, a few days later got him a scholarship in a very fine boys' boarding school. Clifton stayed there about a week and ran away. Professor Nelson then got the boy in three different homes where the people tried to do something for him, but each time Clifton would run away or his mother would take him away.

TWENTY-THREE

WORK at the Research Council with Andrew Nelson, special hobo assignments to investigate female municipal lodging houses, transient camps, relief stations, co-operative colonies, the Hobo College, seemed to fill my life, but I was not completely satisfied.

Then came that awful day when a wire arrived from Ena telling me that mother's house had burned down and that mother herself was so badly burned in the fire that she died a few hours later in a hospital. As a result of this, my baby was being sent on to me. Through the pain which I felt at the realization of mother's death surged a sense of confusion at the thought of living with my own daughter again. I kept wondering what was wrong with me. I felt that I should be glad about that part of it, overjoyed at the thought of being re-united with her again. But I was only vaguely uneasy about it. When I tried to tell myself how glad I was, tried to repeat the things a mother is supposed to say to herself under such circumstances, I knew that I was playing a part, knew that, somehow or other, I had never really achieved motherhood in the full sense of the word.

Nevertheless, it was pleasant when she arrived in charge of a friend from the colony, to see what a sturdy, happy child she was. She seemed glad to see me, but had no special recognition of me as her mother. I was just another woman who was being friendly to her as all of the women at Home Colony had been.

We had a nice little apartment together and, out of the salary I got from my job, I was able to have a colored maid who took care of the apartment and of baby while I was away during the day.

Twelve years before I had promised Lowell Schroeder that I would spend my thirtieth birthday with him. And so, when Andrew Nelson gave me a special assignment which would take me westward again, I welcomed it.

"You're getting to be a typical relief worker, Bertha," Nelson said. "Every time you go out on a hobo trip, your expense account is as large as those who go by first-class train. I'm flying a great deal these days, and I don't spend as much money as you do. Now, Chicago is the most interesting female hobo center in America, and I want you to go there without a cent and see how they treat you. I want you to try and see if they'll give you some clothes."

That night, penniless and ragged, I caught a fast freight for Chicago. Baby was left with the Negro maid, and, far from feeling hesitant about leaving her, I found a secret joy filling my heart as I faced again the freedom of the road.

On that trip I saw a great many men boes, but only four female. Hitch-hiking was becoming easier, apparently!

Blondie had told me that Chicago had a lot of new wrinkles in relief for women and I wanted to see for myself. I got off at the Illinois Central yards without being caught. On Michigan Avenue I stopped the first cop I saw, told him I was broke and had no place to stay, and he directed me to the federal transient bureau at 7 East Harrison Street, where the Broadway car turns.

Such a crowd there was! The intake room is on the second floor there. It was filled to overflowing with men and women. All the chairs were full and they were sitting on window sills and on suitcases. At least half of those waiting were Negroes. I waited four hours before I was called. I gave another name, told them I had hitch-hiked in from Kansas City to meet an uncle from Denver who had written he would take me home with him, but that I couldn't find him. The girl taking the record on a blue card was just out of college. I could see in her eyes that she thought it would be a good case to work on. She gave me an appointment for an interview with a case worker, and after another two hours' wait I was taken into a booth to see her.

She was a nice little Irish girl. I was really hungry by the time I saw her, so that my story was convincing. When she saw I was interested in the way the place worked, she told me all I wanted to know.

Chicago has now only this one federal center for transients, which is a part of the Cook County Bureau of Public Welfare, and which works closely with its other branches of relief. They have given up the Mary Dawes home, and no longer have a shelter for women. The women and families are all dealt with there on Harrison Street, and the men and boys are sent to 363 West Randolph Street, where there is a dormitory for them, and when the cases become "legitimately transient," they are sent to camps; whites to the one near Danville, and Negroes to the one near Cairo.

The women are all given what they call "outdoor relief." That is, they pay for a woman's lodging at a rate not exceeding ten dollars a month (including cooking facilities) and give her ten dollars and thirty-six cents a month for food, exactly the same amount given any single person taken care of by other branches of Cook County Bureau of Public Welfare. When outdoor relief cannot be arranged quickly enough, temporary shelter is provided for a woman at Sarah Hackett Home, or with the Salvation Army, or at the Y. W. C. A.

I was sent to the latter for the night. When the interviewer was finishing my record and showing me how to fill out the single person's affidavit now required, she noticed my clothes were in pretty bad shape and she gave me a card which admitted me to the sewing rooms at 4929 Indiana Avenue where, she said, I could make myself underwear and maybe a dress if I would put in a little time turning out some other garments.

I was jubilant as I heard of this and started out to see it for myself. It was part of the Hobo College for women plan, already bearing fruit!

There were fifty-one women sewing in a dilapidated light warehouse room there on Indiana Avenue. They were making men's shorts, men's shirts, panties for children. They were making clothing for themselves. Several unmarried women, noticeably pregnant, were sewing on layettes. They told me that if they made one layette for someone else they could make one for themselves and also get the materials to make their own hospital gowns and robes. They were all on the same basis as I, on rent and food relief, and they were given a dollar a week for twenty-four hours' sewing and allowed to fit out their own wardrobes.

I made myself underwear and a cotton dress, and got started on men's shirts under the direction of a fine old tailor.

Then one day the case worker called me in and glowered at me, as she shook me by the arm.

"Why did you lie to us?" she said. "The information you gave me was just one pack of lies. When we have helped you, and given you board, lodging and clothes—why did you do it?"

Somehow or other they had found out who I was, and so I was off again. I didn't mind, for it was time for me to leave anyway, in order to keep my engagement with Schroeder.

By hitch-hiking I made St. Louis for my birthday. By a little maneuvering Lowell Schroeder had arranged for his wife (recently acquired) to be out of town, and I had him all to myself. He was greyer and broader than when I last knew him, but of the same gracious manner and authoritative way of speaking.

I told him about my job, about Jordan, the baby, and Big Otto and the Globe. He sat in the big chair in the living room, his fine old face gleaming with understanding and interest.

"Besides my job, I'm secretary—or janitor—for the Unemployed Women's Education Association. I get a small salary out of that, and do about a dozen other things. My chief interest just now is the Women's Hobo College. All of the expenses, about five hundred dollars a month, are paid by the chief. He doesn't want his name known."

"What's he like?" Schroeder asked.

"He robbed the rich; he knows it. Legally, lawfully, legitimately, with the aid and the encouragement of the government. He's interested in saving his soul, and he's got one. And so he pays our Female Hobo College expenses and has left us fifty thousand dollars in his will."

"Bertha," he asked seriously, "how do you explain your polygamous or varietaristic nature? You've had more sweethearts than I've had, and you seem loyal and devoted to all of them. And, although I know you have plenty of men, I am sure they do not fill your life. Do they? Does your child satisfy your nature?"

"No, men don't satisfy me any more than my baby does. I'm afraid of Baby. I don't know why, but just recently I made up my mind to settle down in New York and become a real mother, but I just couldn't do it. Why am I afraid of my child? Why do I want more than one man? I am truly married to the box cars. There's something constantly itching in my soul that only the road and the box cars can satisfy. Jobs, lovers, a child—don't seem to be able to curb my wanderlust."

"I'm in the same boat," he confessed. "The more I learn about unemployment, the more unemployed. The more I contribute to anti-war causes, the more wars. The more college graduates and professors, the more uncertainty. The more we know of the inconsistencies and injustices of capitalism, the more powerful it becomes. You know I've made a lot of money in the last few years— a half a million dollars on one land deal. But it doesn't satisfy me any more than the things you have done satisfy you. As for you, in spite of your agnostic parents, you inherited a deep religious nature. You're a religious mystic, a Christian anarchist riding in a box car to find God. Whenever you go out tramping, on freights or hitch-hiking, you're running away from something, and looking for something at the same time."

"Where can I find it, Lowell?" I asked.

"Go back to New York," he said seriously. "Settle down and let your daughter bring you up."

For a long time we sat in silence. Then I took his hand and held it tightly.

"There's something I want you to do, Lowell," I said. "Something for me and for the thousands like me. You have money. Put our Hobo Colleges and my other schemes in your will."

"And so you've turned gold-digger, have you?" he smiled.

"Yes, if you want to put it that way. I thought I wanted to be a missionary to the hoboes. I see now that outside of feeding and clothing them, nothing can be done worthwhile without changing our economic system. And now the great dear public wants the capitalistic system. I hope it won't always be so. Then I wanted to help the social workers and the social scientists. But the more I investigate, the more convinced I am that they are but cheap, unenlightened tools in the hands of a powerful system."

I stopped, but he put his arm about me, encouraging me.

"Go on, Bertha," he said.

"You said you cleaned up a half million dollars on that big land deal. The first thing you do is to get a hundred thousand dollars in cash, put it in a big scavenger wagon, go down to the hobo district, the slums, the ghetto, the Negro tenements, and have a couple of men shovel the money from the wagon right out into the crowds of poor and let them scramble for it. And, Lord! I want to be there to see it.

"Give a hundred thousand dollars to the Hobo Colleges, men and women. Give them big buildings where they can be warm and comfortable, where they can write poetry and dream, and wash and mend their clothes, bathe and loaf in comfort; and where they can cook their food.

"Give a hundred thousand dollars to buy scholarships to State Colleges and Universities for prisoners. Every year let them have an examination in the State Penitentiary and get the governor to pardon the prisoners who can pass an entrance examination to the colleges. There are thousands of men in jail who ought to be transferred to colleges. It would be an inspiration to all the prisoners and it would do the respectable college students a lot of good."

Schroeder broke in with a laugh. "What would you say to transferring some of the students to the penitentiary?"

"Fair exchange," I said, and went on. "Give your family what you think won't hurt them, but distribute a hundred thousand dollars among the various propaganda movements, the unemployed, the anarchist, socialist, communist, free love, free speech and prisoners' aid movements. Your money won't do them any good, but it will be a fine example. At least you can prove to the world that you weren't a fourflusher and a liar. When a man leaves money to the church, it proves that Christianity was important to him. And if you leave money to the radical movement, it will prove that the radical movement was important to at least one man with money."

Long after Lowell had gone to sleep that night I lay awake staring into the dark, thinking. In my heart I knew, of course, that I must do what he had told me to do—settle down and be a mother to my child. He had said that I had been running away from something and suddenly I realized what it was—I had been trying to escape my own natural need to be responsible for someone, to live for someone else, some special individual person who belonged peculiarly to myself. For years I had told myself that I didn't want to be tied down, that I wanted to keep myself free to help others, to uplift the vast mass of struggling humanity. And I knew now that I had been rationalizing my need to be a mother, dissipating it over the face of the earth when its primary satisfaction lay within reach of my own arms.

Oh, I would go on with my work, with my plans. I

would do bigger things and better things for the poor and the homeless than I have ever foreseen, but first I would set my own house in order. First I would satisfy my need to do my own peculiar job. When I finally went to sleep it was with a feeling of eagerness for a new day, which would take me back to my child—and into a new life.

The next morning when Schroeder said good-bye to me, he handed me an envelope. He had drawn up the will according to my plans, and had made Andrew Nelson and me executors.

"What are you going to do, Bertha?" he asked.

"Oh, darling, I'm going home," I said eagerly. "I'm going home to my baby. It sounds silly, but I feel as though I were going home for the first time in my life!"

"Bless you, dear," he said, and kissed me.

Schroeder provided me with a first-class ticket and a Pullman. I was so glad to be alone, so much in a hurry to get there, and I didn't want any interruptions to my thoughts. Crazily I found one of the Home Colony hymns going through my head: "I'm saved, I am. I know I am. I don't give a damn 'cause I know I am."

Mile after mile, hour after hour, I sat almost in a trance. As the thundering rushing wheels carried me nearer to my child, and it seemed to me that they were carrying me not merely from St. Louis to New York, but from an old and worn-out past, to a new and shining future.

I woke from my reverie as the train came into the Pennsylvania Depot in New York. It was all so strange, but it was true. And it was now all so clear. Everything I had ever struggled to learn I found I had already surmised. Before I had ever hoboed a mile I knew what it was like. All of my experiences with the vagrants, criminals, sex variants, radicals and revolutionists merely clarified that which I had always known or felt.

All that I had learned in these fifteen deep, rich years was a little sociology and economics, types, classifications and figures. A college student could learn it all in a semester, or in a textbook. But I had achieved my purpose—everything I had set out in life to do I had accomplished. I had wanted to know how it felt to be a hobo, a radical, a prostitute, a thief, a reformer, a social worker and a revolutionist. Now I knew. I shuddered. Yes, it was all worthwhile to me. There were no tragedies in my life. Yes, my prayers had been answered.

I was radiant as I stepped off the platform into the arms of the chief. He was holding my baby by the hand. I was startled . . . She was such a large, beautiful, blue-eyed, redheaded, happy young lady, and only eight years old.

Andrew Nelson met us at the gate. "Well, Box Car Bertha, what's new? You look as if you had been riding the cushions over the mountains with a couple of angels."

"I have," I answered, "—with a whole flock of them!"

APPENDIX

WHAT MAKES SISTERS OF THE ROAD?

WHILE working for Andrew Nelson, I gathered and kept, for a book which we were to do together, a great many statistics on the causes of vagrancy in women. The book has not yet been finished, but so much of the material already available for it is pertinent to my own story of sisters of the road, that I have brought a part of it together to include here, with his permission.

The primary factor in the production of vagrants and social outcasts is economic. To be sure, health is a factor.

Many women on the road are sick and diseased. But if they had plenty of money, they wouldn't be on the road. They would be going to the spas of Europe and Hot Springs.

Drink also is listed among the causes of vagrancy. But the rich and the middle class drink much more than the poor women, and they never have to go on the road or apply for charity, no matter how drunk and disorderly they are.

There is really not much more difference between those who become vagrants and others. The upper classes have all the vices of the sisters of the road, and perhaps more, but no matter how lewd, vulgar, promiscuous or immoral they are, they never get on the road or become public charges, and are seldom disgraced.

About five percent of the women of the road are afflicted with psychoses and insanity. But the "Well Offs" have as many mental cases. They are sent to private institutions to be taken care of. They do not burden the taxpayers, and the public never knows of them.

Dromomania, the abnormal desire to travel, is in all classes of people. Women who have money become globe-trotters, and are continually on the go. Poor female wanderers become hoboes, because they have no money.

All other factors can ultimately be traced to environment.

SECONDARY FACTORS THAT MAKE WOMEN TAKE TO THE ROAD

(a) AGE

    (1) The adolescent—the awakening of sex, and the desire to travel.

    (2) The aged—the senile.

(b) ILL HEALTH

    (1) Infectious diseases such as tuberculosis, syphilis, amoebic dysentery, malaria, gonorrhea and tubo-ovarian infections.

    (2) Constitutional diseases—heart, kidney, liver, diabetes, respiratory, dropsy, asthma, cirrhosis of the liver, etc.

    (3) Emaciation, wasting diseases—starvation, general weaknesses.

    (4) Handicaps—blindness, deafness, dumbness, crippled, injuries, paralysis, etc.

    (5) Glandular disturbances—hypo and hyper thyroid; Addison's Disease.

    (6) Insanity and psychoses.

        (a) The hysterical.

        (b) The neurasthenic.

        (c) Flights and fugues.

        (d) Dromomania.

        (e) Melancholia depression.

        (f) Dementia praecox.

        (g) Epilepsy.

        (h) Alcoholic insanity.

        (i) Childbirth insanity.

(j) Illusions, delusions and hallucinations, that constitute misconstrued grievances and persecutions.
Running away from supposed enemies.

(c) THE EXTERNAL APPEARANCE.

(The Ugly Duckling—Deformities and Lack of Physical
Attraction)
(1) Consciousness of lack of attraction and beauty.
(2) Deformities, handicaps and injuries.
(3) Extremes of leanness or stoutness.
(4) Extremes of shortness or tallness.
(5) Extreme awkwardness—"Miss Gawky."
(6) Cross-eyes and eye lesions.
(7) Hyper-trichosis (excessive growth of hair).
and Hypo-trichosis (slight growth of hair).
(8) The tiny and the massive breast.
(9) A natural appearance of being unkempt, tough and
unpleasant.

(d) VICES.

(1) The Drink Habit—the habitual, periodical and the occasional drinker whose addiction to and love for drink
cannot be controlled by will or reason. The woman
who drinks in spite of her determination not to drink.
(2) The Dope Habit—women who are addicted to the use
of morphine, heroin and cocaine—about ten percent,
mostly in the criminal group. There are a large number of marajuana smokers, but these are not dope
fiends.
(3) Addiction to Gambling—women who are possessed
with the idea that they must bet every cent they get
on cards, horses, dice, etc.
(4) Sex irregularities—the nymphomaniacs, the masturba-
tors, those who run away to have an abortion; well-
marked homosexualists, perverts.

(e) FAILURE TO "FIT IN"—WOMEN WITH A NON-COOPERATIVE SPIRIT.

    (1) Inability to get along with family or relatives.

    (2) Feeling of pride which forbids taking help from family or friends.

    (3) General inability to become adjusted.

(f) PREFERENCE FOR THE ROAD AND A HOMELESS, AIMLESS LIFE.

    (1) Many women feel more at home in a box car and on the road than anywhere else.

    (2) Others prefer cheap lodging houses and third-class hotels to their homes.

    (3) Many women prefer to live in Shelter Houses and Transient Bureaus. They like to be taken care of, and don't like to take the chance of going hungry, sleeping out or hoboing.

    (4) There are some women on the road, and in Transient Bureaus because they say "What else can I do? Where can I go or hide?" They can think of no other place to live or method of existing.

OTHER FACTORS AS TO WHY WOMEN WANDER

(a) To escape from reality, to get away from poverty, misery and unpleasant surroundings.

(b) To seek freedom from parental and family discipline.

(c) To run away from husbands, lovers and admirers.

(d) Inability to find expression at home.

(e) Religion—the Search for God.

(f) To get new and better clothes. Silk stockings! Oh, what tragedies have taken place for thy sake!

(g) Climate and weather—the monotony of Nature.

(h) Hatred of farm, burg or city.

(i) **Freedom** and adventure.
(j) Romance—to find lovers and a husband.
(k) To get experience.
(l) "A place in the sun."
(m) To see family and relatives.
(n) "The push and the pull." Some drive compelling them to go away, and some call beckoning and seducing them.

WHAT STAMPS WOMEN SISTERS OF THE ROAD?

(a) The Law.
(b) The Church.
(c) Public Opinion, Custom and Mores.
(d) The women themselves, those who choose to be known as Sisters of the Road.

FOUR MAIN GROUPS OF SISTERS OF THE ROAD

(a) The economic or unemployed.
(b) The anti-social or criminal.
(c) The over sex-conscious group.
(d) The rebels.

HAZARDS OF A WOMAN ON THE ROAD

(a) Disease, injury and pregnancy.
(b) Developing into a thief, prostitute and beggar.
(c) Developing the "get-by" philosophy; thinking the world owes her a living; learning that the public will support her by charity or crime.
(d) Becoming tough and hardboiled and caring nothing for home, family, children or the good life.
(e) Finally—developing into an enemy of society and the government.

GROUP CLASSIFICATIONS OF OCCUPATIONS OF WANDERING WOMEN. LEGITIMATE

a. THE ECONOMIC GROUP.

    1. Member of poverty-stricken family.

    2. Unemployed woman.

    3. Woman on relief.

    4. Searcher for work.

    5. Desire to better condition.

    6. The never-had-a-job.

b. THE UNTRAINED WORKER.

    1. Servant girl.

    2. Agricultural worker.

    3. Factory worker.

    4. Housewife whose home has been broken up.

    5. The nursemaid.

c. THE TRAINED WORKER.

    1. Saleswoman.

    2. Stenographer and clerical worker.

    3. Professional and semi-professional woman.

    4. Research worker.

    5. Waitress.

d. THE PROFESSIONAL GROUP.

    1. Actress.

    2. Musician.

    3. Artist.

    4. Dancer.

    5. Teacher.

    6. Traveling student.

e. THE RADICAL GROUP.

    1. The traveling propagandist.

    2. The migratory radical worker.

3. The fighter. (Those who travel to strikes and free-speech fights.)

THE ANTI-SOCIALS. ILLEGITIMATE

a. VICE GROUP.
1. The amateur—anything to get by.
2. The prostitute—working en route.
3. Migratory hustler.
4. The worker in the joint.
5. The prostitute with a pimp.

b. TAVERN HABITUE.
1. The booze-hound.
2. The jack-roller.
3. The barmaid.
4. The good fellow—the saloon loafer.
5. The percentage girl.
6. The battle ax—the female bum.

c. THE DRUG ADDICT.
1. The pipe smoker.
2. The morphine, heroin user.
3. The cocaine sniffer.
4. The marajuana smoker.

HOW PENNILESS WOMEN CAN EARN FOOD AND SHELTER

1. Work in restaurants and hotels in exchange for food.
2. Work in homes and hotels in exchange for board and lodging.
3. Work in store or factory; obtain advance at end of day.
4. Get job, then get credit at hotel or boarding house, or restaurant and arrange to settle on pay-day.
5. Leave watch, jewelry, clothes as security for board.

HOW PENNILESS WOMEN USE THEIR SEX TO OBTAIN FOOD, SHELTER AND CLOTHES

1. By flirtations.
2. By promising men favors.
3. By intimacies.
4. By prostitution.
5. By homosexual relations.

CRIMINAL METHODS THAT WOMEN USE IN OBTAINING NECESSITIES

1. Stealing and confidence games.

THE KIND OF HOMES FEMALES ON THE ROAD COME FROM, IN ORDER OF THEIR IMPORTANCE

a. Broken homes, mother or father dead, divorced or absent.
b. Orphan homes, graduates from juvenile jails and institutions, poor houses and adoption homes.
c. Poverty-stricken homes, ex-prisoners and paroled, some feeble-minded and insane institutions.
d. Lamsters—runaways from penal institutions, or own home, or other institutions.

HOW WOMEN TRAVEL WITHOUT MONEY

a. Walk.
b. Hitch-hike.
c. "hobo"—Steal rides on passenger and freight trains.
d. Travel in their own or friend's automobile.
e. Motorcycle and bicycle.
f. In trailers.

WHERE WOMEN GET FREE FOOD, SHELTER AND CLOTHES AGENCIES

a. Federal, State and Municipal Relief Stations.

b. Religious charities:
> Y. W. C. A.
> Salvation Army
> Rescue Missions
> Protestant, Catholic and Jewish organizations

c. Private charities:
> Travelers Aid
> Working Girls' Homes
> Endowed Homes

d. Organizations:
> Labor Unions
> Clubs
> Fraternities
> Organizations they or their families belong to

e. Radical organizations.

f. Obtain credit here and there.

g. Beg.

h. Steal.

i. Pick up food and garbage from street and ash cans.

j. Sleep in alleys and box cars.

k. Starve and "Carry the Banner."

FEDERAL EMERGENCY RELIEF ADMINISTRATION, FEDERAL TRANSIENT BUREAU, CENSUS OF TRANSIENTS UNDER CARE BY STATES

State	Unattached Individuals Total		Families No. of Families	Local Homeless Unattached		Total Individuals Under Care Sept. 15
	Male	Female		Male	Female	
Alabama	2,531	136	1,224			6,781
Arizona	4,429	34	224			5,250
Arkansas	2,607	295	669			5,380
California ...	10,202	616	3,673			23,321
Colorado	2,210	133	1,057	15	....	5,635
Connecticut .	1,086	5	28			1,172
Delaware	252	...	50			469
Dist. Columbia	1,348	74	282			2,322
Florida	2,066	219	1,113			6,933
Georgia	2,565	160	918			5,841
Idaho	1,154	44	1,075			4,510
Illinois	6,127	220	960	611	7	9,995
Indiana	1,894	41	339	998	7	4,162
Iowa	1,653	7	232			2,544
Kansas	1,975	91	832			5,035
Kentucky ...	1,223	10	42			1,387
Louisiana	3,531	78	559			5,305
Maine	717	1	19			809
Maryland	4,093	20	172			4,989
Massachusetts .	1,414	14	110			1,803
Michigan	1,607	97	880	2,803	588	8,606
Minnesota ...	4,064	44	505	778	...	6,620
Mississippi ...	630	17	120			1,040
Missouri	3,586	218	2,062			11,100
Montana	2,112	8	37			2,234

State	Unattached Individuals Total		Families No. of Families	Local Homeless Unattached		Total Individuals Under Care Sept. 15
	Male	Female		Male	Female	
Nebraska	1,489	19	190	737	...	2,896
Nevada	1,489	...	33			1,585
N. Hampshire.	689	16	172			1,282
New Jersey ..	1,132	36	485			2,964
New Mexico .	1,299	16	353			2,676
New York ...	9,057	258	1,182			13,655
No. Carolina .	1,113	17	48	2	...	1,290
No. Dakota ..	1,520	3	7			1,542
Ohio	8,276	176	1,193			12,644
Oklahoma ...	200	11	312			1,987
Oregon	1,524	63	488			3,309
Pennsylvania .	4,986	80	582	5,307	634	13,043
Rhode Island .	618	6	44			790
So. Carolina ..	1,001	22	167			1,596
So. Dakota ...	782	9	56	45	...	1,044
Tennessee	3,233	69	785			5,955
Texas	7,284	155	980			10,529
Utah	849	37	162			1,487
Vermont						
Virginia	2,193	47	473			4,116
Washington ..	2,736	291	1,371	1,767	...	9,900
W. Virginia ..	1,181	24	47	48	30	1,413
Wisconsin ...	4,315	133	1,477			6,220
Wyoming ...	618	11	88			936
Grand Tots.	124,050	4,070	26,877	13,111	1,266	236,111

(1) ANALYSIS OF NEWLY REGISTERED UNATTACHED FEMALE TRANSIENTS

1. BY RACE

	White	Indian	Mexican	Negro	Oriental	Misc.	Total
Dec..	1753	6	8	130	1	3	1901
Jan. .	1710	12	4	261	2	..	1989
Feb. .	1481	10	3	186	..	..	1680
Mar..	1989	5	11	325	1	3	2334
Apr..	1527	7	6	180	3	..	1723
May .	1796	9	4	202	2	..	3013
June.	2018	7	6	234	1	50	2316

2. BY AGE

	Under 16	16-20	21-24	25-34	35-49	50 and Over	Unknown	Total
Dec..	24	287	634	413	374	155	6	1893
Jan. .	28	328	322	510	484	313	5	1990
Feb. .	37	280	324	352	379	307	2	1681
Mar..	53	353	349	458	450	317	354	2334
Apr..	37	340	304	392	391	257	2	1723
May .	25	399	385	495	382	323	4	2013
June.	48	457	404	528	449	379	51	2316

(2) REPORT OF THE TEMPORARY SHELTER OF HOMELESS WOMEN IN NEW YORK CITY

Number of Registrations:

The total number of new registrations at Central Registration Bureau in April was 149 as compared with 239 in March. The number of people accepted directly at agencies during April was 796 as compared with 826 in March.

Disposition of Cases:

The disposition of cases is as follows: (All percentages are based on total of new and old cases.)

	March No. for Month	% of Cases	April No. for Month	% of Cases	% of new & old cases for 1st quarter of 1934	
Family Agencies	137	10	28	1	306	9
Home Relief	766	54	703	59	1717	52
Shelters	161	11	145	13	512	16
Other continued care	138	10	148	13	235	7
Emergency Work Bureau	4	1	29	1	101	3
Others	200	14	145	13	487	13

Includes hospitals, food stations, and various agencies not giving continued care, and those people who have been able to manage with advice only.

The total number of women accepted for any kind of continued care in March was 1041 or 74% of the total, in April was 879 or 73% of the total.

Social Statistics:

In March there were 143 women under 25 years of age, representing 12% of the total for the month; in April there were 114 representing 11% of the total for the month. This shows a decrease of 1% in the number of younger women.

A study of the living arrangement of the women reveals that in March 479 or 42% of the total groups were living in furnished rooms; in April 386 or 37% were living in furnished rooms. 90 or 8% of the March group were living in shelters at the time of registration; 60 or 6% in April were living in shelters. Of the remaining 57%, 247 have been living in their own apartments, 129 were living with relatives or friends.

	Old	New
AGE GROUPS		
16-20	3	34
21-24	5	72
25-29	4	78
30-34	13	71
35-39	14	96
40-44	10	91
45-49	8	86
50-54	15	84
55-59	8	69
60-64	9	66
65-69	6	49
70 and over	1	32
Unstated	2	117
Total	98	945
MARITAL STATUS		
Single	53	355
Married	2	12
Separated	9	50
Widowed	27	317
Divorced	3	16
Deserted	2	78
Unmarried mother .	1	4
Unstated	1	113
Total	98	945
RELIGION		
Catholic	43	258
Jewish	38	101
Protestant	16	431
None		2
Unstated	1	153
Total	98	945

	Old	New
LIVING ARRANGEMENTS		
Unfurnished room ...	6	14
Unfurnished apt.	36	241
Furnished room	1	350
Furnished apt.	24	25
Shelter	20	36
Relatives or Friends ..	4	109
Homeless	7	19
Unstated		151
Other		
Total	98	945
LENGTH OF TIME IN NEW YORK STATE		
Less than 1 yr.		26
1 yr. less than 2 yrs..	3	10
2 yrs. less than 10 yrs.	15	285
10 yrs. and over	76	482
Unstated	4	142
Total	98	945
LENGTH OF TIME IN NEW YORK CITY		
Less than 3 mos.		21
3 mos. less than 1 yr..		5
1 yr. less than 2 yrs..	3	10
2 yrs, less than 5 yrs.	4	78
5 yrs. less than 10 yrs.	11	207
10 yrs. and over	76	482
Unstated	4	142
Total	98	945

	Old	New

TYPE OF OCCUPATION	Old	New
Professional	5	60
Office Worker	17	91
Industrial Worker	17	137
Domestic and Personal Service	52	439
Hotel and Restaurant		25
Saleswoman	4	34
Other		
Unstated	3	140
Never previously employed		19
Total	98	945

LENGTH OF TIME UNEMPLOYED	Old	New
Less than 3 mos.	21	128
3 mos. to 1 year	23	235
1 year and over	44	323
Unstated	10	259
Total	98	945

CITIZENSHIP	Old	New
Citizen	70	664
Alien	25	166
Unstated	3	115
Total	98	945

S.S.E. (New Cases Only)	
Identified	266
Not identified	679
Total	945

EMPLOYABILITY (C.R.B. Cases Only)	
Employable	125
Not employable	24
Total	149

C.R.B. CASES ONLY	
Mental Difficulty Suspected	13
Mental Difficulty Diagnosed	2
Total	15

(3) REPORT ON TRANSIENT AND HOMELESS WOMEN IN PENNSYLVANIA

Pennsylvania plays host to approximately 600,000 people yearly, who find it necessary to ask for food and lodging for which they cannot pay.

Experience has shown what the transient population corresponds in character and content with the resident group. It includes men and boys, women and girls and families.

Philadelphia and Pittsburgh furnish the largest number of problem men and women. The transient age group are:

Age	Total Number Transients	Percent
	24,805	100.0
Under 21	3510	14.1
21-24	4521	18.2
25-34	7882	31.8
35 and over	8892	35.9

We have found that 80% of the Pennsylvania transients are white, and 20% are Negroes, and about 15% are foreign-born. As to the Marital Status 90% say they are married, and 10% single.

The transient group appear to be more venturesome and intellectually superior to the resident homeless.

No comparable or definite information is available regarding the transient movement for women and families. Recent studies indicate a surprising growth in the number of women and girls on the road necessitating a more constructive consciousness of their problem. It is reasonable to expect that large numbers of them will react to the conditions which men encountered as the original swoop of declining employment overtook them. Families offer a more perplexing problem.

CLASSIFICATION OF SPECIAL CHARACTERISTICS OF VAGRANTS AND SISTERS OF THE ROAD

Each of the types of the Social Outcast have distinct and definite characteristics which stamp them as belonging to their class.

Ordinary Vagrants   *Criminal Sisters of the Road*

1. HEREDITY

Poor.   Fairly good.

2. RESOURCES

None—dependent.   Have money and possessions.
Society must support them.   Permanent homes and families.
Homeless. Friendless.   Friends. "Fall jack" "mouth
Adrift from family.   pieces."
                               Pay their way through life.

3. ECONOMIC ATTITUDES

Live from hand to mouth.   Concerned about future.
Do not save, invest nor insure. Save, invest, insure and bribe.
Do not belong to labor or so- Members of labor, social and
  cial organizations.   political parties.
No provision for sickness, jail, Provide for sickness, unem-
  old age or death.   ployment, old age, arrests
                                 and death.

4. INDUSTRY

Dislike work. Look for snap.   Hard workers. Nothing too
Temperamental workers.   difficult or hazardous if pos-
Think they can live without   sible.
  working.   Will work at all times, day or
Have little pleasure in work.   night.
                               Joy in accomplishment. Are
                                 go-getters, able to crush
                                 competitors and enemies.

Ordinary Vagrants　　　　　　*Criminal Sisters of the Road*

5. ADJUSTABILITY

Non and mal-adjusted.

New or difficult situations floor them. Seek escape in day dreams, drink and drugs.

Run away from hardship, trouble.

Unable to fit in.

Easily adjustable to all situations.

Ready for hazardous, difficult experiences.

Easily adjust themselves to the inevitable — jails, jams and death.

6. INHIBITIONS

Poorly developed.

Victims of their own weaknesses.

Drink heavily, use drugs.

Indulge in vices, float with the tide.

Well developed.

Drink modestly, gamble cautiously, and only when they can cheat.

Guard against passions and weaknesses.

7. CO-OPERATION

Non-cooperative. Rebel against routine and discipline.

Shirk responsibility. Try to avoid doing their duty.

Most co-operative. Will serve, help, pay, bribe, protect anyone who will help them.

Loyal to their group, dependable and competent.

8. HEALTH

Insanity, morbidity and mortality rates high.

Live on low level.

Food irregular and insufficient.

Neglect personal hygiene.

Spread disease and vermin.

No interest in public health.

Birth rate low.

Insanity and morbidity low.

High violent death rate.

Live on high level.

Eat proper food.

Care of personal hygiene.

Interested in public health and athletics.

Birth rate high.

Ordinary Vagrants   *Criminal Sisters of the Road*

9. ENEMIES

Ordinary Vagrants	Criminal Sisters of the Road
Their own worst enemies. Unable to protect themselves from hostile forces. Easily abused, robbed and exploited. Servile to those who enslave them.	Cunning and careful about making enemies, but when principles of profits are at stake, they are prepared to protect themselves against the most powerful enemies, including the law and police.

10. RELIGION AND IDEALS

Ordinary Vagrants	Criminal Sisters of the Road
Non-religious. Skeptical. Faithless. Indifferent. Unloyal and disloyal. Little concern in civics, community welfare or a new society.	Faithful to the church, devoted to family. Loyal to their group. Steadfast to her standards of others.

If any group is to survive, they must have survival qualities, and the fact is that many of the well-known criminals of the gangster type are dead or in jail. It is self-evident they are not successful or their successes did not last very long. "The way of the transgressor" may not be very hard, but the life of the average gangster in the limelight is short. Every modern gang is made up with one or more women. Often one-half of the mob are women.

SOCIOLOGICAL CLASSIFICATION OF WOMEN BEGGARS

Vagrancy, poverty, unemployment, charity, relief, missions, desertions, illegitimacy, have always more or less been associated with beggars. The history of the poor is the history of beggars.

Formerly when a women was homeless, penniless and friendless she existed by begging. And until recently most individuals who applied for relief felt they were beggars and were considered by a large part of the populace as being such. In so many cases the woman states that she felt humiliated; like a beggar when she first came to the Women's Service Bureau to apply for help.

A beggar, "panhandler" or "moocher" is one who solicits food, money, clothing and shelter from individuals or institutions and gives nothing in return. She is one who thinks that society should support her. Here is a list of the most common types:

a. Panhandlers: those who beg money on the street. "Mister please give me a dime."
b. Moochers: those who ask for food in stores or back doors.
c. Peddling Panhandlers: those who offer for sale papers, pencils, etc., not with the thought of selling them, but as a stall to beg money.
d. The old clothes moocher: one who begs clothes and sells them.
e. The Panhandling Con: the woman who begs for an organization, saying it is for charity or some good cause, and then pockets all of the money.
f. The Panhandling Mother: the woman with a baby in her arms or one or two children by her side. Sometimes these panhandling mothers call attention to the fact that they are pregnant.
g. The Chiseling Panhandler: the woman who begs from her friends and acquaintances; who goes to a meeting, lodge or church and tells a hard-luck story; never begs outright, but by innuendo. The hitch-hiker is a notorious chiseler who tells the person who gave her a ride that she hasn't eaten for days. They have all kinds of pathetic sob stories.

Beggars are divided into many types. The woman on the road usually begs for food, but often asks for money. Her begging is a natural outgrowth of the peculiar get-by philosophy that has developed amongst most beggars.

They may be further sub-divided into groups:

a. Blinkey (blind)
b. Deafey (deaf)
c. Dummy (dumb)
d. D. & D. (deaf and dumb)
e. Army or wingey (armless)
f. Peggy (legless)
g. Crippy (paralyzed)
h. Fritzy (epileptic)
i. Nuts (feeble-minded or insane)
j. Shaky (with pronounced tremors)

The above groups are true types of handicapped women. There is also a group of professional beggars who are phoney or pseudo-handicapped. They imitate practically every type listed above and some are so able to imitate a blind, deaf or crippled person so well that only an expert can detect them. The most common types of pseudo-handicap beggars are:

1. BLISTERS. (Those who put acids or alkalis on the limbs to create the impression of ugly sores.)
2. TOSSOUTS. (Those who distort and throw joints out of order. Many are experts at this.)
3. HIDDEN HANDS. (Those who hide and bind hands.)
4. FLOPPERS. (Those who sit or flop down in front of a church or building and give the impression of being cripples.)
5. GHOSTS. (Those who simulate pallor, haggardness, or coughing to imitate a tubercular patient.)

The professional beggars have devised hundreds of ways of deceiving the public. The woman beggar and the sister of the road is not necessarily identical, but the woman who is broke part of the time is apt to become the woman who is broke most of the time and gradually acquires a technique of supplying her intimate needs. The casual vagrant woman that lives from day to day, getting just enough to see herself through the day, is a potential beggar. Practically all of the women of the road say they do not get enough to eat, or enough clothes, and they see no reason why they should not beg. Comparatively very few women survive a prolonged stay on the road, without becoming some type of a beggar.

HOW WOMEN HOBOES BEG

1. Stimulate Pity—by whining, apologizing, emphasizing their hunger, disease or distress.
2. Stimulate Sympathy—by telling hard-luck stories.
3. Stimulate a sense of Comradeship—by appealing to a fellow-worker, union member, lodge sister, member of an organization, church, etc.
4. Chisel—by edging in on gamblers or racketeers—being with friends when they are paid off—by horning in here and there.
5. Stimulate Fear—by meeting a woman who is alone and frightening her, by insinuating they must have help—going to a back door when the woman is alone and demanding food.
6. Work Confidence Games—by requesting a loan and promising to return it—by flashing a telegram saying that they are going to get money—stating they are related to someone whom the person knows.

CHISELERS, CHEATERS, BEATERS AND CREDIT SEEKERS

The women of the road have comparatively little difficulty in "getting by," any more than the average woman elsewhere has. Just as the father and the husband and the family have provided down through the ages, there are those who provide for sisters of the road.

It has been comparatively recent that women have been obliged to shift for themselves, to vote for themselves, to make their own paths in life, and naturally when women leave home and think and do for themselves, they choose the easiest way—and the easiest way may be the crookedest way. Whether the women are instinctively liars and cheats and crooks, has yet to be proved or disproved.

Whether for selfish, sexual, or other reasons man enjoys coming to the rescue of a woman in distress, it permits him to be gallant, to be strong, to rescue the weak. Many men who would let another man starve to death will give all they have to some woman in a panic of real or simulated distress.

The three things that penniless women do beside starve are work, beg, and steal, but we must add another method whereby women can easily get money, food, shelter, and clothes, without working, begging, stealing or selling their bodies. Various names are given to those who follow this method of getting assistance.

1. Chiselers.
2. Cheaters.
3. Beaters.
4. Credit Seekers.

These might be listed under the term of racketeers or confidence women—the so-called "Cons." But modern hoboing has developed so many new angles that it may aid in understanding to define these terms.

1. THE CHISELERS.

A chiseler neither begs, borrows, nor steals; she just horns in, tells a pathetic story of want and distress in such a way that the hearer feels guilty or uncomfortable if he doesn't come to the rescue. She never directly asks for anything and claims friendship with the individual she chisels.

"How do you do, Mr. Smith," she says. "I'm Miss Jones. I just came from the University of Ohio. I knew your daughter, Priscilla, and we were such good friends. She's such a wonderful girl, and, and, and. . . . I'm just so embarrassed; I expected a check at the post office and it didn't come."

Or she tries another tack.

"I'm so glad to meet you. Father is a thirty-second degree mason and I see you're a mason also. I'm in a terrible predicament. I live over at the Palmer House and I want to move. It's so expensive over there; but I owe a little bill of twenty-two dollars. I expect dad in town next week and he'll scold me for being so extravagant."

The favorite method of the chiselers is to be in a gambling room and to horn in with the winners; to be with some acquaintances when they get paid. There are many other methods.

2. THE CHEATERS.

A cheater is one who misrepresents herself, who lies and deceives and makes false promises in order to obtain money, food or shelter. "My name is Sadie Bolliver, I live at 2742 Grand Avenue. My father is the foreman at Sears Roebuck."

3. THE BEATERS.

A beater brazenly obtains credit in her own name and gives the impression that she is responsible and will pay the bill. A woman registers at a hotel and at the end of the week "beats it out." At stores she says: "Send me a statement at the end of the month and I'll send you a check. I always deal this way."

4. THE CREDIT SEEKERS—THE BORROWERS.

This group cannot be called properly, crooks, racketeers or confidence women. They seek to obtain credit, they ask for loans or they ask for credit in stores, hotels or restaurants and honestly intend to pay their debts. They must be clearly differentiated from the dead beats, or confidence women, who have not the slightest intention of paying, they honestly intend to pay their bills and it is surprising how easy it is for a woman on the road, homeless and penniless to obtain credit. Most any woman, fairly-well dressed, with a little baggage can go to a hotel and register and say: "I'm expecting a check in a few days," or to a rooming house and say: "I'm sorry but I haven't any money now but I expect to get a job. I can pay you in a week," or "I expect a letter from home with a money order."

There are very few restaurants who will turn down a woman who will say, "I'm sorry but I haven't any money and I'm hungry. If you'll give me my dinner I'll pay you later." The merchants, especially the small merchants, do not hesitate to take a chance in giving a woman a pair of stockings, or a pair of shoes, or a cheap dress, on credit. It's absolutely amazing how women can live on credit.

A number of women among my friends have gone into banks, total strangers with absolutely no security, and have been able to secure loans of ten, twenty or fifty dollars. There are some women, as well as men, that you simply can't turn down when they ask for credit. Women who belong to labor unions, organizations, churches, find it very easy to borrow money.

If a woman has a domicile other than a shelter house or relief station, she has comparatively little trouble in opening up an account at the neighborhood shops and large department stores. A small payment down enables one to furnish her house with radio, piano and even an automobile. It is true, "Ask and you shall receive."

SOCIOLOGICAL CLASSIFICATION OF THE CRIMINAL OR ANTI-SOCIAL GROUP OF WOMEN

A small percent of the "Sisters of the Road" are active criminals or grafters. Most of the girls who fall into the hands of the law are arrested for vagrancy, disorderly conduct, or drunkenness.

There are very few women of the road who are full-time professional thieves or crooks. The criminal Sisters of the Road fall into the following types:

1. PETTY LARCENY THIEF.

The girl who steals food from grocery stores, fruit from fruit stands, clothes from lines, automobile accessories from automobiles, the mat from a door, umbrella from a stand, etc. She will steal anything that is easy to steal and where she thinks she is not taking much of a chance. There are three types of these women:

a. *Professional*—the girl who makes a practice of and who makes a living from stealing.
b. *Amateur*—the girl who steals occasionally, who has no intention of continuing to steal.
c. *Accidental or Hungry Thief*—the girl who steals food because she is hungry—a small article to sell in order to obtain a night's lodging—who steals clothes because she needs them. She only steals in desperation.

2. SHOP-LIFTER, BOOSTER, DERRICK OR CLOUT.

The girl who steals things from stores. The professional shop-lifter makes a practice of stealing from department stores; the sisters of the road who practice shop-lifting confine themselves to second-hand stores, junk shops, neighborhood stores. They are not very clever and most of them are amateurs. If a girl is a good thief, she can steal enough to live well and pay her way.

3. THE JACK-ROLLER.

One who robs or "rolls" a drunken person. From time immemorial the drunk always spent or lost money, and it is a theory that you do a drunk a favor if you take his or her money away. This is the way to keep him or her sober. Sailors, miners and lumber-jacks and even skilled union men and women, when drunk, are very often robbed. Many women who are apparently honest and decent and would never think of stealing anything, appear to have no compunction about robbing a drunk and it is usually true of sisters of the road. Nearly every drunk locked up in a police station with money, wakes up robbed, so jack-rolling is part of the life of a drunkard.

4. THE STRONG-ARM ROBBER

Strong-armed robbery is probably the most common kind of robbery that occurs among female hoboes. The technique is very simple. No firearms are required and hence the danger of a charge of robbery with a gun is not incurred. The robber, in strong-arming a victim grips the victim's neck and chokes him. As she is doing that, she has at least one accomplice—usually two —who go through the pockets of the victim and punch him either in the abdomen or in the head and knock him down and run. In a crew of strong-arm robbers there is often a woman. She lures the victim into an alley or hallway.

5. BURGLARS.

Burglary is rather rare for a woman, but sometimes women break into empty buildings, steal plumbing, etc., or into a home and steal furniture or jewelry. Quite often they break into a bootleg joint or liquor store in order to steal liquor. Often they "crash" (break into a store window).

6. HOLD-UP OR "HOIST" WITH A GUN.

The woman who uses a gun for robbery is very uncommon, but a number of females have been arrested for this crime.

7. HUSTLING OR SELLING OF FAKE OR STOLEN GOODS.

Slum hustling—Selling fake jewelry.
Weave hustling—Selling spurious cloth.
Skin hustling—Selling fake fur.
Worm hustling—Selling fake silk.
One can "hustle" almost anything that is crooked, and many sisters of the road hustle one thing or another.

8. PICKPOCKETS, CANNONS, WHIZZES OR GUNS.

There are many professional and amateur pickpockets who work the road.

a. Moll-buzzers: Women who specialize in robbing the pockets or purses of other women. Many sisters of the road belong to this class.

9. CONFIDENCE WOMEN.

Many women have been the victims of confidence women and not a few sisters of the road practice the confidence game. The most common type seen around the roads is that in which a confidence woman says to a female hobo, "For two dollars I'll get you a job," or "For three dollars I know where you can buy a new dress." There are many angles to this game, and women of the road are easily duped.

Types of "Cons":

    a. Solicitors for fake magazines (sheet writers).
    b. Solicitors for fake charities, etc.
    c. The carnival workers.
    d. Pitch women.

10. SHORT CHANGE ARTIST OR HYPE.

There are various methods by which a woman tries to confuse or frighten or cheat others in making change.

11. THE GAMBLER—CROOKED GAMBLER.

The most common is the "duke player," the person who cheats at cards or checkers. Women on the road gamble considerably and there are not a few sisters of the road who try to cheat the other women. Another common trick of crooked gambling on the road is the "match" or the "smack," in which three women match pennies or nickels and often two of them will cheat the other woman.

12. THE CHARLATAN.

A charlatan quack is a real, or phoney professional woman, such as a bona fide doctor, lawyer or educator, who uses her real or supposed knowledge to fool or bluff the public, in order to exploit her clients.

13. THE FAKER.

Fakers include the street corner or doorway "pitch women" eulogizing their corn cure, razor blades, Indian herb tonic, etc. All games and concessions at the carnivals, fairs, bazaars, etc., come under this heading.

These forms of modified larceny are not condemned as they provide more amusement than harm. The average person attends these affairs for the sole purpose of being "taken." If after spending a dime at each of the attractions he arrives home with some money, he feels that he did not fully enjoy himself. There is, however, a vicious gambling element connected with some touring carnivals which is very expensive and harmful.

CLASSIFICATION OF SISTERS OF THE ROAD, AMOUNT OF MONEY REQUIRED FOR THEIR MAINTENANCE, ACCORDING TO THEIR NEEDS

Necessity, the mother of invention, is also the mother of many types of social outcasts, and quite often the amount of harm the outcast does to society is in direct proportion to her unsatisfied needs.

A vagrant who depends upon the charities or the missions or a few dimes that she begs on the street for her bed and board does little harm.

A bum who is addicted to drink and is satisfied with cheap moonshine or "canned heat" can keep soused for about a dollar a day. This she obtains by begging and petty larceny. She injures society little.

A drug addict needs from three to ten dollars a day, and if she is a shop-lifter, would have to steal at least thirty dollars' worth daily, for a "fence" could give her only about a third of the actual value of the articles. A dope fiend must have her dope and will stop at nothing to obtain it.

A high-class grifter living on the Gold Coast, keeping a couple of new cars, with a cabaret habit and supporting a bunch of hangers-on, would need a thousand dollars a week.

CLASSIFICATION III

CLASSIFICATION OF WOMEN HOBOES WHO ARE RADICALS, REVOLUTIONISTS, REBELS, AND DISCONTENTS; THESE ARE COMMONLY KNOWN AS REDS

A large number of the girls on the road live in an environment where radical propaganda is most common. Many of the women have belonged to various labor organizations, I. W. W., Socialist Parties, Communist Party, and anarchist groups. The most common organizations and groups that the women have belonged to are:

RADICAL ORGANIZATIONS

1. The I. W. W.—the Industrial Workers of the World.
2. Socialists—Socialist Labor Party.
3. Communists—Communist Party—the Trotskyites—the Left Wingers. There are several different parties, but the large and most important are the Communist Internationales or the Bolshevists.
4. Anarchists—Anarchist Communists of the Emma Goldman, Alexander Berkman, Peter Kropotkin types. Individualist anarchists of the Max Stierner, Tucker, and Frederick Nietzsche types.
5. The Single Taxers.
6. Hobo Organizations—International Sisterhood Welfare Association— I. S. W. A.—The Down-and-Outers—The Zeros managed by Urban Ladue—The Hobo Colleges.
7. The Itinerant Workers Union—The Hoboes of America.
8. Unemployed Councils.
    a. Unemployed councils—Communists.
    b. Committee of the unemployed—Socialists.

c. The unemployed committee—I. W. W.
d. The unemployed committee—A. F. of L.
e. Unemployed groups of many other kinds.

9. The League for Industrial Democracy—Socialists.
10. The International Labor Defense—Communists.
11. The General Defense Committee—I. W. W.
12. The Technocrats.
13. Special organizations such as The Plebeian Forum—The Worker's Forum—The Vagabond Club—The Bug Club— The Dill Pickles—The Direct Actionists—The Kill the Rich —The Secret Thirteen, etc.

All the above organizations and groups can be divided under four general headings, depending on their purposes and aims and tactics and methods of action. It is the primary purpose of all these groups to do away with poverty, to abolish unemployment and to better the conditions of the workers. Some of these organizations have as their chief object the abolition of the capitalistic system—the profit system.

CLASSIFICATION OF RADICALS ACCORDING TO THE TACTICS THEY ADVOCATE

1. Those who advocate education, organization.
2. Those who advocate political action.
3. Those who advocate mass action—strikes—Hunger marches —demonstrations—make demands upon the government for benefits such as old age and unemployed insurance.
4. Those who advocate revolution, violence, appropriation, confiscation—the taking over of the warehouses, the mills, the mines, the factories—those who would kill the rich and the tyrants and bomb anyone who stands in the way of the workers getting the full product of their labor—those who are willing to use every method to destroy their supposed enemies and put their class in power.

CLASSIFICATION OF TYPES OF RADICALS

1. The professional agitator—the soap-boxer—the propagandist who spends most of her time trying to win converts. She may be on a small salary but most of the time is unpaid.
2. The peddler of radical literature—she sells the official papers of the organization—distributes pamphlets—pastes up leaflets on shelter houses and telegraph poles. She usually gets a commission on selling literature.
3. The active member—the active worker—the woman who takes her organizaton seriously and attends meetings regularly —tries to win converts and her ideals are her religion.
4. The sympathizer—the one who is sympathetic towards radicalism, but is not especially active, will go to meetings, give in the collection, but will not join a demonstration or say very much about what she believes.
5. The indifferent—She has a slight interest in radicalism but no particular admiration for it. If she thought they would win she would go with them, but she is just as willing to join the Democrats.

Down through the centuries, the vagrant, the wanderer, the homeless, unattached woman has been associated with drunkenness. Vagrants and mendicants are usually thought of in terms of alcoholics.

The theologians and a large percent of the lay population have associated vagrancy, unemployment, delinquency, and poverty with alcohol. It has been thought by many and is believed yet by not a few that alcohol is responsible for all of the unemployment, prostitutes, crime, and evil in the world.

We need to be reminded that a large percent of the women that are employed in all walks of life—saleswomen, servants, professional women, actresses, artists, drink to excess, and yet, for the most part, are able to do their day's work. There are thousands of factory workers who get drunk and still do good work. The same can be said about newspaper women who drink a considerable portion of the time and still work well. Many of the drunkards in the shelter houses, if they were working, might drink the same amount of liquor and not be a menace. And so it is well to understand the liquor consumed is quite apt to affect a sister of the road somewhat differently than it would an employed woman.

Three Kinds of Booze Consumed by Sisters of the Road

1. *Legal Liquor.* 2. *"Moonshine."* 3. *Denatured Alcohol.*

The Psychic Effects of Drinking Alcohol

Last year about 5,000 supposedly mental cases passed through the Psychopathic Hospital in Chicago. About 15% were diagnosed as alcoholic. The majority of these were not committed to the insane asylum, but were discharged, apparently recovered. The records in the Chicago Hospital suggest that alcohol, whether methyl or denatured, is responsible for apparently little insanity. Alcoholism and psychoses have always been associated. Whether the psychoses is responsible for alcoholism or alcoholism is responsible for psychoses, we are not able to say at this time.

SOME NEW TYPES OF SISTERS OF THE ROAD— MIGRANTS, TRANSIENTS, AND REFUGEES

Since the government has become socialized, humanized and "New Deal" there are appearing some new terms in sociological literature.

TRANSIENT. A transient is a sister of the road who applies to a government relief organization for assistance and whose residence is in another state or county.

MIGRANT. A migrant is a person who is traveling around the country seeking to make a living by honest work. These were formerly called "hoboes."

REFUGEE. Refugees are those women who have lost their homes because of droughts, floods, and other catastrophes over which they or their family or the community have no control. The recent drought in the west and the floods in the east are responsible for thousands of women being on the road.